ECONOMIC REFORM
IN
EAST GERMAN INDUSTRY

Economic Reforms in East European Industry:

General Editors
ALEC NOVE AND J. G. ZIELINSKI

Other volumes in this series
Janusz G. Zielinski on POLAND
Iancu Spigler on RUMANIA

INSTITUTE OF SOVIET AND EAST EUROPEAN STUDIES

University of Glasgow

ECONOMIC REFORM IN EAST GERMAN INDUSTRY

GERT LEPTIN AND MANFRED MELZER

TRANSLATED FROM THE GERMAN BY
ROGER A. CLARKE

Oxford   London   New York
OXFORD UNIVERSITY PRESS
1978

Oxford University Press, Walton Street, Oxford OX2 6DP

OXFORD   LONDON   GLASGOW
NEW YORK   TORONTO   MELBOURNE   WELLINGTON
KUALA LUMPUR   SINGAPORE   JAKARTA   HONG KONG   TOKYO
DELHI   BOMBAY   CALCUTTA   MADRAS   KARACHI
IBADAN   NAIROBI   DAR ES SALAAM   CAPE TOWN

British Library Cataloguing in Publication Data

Leptin, Gert
   Economic reform in East German industry.
   —(Economic reforms in East European industry).
   1. Industry and state—Germany, East
   2. Germany, East—Industries
   3. Germany, East—Economic policy
   I. Title   II. Melzer, Manfred   III. Series
   388.9431   HC290.78   77–30589

ISBN 0–19–215346–3

Printed in Great Britain by
John Wright & Sons Ltd.,
at the Stonebridge Press, Bristol.

CONTENTS

TABLES

viii

MAPS

FOREWORD

In contrast to what we know of economic changes in the Soviet Union, our knowledge of economic reforms in Eastern Europe is very fragmentary, yet some of these countries have embarked on economic changes more far-reaching than the Soviet Union and/or have put forward proposals and started discussions of greater theoretical sophistication and practical potential than anything we can find in the Soviet Union itself. Also, taken as a whole, communist Eastern Europe represents substantial economic, political, and military potential whose importance within the Soviet Bloc is likely to grow. In sum, Eastern Europe represents a significant and interesting subject, on which we know too little. Taking a broad view, one can argue that there may be overconcentration on research on the Soviet Union, while research on East European countries is neglected.

As a result of this conviction, the Institute of Soviet and East European Studies in the University of Glasgow took the initiative in starting a comprehensive project on Economic Reforms in East Europe. The fact that owing to the political events of 1968 in Poland and then Czechoslovakia a substantial number of East European economists, with first-hand knowledge of their countries, had to seek refuge in the West influenced the timing of our undertaking. This was an opportunity created by most regrettable events, but one which we could not miss.

The present volume marks the end of the series which has also included works on Poland and Rumania. Initially it was hoped to provide additional studies on Yugoslavia, Bulgaria, Czechoslovakia, and Hungary, as well as a separate volume devoted to comparative analysis of economic reforms in Eastern Europe as a whole; but unfortunately, for reasons beyond the editors' control, this has proved impossible.

The Institute's initiative to start the project, of which this book is a part, was supported by a grant from the Social Science Research Council, which is gratefully acknowledged. The readiness of Oxford University Press to publish the results of our research in the form of this series helped us greatly in the organization of the project. We want to express our heartfelt thanks for their collaboration and co-operation.

CO-EDITORS
Alec Nove
Janusz G. Zielinski

A BRIEF STATISTICAL PROFILE

Unless otherwise stated, figures are for 1974. The main source is the 1976 GDR Statistical Yearbook. The figures in brackets are for comparison and relate to the UK and the Federal Republic respectively. Sources for these are the Federal Republic Statistical Yearbook for 1976 and that of the GDR and their international sections, data from the Federal Government Report on the State of the Nation, 1971 and 1974, and *Leistung in Zahlen '75* (Bonn, 1976).

Population: total 16·9 m. (56·0; 62·0), of which male 46·4 per cent (48·6; 47·9), proportion under 15 years of age 22·0 per cent (24·0; 22·0), proportion over 65 years of age 16·0 per cent (14·0; 14·0), density 157 per square km (229; 250), proportion urban-dwellers 75·4 per cent (77·4; —), births minus deaths per 1,000 of population −3·0 (1·3; −1·6), average life expectancy in 1973 (1970–2; 1972–4): men 68·8 years (68·9; 67·9), women 74·2 (75·1; 74·4).

Area and land use: total area 108,178 square km (244,000; 248,600), of which agricultural land 58·1 per cent (77·2; 54·5). Of the agricultural land 77·0 per cent (38·4; 60·0) is arable and 23·0 per cent (61·6; 40·0) pasture.

Employment: proportion of population in employment 49 per cent (45; 1975: 43), of which in manufacturing industry and handicrafts 42·2 per cent (1971: 35·5; 1975: 41·0), construction 7·4 per cent (6·7; 7·1), agriculture and forestry 11·1 per cent (2·5; 6·4) and trade and transport 18·2 per cent (21·1; 20·3).

Contributions of sectors of the economy to national income, 1972 (net material product by Marxist definition): manufacturing industry 61·1 per cent (—; 59·4), construction 8·2 per cent (—; 9·4), agriculture 11·1 per cent (—; 4·2), trade 12·8 per cent (—; 18·1), transport 5·3 per cent (—; 6·7), other productive sectors 1·5 per cent (—; 2·2).
Investment: proportion of 1972 national income (NNP) excluding inventory charges 28·5 per cent (—; 29·1). Structure of investment (1971): manufacturing industry 53·4 per cent (—; 29·0), construction 3·2 per cent (—; 3·5), agriculture and forestry 13·0 per cent (—; 3·2), transport 8·5 per cent (—; 9·1), trade 4·1 per cent (—; 5·7), services 17·8 per cent (—; 49·6). Comparability is affected by differences in the price system.

Consumption and provision of services (per 1,000 inhabitants in 1973): railway network 0·842 km (0·360; 0·522), passenger cars 91 (265; 286), radios (1972) 355 (1970: 330; 307), TV sets (1972) 283 (298; 274), newspapers (1972) 423 (1969: 488; 374), new book titles 0·31 (—; 0·69), doctors 1·72 (1969: 1·22; 1972: 1·84), dentists 0·45 (1969: 0·26; 1972: 0·50), hospital beds 10·9 (1969: 19·8; 1972: 11·3), university students (1972) 6·44 (1969: 6·4; 10·7), dwellings per family 0·98 (—; 0·98).

Food consumption in kilogrammes per head in 1972 (1970–1; 1971–2): grain products 96·3 (73·0; 65·0), potatoes 133·6 (101·8; 101·0), meat 70·8 (76·3; 80·2), fats 26·9 (23·0; 29·5), sugar 35·2 (49·6; 34·0); fresh fruit 37·2 (56·6; 95·9), tropical fruit 14·6 (—; 22).

		GDR		Fe
		1972	1975	197
Area	square km	108,178	108,178	248,5
Population	000	17,043	16,925	61,6
Inhabitants	per square km	158	156	24
Natural increase rate	per 000	−2·0	−3·5	—
Employed population	000	8,266[2]	8,355[1]	27,06
Production of:				
Electric power	mlrd kWh	73	84	27
Gas	million cubic metres	4,794	4,915[1]	17,23
Hard coal	000 tons	816	540	102,47
Brown coal	000 tons	248,451	246,612	110,41
Oil	000 tons	—	—	7,09
Iron ore	000 tons	268[5]	53[5]	6,11
Pig iron[10]	000 tons	2,151	2,420	32,00
Steel[11]	000 tons	6,065	6,445	43,70
Cement	000 tons	8,857	10,656	43,14
Petrol	000 tons	2,507	2,882[1]	15,13
Sawn timber[12]	000 cubic metres	1,952	2,040[1]	9,58
Paper	000 tons	735	794[1]	4,78
Synthetic fibres and thread	000 tons	70	104[1]	64
Nitrogenous fertilizers	000 tons (N)	428	436[1]	1,32
Passenger cars	000	140	159	3,51.
Lorries	000	27	36	30
Diesel oil	000 tons	3,785	4,853[1]	10,08
Radios	000	1,041	1,068	5,49
Washing machines	000	296	369	1,59
Refrigerators	000	442	526	2,66
Beet sugar	000 tons	662	730	2,102
Butter	000 tons	249	273	48
Railway waggons	units	4,432	4,881[1]	—
Ships	000 GRT	1,198	—	1,60
Fish catch	000 tons	323	333[3]	42
Livestock numbers				
Cattle	million	5·38	5·59[1]	13
Pigs	million	10·36	11·52[1]	19
Poultry	million	43·75	45·67[1]	99
Agricultural area	000 hectares	6,291	6,293[1]	13,476
Net agricultural output				
Wheat	000 tons	2,744	2,736	6,608
Rye	000 tons	1,904	1,563	2,914
Barley	000 tons	2,592	3,681	5,997
Potatoes	000 tons	12,140	7,673	15,036
Sugar beet	000 tons	7,223	6,414	14,656
Foreign trade				
Imports	million DM	22,851[16]	39,289[16]	131,133
Exports	million DM	23,931[16]	35,105[16]	151,950

[1] 1974; [2] incl. members of production cooperatives (in agriculture only working members a 27 per cent; [7] metal content 28 per cent; [8] metal content 32 per cent; [9] metal content 50 railway sleepers; [14] 1971; [15] 1970; [16] incl. intra-German trade; [17] 1972.

ublic 1975	Great Britain and Northern Ireland 1972	1975	France 1972	1975	Italy 1972	1975
599	244,044	244,044	547,026	547,026	301,225	301,225
832	55,790	55,962	51,742	52,910	54,345	55,810
249	229	229	95	97	180	185
−2·4	+2·8	+0·6	+6·3	+3·5	+6·7	+6·1[1]
878	25,377	25,310[1]	21,468	22,414	19,028	19,436
302	243	254	163	178	130	141
282[1]	9,315	10,788[3]	6,072	5,988[3]	2,928	3,400[1]
393	119,506[4]	127,800	29,762	22,414	151	4
377	—	—	2,962	3,085	839	1,176[1]
741	84	1,130	1,500	1,076	1,200	1,030
671[6]	9,564[7]	3,324[7]	54,252[8]	54,264[8]	616[9]	658[9]
074	15,317	12,042	18,988	17,924	9,446	11,410
415	25,321	20,012	24,054	21,524	19,813	21,852
516	18,048	16,896	30,114	29,212	33,461	36,309[1]
926[1]	14,054	14,554[1]	15,189	16,848[1]	13,981	14,856[1]
905[1]	627[14]	935[3]	9,500	9,700[1]	2,161	2,102[1]
406[1]	3,289	3,372[1]	3,565	4,154[1]	2,987	3,471[1]
767[1]	374	396[1]	234	238[1]	325	339[1]
473[1]	772	984[1]	1,472	1,694[1]	1,045	1,124[1]
905	1,921	1,268	2,719	2,544	1,719	1,350
286	408	381	298	305	107	113
201[1]	25,133	27,204[1]	9,056	13,063[1]	25,190	29,100[1]
415	1,475	768	2,936	3,547	3,300[15]	1,800[1]
491	1,249	992[1]	1,176	1,862	2,996	2 898
633	984	1,178[1]	652	—	5,424	5,019
238[1]	1,055	758[1]	3,604	3,147[1]	1,141	1,015[1]
518	94	47	514	540	83	76
—	—	6,352[1]	20,415	9,840[1]	1,885	540[1]
109[1]	1,233	1,262[1]	1,129	1,343[1]	948	868[1]
473[3]	1,082	1,144[3]	783	797[3]	414	390[3]
14·36[1]	13·48	15·23[1]	21·75	22·86[1]	8·61	8·41[1]
20·45[1]	8·62	8·62[1]	11·39	11·37[1]	8·20	8·20[1]
96·69[1]	133·21	132·32[1]	190·00	200·00[1]	110·00	110·00[1]
303	18,831[14]	18,683[3]	33,035[15]	32,515[17]	17,649[14]	17,484[3]
014	4,760	6,126[1]	18,123	19,100[1]	9,423	9,577[1]
125	—	14[1]	328	312[1]	—	37[1]
971	9,239	9,126[1]	10,426	9,972[1]	—	552[1]
853	6,441	6,791[1]	7,966	7,592[1]	3,002	2,896[1]
203	6,350	4,609[1]	18,669	22,114[1]	10,685	7,800[1]
655[16]	89,688	131,001	85,535	133,434	62,045	94,375
511[16]	78,383	107,646	82,881	128,440	59,683	85,681

lidates); [3] 1973; [4] excl. Northern Ireland; [5] metal content 25 per cent; [6] metal content
; [10] incl. ferro-alloys; [11] in billets and liquid for casting; [12] excl. railway sleepers; [13] incl.

MAIN POLITICAL EVENTS
IN THE GDR SINCE 1949

7 October 1949

The German Democratic Republic (GDR) was founded on 7 October 1949. On that day the Second German People's Council, essentially dominated by the Socialist Unity Party of Germany (SED), was constituted as a 'provisional national chamber', i.e. as the parliament envisaged in the constitution worked out for the GDR by the First German People's Council. Thereby, following the foundation of the Federal Republic of Germany in the Western zones, independent statehood commenced in the Soviet occupation zone too, and thus Germany was divided into two states. The cause of this development was presumably less a conscious policy of division by East or West—as both sides subsequently asserted again and again—but rather the inability of the two principal victorious powers of the Second World War, the USA and the USSR, to balance their conflicting interests and agree on a common policy towards Germany.

17 June 1953

As a consequence of the announcement of increases in work norms there were strikes and demonstrations in East Berlin and the surrounding districts on 16 June 1953. After a demonstration march to the 'house of ministries' in East Berlin, which was basically started by construction workers and which other workers joined, the protests became a general demand for improvement of living conditions and finally for free elections. On 17 June the demonstrations increased—in particular with the march of 12,000 workers from the Henningsdorf steel works to Berlin—to a general uprising of the people demanding the removal of the communist régime. Simultaneously uprisings developed in all the major cities of the GDR. By declaring a state of emergency and putting Soviet troops into Berlin and more than 120 other cities the uprising was put down.

13 August 1961

The increasing political pressure on Berlin since Khrushchev's ultimatum of 27 November 1958, and the measures against farmers (the conclusion of agricultural collectivization in 1960), had led to a renewed rise in the movement of refugees from the GDR to West Germany since 1959 (1959: 144,000; 1960: 199,000). In the first seven months of 1961 the number of refugees swelled to over 155,000, and early on the morning of 13 August the Berlin sector frontiers were blocked by police and enterprise task forces and movement from East Berlin to West Berlin was forbidden for East Berliners and inhabitants of the GDR. The measures were allegedly carried out at the suggestion of the member countries of the Warsaw Pact. Ten days later, on 23 August 1961, entry to East Berlin by West Berliners was also forbidden or made subject to special permission which was only granted in rare exceptional cases.

19 March and 21 May 1970

The meetings between the Federal Chancellor, Willy Brandt, and the Chairman of the GDR Council of Ministers, Willi Stoph, in Erfurt (GDR) and Kassel ushered in a new phase in intra-German relations. The conclusion that, because of the world political situation and, particularly, relations between the USA and the USSR, reunification of Germany could not be brought about in the foreseeable future, but that the easing of tension between the great powers should be used to benefit the population in both parts of Germany, led to the attempt to achieve concrete improvements in mutual relations, especially in the so-called 'humanitarian field', while maintaining their respective basic political positions. These efforts and the simultaneous improvement in relations between the Federal Republic and the East (treaties with the USSR and Poland) were at the same time an essential element in the general relaxation of East–West tension.

3 May 1971

The retirement of Walter Ulbricht from the office of First Secretary of the SED and his replacement by Erich Honnecker marks the end of a political epoch in the GDR and its significance extends beyond the actual grounds for this retirement—increasing economic difficulties in the GDR and resistance, in the form of delaying tactics, to the easing of East–West tension which he regarded as being at the expense of the GDR. The significance of the 'Ulbricht era' for the GDR is somewhat comparable to that of the 'Adenauer era' for the Federal Republic, to which it displays certain basic structural similarities: starting from the interests of the occupying power and adhering closely to their respective policies, both men sought to extend their own scope for political manœuvre and make use of it for the benefit of the part of the German population for which they bore direct responsibility.

3 September 1971

After months of stubborn negotiations in the building of the former Allied Control Commission the four-power agreement on Berlin was signed in Berlin. This agreement is the kernel of the East–West treaties and is closely and also formally connected with the treaties between the Federal Republic and the USSR and Poland as well as with the treaties concluded later between the GDR and the Federal Republic. The four-power agreement on Berlin (the 'Berlin Agreement') regulates both relations between the two parts of Berlin and between West Berlin and the GDR and also between Berlin and the Federal Republic ('. . . as hitherto not a constitutional part . . .'). As well as this, the agreement contains the first treaty regulations on rights of access to Berlin and thus gives a framework for the additional agreements between the GDR and the Federal Republic which were concluded later in the traffic treaty and the treaty of principles.

21 December 1972

The signing of the treaty on the principles underlying relations between the Federal Republic of Germany and the German Democratic Republic created the basis for a whole series of negotiations which were subsequently entered into with the aim of producing new regulations on substantial areas of mutual relations. Even though the nature of these negotiations and their results is like that of negotiations between two states, their effect on how men live together in both parts of Germany is of considerable internal political importance.

ABBREVIATIONS

BWR (Bezirkswirtschaftsrat)—Regional economic council

CC—Central Committee (of the SED)

DIW (Deutsches Institut für Wirtschaftsforschung)—German Institute for Economic Research (West Berlin)

DM—Deutsche Mark

FDGB (Freier Deutscher Gewerkschaftsbund)—Free German Trade Union Association

ESS—Economic System of Socialism

GDR—German Democratic Republic

LPG (Landwirtschaftliche Produktions Genossenschaft)—Agricultural Production Cooperative

MVN (Materialverbrauchsnormen)—Material use norms

MW—Megawatt

NES—New Economic System

SED (Sozialistische Einheitspartei Deutschlands)—Socialist Unity Party of Germany (Communist Party)

VEB (Volkseigener Betrieb)—Nationalized enterprise

VEK (Volkseigener Kombinat)—Nationalized combine

VVB (Vereinigung Volkseigener Betriebe)—Association of nationalized enterprises

DEFINITIONS

Accounting unit: agreed accounting basis for intra-German trade. Its value corresponds to the (Western) DM.

Age breakdown, age structure: division of the population into age groups.

Balance of payments: trade balance plus services and net capital movements.

Capital intensity: gross capital stock per employee.

Capital productivity: gross production per unit of gross capital stock.

Consumption rate: proportion of private and public consumption in gross social product; in the narrower sense: proportion of consumption by private households (private consumption) in gross social product.

Cooperation community: form of cooperation between combines and enterprises of the same or different organizational subordination, in order jointly to shape the production process or individual phases of it. The principal application is in provincially managed industry to overcome diffusion of production facilities. The basis of the cooperation community is the cooperation agreement. Its primary purpose is improvement of the quality of the products, reduction of costs and adoption of better techniques.

Cooperation union: contractually fixed form of cooperation between producers of finished products and important suppliers to ensure production of important products. The purpose is both to achieve higher quality of the final products and also cost savings, reduction of delivery times, and maintenance of even quality in the products. The juridical basis of cooperation in the cooperation union is a cooperation agreement which lays down both the rights and duties of the participating enterprises and the tasks and the mode of operation of the organs (cooperation council, working groups).

Cost-benefit thinking: thinking oriented towards profitability, concentrating on the comparison of cost and revenue for every economic transaction.

Disposable income of private households: total amount of net wages and salaries, public and private transfer payments (e.g. pensions, sick pay) and distributed profits and private income from capital.

Factor productivity: labour productivity and/or capital productivity.

Foreign currency Mark: accounting magnitude for the statistical returns on GDR foreign trade. It corresponds to the (Western) DM before the 1961 revaluation.

Foreign trade intensity: foreign trade as a proportion of social product.

Foreign trade turnover: imports and exports.

Gross capital investment: total value of the new plants added to the available gross capital stock in a period (buildings and equipment).

Gross capital stock: value of all plant available in a period (buildings and equipment).

Gross social product: sum of the net value of production (gross value of production less the goods and services used in production) received by residents (permanent inhabitants of a state) at home and abroad, valued at market prices.

Gross value of production: sum of sales, self-produced equipment, plus or minus change in stocks; it contains all domestic and foreign payments.

Industrial structure: proportion of individual branches of industry in gross value of production, in number of employees and in the capital stock of industry as a whole.

Intra-German trade: earlier intra-zonal trade; trade between the GDR and the Federal Republic.

Investment rate: proportion of gross capital investment in gross social product.

Labour productivity: value of production per employee.

Net profit: difference between total profit and production capital charge.

Net profit deduction: part of net profit payable to the state (via the VVB).

Net social product: gross social product less depreciation allowance according to usage.

Participation rate: proportion of persons gainfully employed or capable of working (actually employed plus unemployed) in the resident population.

Population density: inhabitants per unit of area.

Potential labour force: persons gainfully employed and others capable of working.

Principle of earning one's own resources: whereby enterprise is responsible for procuring and earning the financial resources to finance its investment.

Principle of economic accounting: recording and presentation of enterprise performance according to costs, in money form, with increased consideration of cost-benefit thinking.

Production capital charge: interest rate of 6 per cent levied by the state on all enterprise gross capital goods and working capital, which may not be charged as a cost but is payable out of profit.

Purchasing fund: part of the available income which is used by the population within a definite period for the purchase of consumer goods and services.

Social product: see Gross social product.

Structure-determining tasks: tasks which are crucial for the development of the future structure of the national economy.

Supply industries: enterprises which produce raw materials or basic and auxiliary materials or semi-finished products. They provide partial assemblies or semi-finished products for the enterprises which undertake the further processing.

System of economic levers: inter-coordinated system of economic policy measures.

Trade balance: comparison of imports and exports.

Working capital: resources for financing enterprise circulation (e.g. for materials, stocks of production, unfinished products).

IMPORTANT GDR PERIODICALS

Die Arbeit (Labour). On the theory and practice of trade unions. Published by the federal board of the FDGB. Berlin.

Arbeit und Arbeitsrecht (Labour and labour law). On socialist labour and labour law. Berlin.

DDR Aussenwirtschaft (GDR foreign trade). Information, documents, and trade fairs bulletin. Berlin.

DDR—Verkehr (GDR transport). On complex problems of planning and management of transport. Berlin.

Einheit (Unity). On the theory and practice of scientific socialism. Published by the Central Committee of SED. Berlin.

Der Handel (Trade). On the theory and practice of internal trade in the GDR. Berlin.

IPW Berichte des Instituts für Internationale Politik und Wirtschaft (Reports of the Institute for International Politics and Economics). Berlin.

Kommunale Dienstleistungen (Communal services). Specialist periodical on theory and practice. Organ of the Institute of Communal Services. Dresden.

Kooperation (Cooperation). On socialist agriculture and food production. Berlin.

Marktforschung (Market research). Reports of the Institute of Market Research. Leipzig.

Neue Deutsche Bauernzeitung (New German farmers' newspaper). Organ of the Central Committee of the SED. Berlin.

Sozialistische Arbeitswissenschaft (Socialist labour studies). Theoretical periodical for the scientific study of labour. Berlin.

Sozialistische Finanzwirtschaft (Socialist finance). Berlin.

Sozialversicherung/Arbeitsschutz (Social insurance/labour protection). FDGB periodical. Berlin.

Staat und Recht (State and law). Published by the 'Walter Ulbricht' German Academy for political and legal studies. Berlin.

Statistische Praxis (Statistical practice). On accounting and statistics. Published by the State Central Administration for Statistics. Berlin.

Die Technik (Technology). Scientific and technical periodical on fundamental and sectional questions. Berlin.

Die Wirtschaft (The economy). On politics, economics, and technology. Berlin.

Wirtschaftsrecht (Economic law). On the theory and practice of socialist economic law. Berlin.

Wirtschaftswissenschaft (Economic science). Berlin.

Wissenschaftliche Zeitschrift der Hochschule für Ökonomie (Scientific journal of the Higher School of Economics). Berlin.

Regional structure of employment in the GDR

Source: *Ökonomische Geographie der Deutschen Demokratischen Republik,*
2nd Edition, Leipzig, 1970, 93

Majority of labour force in district:

in industry

<40%

40–50%

>50%

in agriculture, forestry, or water supply

<40%

40–50%

>50%

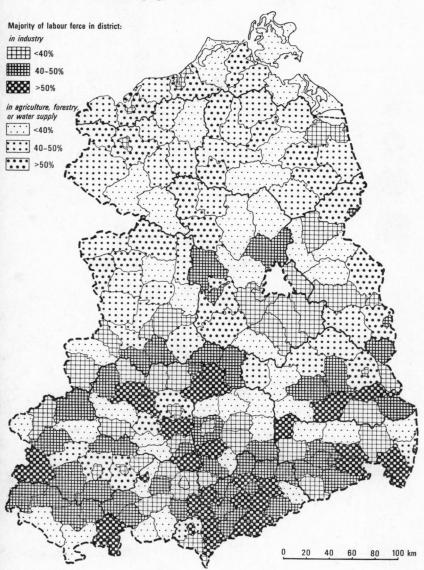

0   20   40   60   80   100 km

Settlements of over 5000 inhabitants in the GDR

Source: *Ökonomische Geographie der Deutschen Demokratischen Republik*, 2nd Edition, Leipzig, 1970, 109

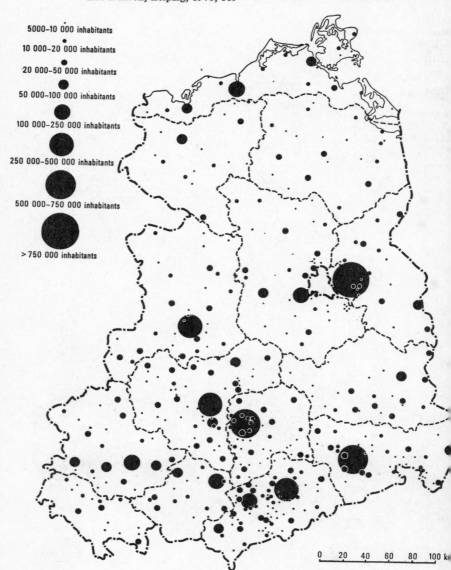

5000–10 000 inhabitants

10 000–20 000 inhabitants

20 000–50 000 inhabitants

50 000–100 000 inhabitants

100 000–250 000 inhabitants

250 000–500 000 inhabitants

500 000–750 000 inhabitants

> 750 000 inhabitants

0   20   40   60   80   100 km

Provinces and Districts in the GDR

Source: Ökonomische Geographie der Deutschen Demokratischen Republik,
2nd Edition, Leipzig, 1970, 17

Boundaries:
- - - - Provincial boundaries (from 1946)
- · - · - State boundaries
———— District boundaries (from 1952)

Rostock

MECKLENBURG

Neubrandenburg

Schwerin

BRANDENBURG

West Berlin

East Berlin

Magdeburg

Potsdam

Frankfurt

SACHSEN-ANHALT

Cottbus

Halle

Leipzig

SACHSEN

Dresden

Erfurt

THÜRINGEN

Gera

Karl-Marx-Stadt

Suhl

0   20   40   60   80   100 km

CHAPTER I

THE BACKGROUND AND CAUSES OF THE REFORM

I.1 Introduction

The statement that the history of the Soviet economy is the history of its reforms is neither new nor original. This does not mean, however, that it is incorrect. Furthermore, the same statement can be made with equal justification for the German Democratic Republic, and indeed for most of the other East European countries too. This conformity in their development raises questions as to whether and how far the same causes determined the economic reforms in these countries, where special factors were at work, and what common or particular solutions were found for the problems arising.

Within the framework of the economic reforms begun in Eastern Europe at the beginning of the 1960s there are several reasons for claiming the GDR reform to be of particular interest. For one, the GDR, as early as 1963, was the first state in the Eastern Bloc to draw concrete conclusions for the shaping of its own economy from the Soviet Liberman discussion of the summer and autumn of 1962. Furthermore, the external effects of the GDR reform—particularly on the Soviet economic reform of 1965—were so obvious that not only was it seen as a general prototype but, in Federal Germany at least, the question was seriously discussed whether the Soviet Union had used the GDR and its economy as a field for experiment—like the famous experimental enterprises Bolshevichka and Mayak in the Soviet Union itself later. And finally the GDR reform deserves special investigation because, after some fundamental corrections to its conception of reform in 1968 and 1969, the GDR took a number of measures at the end of 1970 and more in 1971 which, taken together, amount to a complete break with the conceptions of reform embodied in the 1963 'New Economic System' (NES) and must thus be seen as an unequivocal and presumably final termination of the reform. The question whether this reversal of the GDR reform is also a prototype for any further reforms in other East European countries can only be answered if the factors in the GDR economy that led to the reform are analysed. The common factors which are valid for all East European countries and the specific ones which apply only to the GDR must be distinguished and weighed up against each other.

The political background of the GDR must be examined and the economic situation at the end of the 1950s and beginning of the 1960s set out. Finally, we shall describe the background and the beginning of the reform and give a characterization of the 'New Economic System'.

I.2 The conditions of development of the GDR economy until the beginning of the 'New Economic System'

GENERAL AND SPECIFIC CONDITIONS OF DEVELOPMENT IN THE GDR

The general problems of socialist economies, which in the GDR, as in other countries of Eastern Europe, have recently compelled reforms, will be mentioned only briefly. These are—apart from the permanent need for organizational adaptations—primarily difficulties which stem from the common economic system, extensively modelled on the Soviet prototype. They include problems of rapid and precise information at the different levels of decision-making; problems of choice of goal and the associated conflicts of interest which are coming more and more clearly to light between different social groups, in particular between the political leadership and the mass of workers and consumers; planning problems; and problems of management, control, and bonuses. Among the planning problems the principal difficulties are the forecasting of the structure of the economy; the ensuring of balanced growth; the connection between branch and regional planning; the harmonization of physical and monetary planning; price problems; the balancing of material balances; and in particular the ensuring of material-technical supplies. The problems of management include the translation of aggregate economic planning, in a direct or indirect way, into enterprise plans; ensuring the consistency of the system of indicators for enterprises; enterprises' striving for 'soft plans'; the creation of hidden reserves of materials and capacity; and the middle managers' and functionaries' fear of undertaking responsibility. This list is by no means exhaustive and can always be further expanded.

Besides these difficulties, which are more or less common to all East European countries, each individual country has its particular development problems, which stem essentially from its geographical position and its history. The particular problem of the GDR is her position *vis-à-vis* Western Europe: she is the most exposed to Western Europe, has the closest economic and cultural links with this region and—like Czechoslovakia—the highest level of economic development. This combination of factors gave the GDR its role as western outpost of the 'socialist camp'. This function as an outpost conflicts to a certain extent with the consequences of her historical development: even though the GDR always behaves internally and externally as a liberated socialist state and one of the victorious powers of the Second World War, she cannot escape the consequences of her origin in the German Reich. This was shown in the early post-war years in the massive dismantling and removal of production capacity and infrastructure, which surely exceeded the corresponding measures in West Germany; it continued with extensive drawings on current production for reparations purposes, and is expressed today in the one-sided concentration of GDR foreign trade on the Soviet Union (with about 30 per cent of the total trade turnover). Approximately half of GDR exports to the Soviet Union consists of machinery and equipment, and more than one-quarter of Soviet imports of machinery and equipment comes from the GDR. The satisfaction of Soviet requirements for these goods must be seen as one of the dominant and constant factors in GDR economic policy and indeed in her overall general political objectives.

The other dominant constant factor in the development of the GDR, which distinguishes her from all the other socialist countries of Europe, stems from the division of Germany. Even though this division seems to have been stabilized for the foreseeable future by the Eastern Treaties of the Federal Republic, and the existence of the GDR is therefore no longer directly in question, she is nevertheless in a special situation: 'competition between capitalism and socialism' is something different for the GDR and her political leadership than for the other countries of Eastern Europe, including the Soviet Union. It is not so abstract, not so cut off from the real life of the political leadership and, what is more important, of the population. In the GDR competition means direct comparison with the Federal Republic, with the 'West German economic miracle'. This competition takes place before the eyes of the population of both parts of Germany. The GDR can restrict and impede personal contacts and correspondence, but radio and television from the Federal Republic, and particularly commercial television advertising, provide the citizen of the GDR with extensive information. This had political consequences for the GDR leadership which no other communist leadership in Europe faced: however strained the relationship in these other countries between the population and the political leadership, the leadership still served as the champion of the population's national interests *vis-à-vis* the outside world and particularly *vis-à-vis* the Soviet Union. In the GDR this was only partly so. There—at least in the consciousness of the population, if not in reality—there was always a national alternative, namely the Federal Republic. This basic factor was a permanent element making the

GDR leadership insecure and increasing its dependence on Soviet support, which in turn was seen by the population as confirmation of its doubts about the leadership. The GDR and her leadership may have succeeded, by dint of their economic efforts and progress, in reaching a favourable economic situation in comparison with other East European states. Yet this is certainly not sufficient to compensate for the difficulties which stem from the GDR's political situation.

THE POLITICAL BACKGROUND OF THE REFORMS

During the greater part of the GDR's development an additional element of political disintegration was the existence of the 'open frontier', that is, of free movement between East and West Berlin. This offered the population of the GDR the possibility of a relatively simple way of escaping the intensity of political pressure and the economic gap between East and West Germany. Between 1949 and 1969 around 2·9 million [1] mostly younger citizens of the GDR took advantage of this possibility, with the peaks in 1953 and 1960–1 undoubtedly caused by political events. In 1953 indignation over an administratively decreed increase in norms produced a general uprising, the suppression of which led to the number of refugees swelling from 182,393 in 1952 to 331,390 in 1953. In 1960–1 both the conclusion of agricultural collectivization and the increasing pressure being brought on West Berlin caused a new climb in the number of refugees. The increasing external pressure on West Berlin from the Soviet Union was prompted by two main factors: the refugees and the growing strain on the labour supply in the GDR, and the effect which the possibility of easy departure had on some of those who remained—since in principle this way was open to them too they did not feel compelled to adapt to the existing conditions in the GDR. It is therefore understandable that both the GDR leadership and the Soviet leadership were concerned to eliminate these disruptive influences which stemmed from the existence of West Berlin. Just as the Soviet Union had tried in 1948 to drive the Western Allies out of Berlin by the blockade of the city, Khrushchev now tried to solve the Berlin problem as he saw it by the ultimatum of 27 November 1957, which described the Allied agreements over the occupation zones of Germany as 'no longer in force' and demanded the transformation of West Berlin into a 'free city' within six months. The pressure on Berlin continued after the expiry of the six months and was reinforced by repeated threats of the conclusion of a 'separate peace' between the Soviet Union and the GDR. As a result of these threats the number of refugees to West Berlin grew—from 143,900 in 1959 to 199,200 in 1960. In the first seven and a half months of 1961 alone there were a further 155,000. On 13 August 1961 the 'open frontier' was closed by the building of the Berlin wall.

Another reason for the increasing numbers of refugees at the beginning of the sixties was the intensification of the policy of socializing craftsmen and particularly farmers. Following the establishment of the first agricultural production cooperative (LPG) in 1952, some 10,000 LPGs had been formed with state support by the end of 1959, working 45 per cent of the agricultural land area of the GDR. In the first three and a half months of 1960 the remaining farmers were induced, by a large-scale state campaign, to enter cooperatives 'voluntarily'. The number of LPGs had doubled by 31 May 1960, to almost 19,300 and their share of the agricultural land area rose to over 84 per cent. These measures not only produced a sharp increase in the proportion of farmers among refugees but also led to a clear set-back in agricultural production (yields per hectare, labour productivity) and to a deterioration in supplies to the population.

THE ECONOMIC BACKGROUND OF THE REFORMS

Although these political factors had an undoubted influence on the GDR economic reform of 1963, economic policy decisions and economic developments were the principal determinants of the reform. It is very difficult to establish the beginning of the chain of events which led to the reform, but it may be expedient to start with the directive of the Third Socialist Unity Party (SED) conference (23 and 24 March 1956) for the second GDR five-year plan for the years 1956–60. The objectives set by this directive were relatively demanding. National income (net social product in the material production sphere) was to rise by 45 per cent; production of manufacturing industries by as much as 55 per cent. Since simultaneously a growth of 50 per cent in labour productivity in the manufacturing industry was planned it is clear that at that time the planning authorities were still counting on an increase in the industrial labour force. As the plan at the same time provided for intensified cooperation with the Comecon countries it is no wonder that the course of the GDR economy was also affected by the disturbances which emanated from the Polish and Hungarian events of 1956. At any rate, a year and a half after passing the directive for the second five-year plan the leadership of the SED felt itself compelled, at the 33rd meeting of the Central Committee (16–19 October 1957), to set new and substantially reduced plan targets. On the basis of these resolutions the law on the second five-year plan was drafted and published on 9 January 1958, two years after the beginning of the plan period.

Despite this delay it was still overtaken at the moment it was published. In the second half of 1957 and in 1958 economic development proceeded far more favourably than had been anticipated. As the Soviet Union had abandoned her sixth five-year plan and replaced it by a seven-year plan for 1959–65, and as the second post-war boom was coming to an end in the Federal Republic and growth rates were sinking, it seemed expedient to the political leadership of the GDR, in order to synchronize its plans with those of the Soviet Union, and in view of its improved position in the competition with the Federal Republic, to get rid of the five-year plan which was no longer suitable and, like the Soviet Union, work out a seven-year plan for 1959–65. The appropriate resolution was adopted at the Fifth SED Congress which took place on 10–16 July 1958. The 'principal economic task' set was to catch up and overtake West Germany in *per capita* production of the major foodstuffs and consumer goods by 1961—an aim which, in view of the GDR's favourable development and the faltering growth in the Federal Republic, seemed by no means unrealistic. Of course a condition for success was the stabilizing of the employment situation and a further increase in labour productivity. This was what was meant by 'the principal economic task'. In practice it was a challenge to the population: 'Stay here, make an effort, and soon it will no longer be worth going to West Germany.' The success of the whole seven-year plan depended on the response to this challenge.

The actual development was quite different from what the SED leadership had expected. The economic setback in West Germany was very short, and quickly and smoothly passed into a new upswing with rising growth rates. On the other hand, long years of experience of broken promises had made the population of the GDR sceptical and hard to convince. In addition, the political measures against West Berlin which we have described and the collectivization of the farmers, with the consequent flight of farmers, were not calculated to create the necessary confidence. Migration to the West continued and the growth of labour productivity in the GDR fell further behind that of the Federal Republic; whereas a gap of 15 per cent was mentioned for 1958, Ulbricht put the productivity gap of GDR industry in 1963 at 25 per cent.[1] Thus the conditions for the success of the seven-year plan and of the principal economic task were not fulfilled. The principal economic task was dropped in 1961 and the seven-year plan, which in practice collapsed in 1961, was formally annulled at the Sixth Congress of the SED early in 1963 with the announcement of a new long-term plan for 1963–70.

[1] According to West German calculations the gap in 1970 amounted to at least 35 per cent: see [2].

The variations in the GDR's economic growth rates can be seen in Table 2, which shows the stagnation of investment and the development of national income and of the gross output of the manufacturing industry.

Table 2: *National income, gross output of manufacturing industry, and investment*

| | National income | | Gross output of manufacturing industry | | Investment | |
	mlrd M	percentage increase	mlrd M	percentage increase	mlrd M	percentage increase
1955	52·6	—	44·8	—	8·0	—
1956	54·7	4·0	47·6	6·2	10·0	25·0
1957	58·5	6·9	51·2	7·6	10·8	8·0
1958	64·9	10·9	57·0	11·3	12·1	12·0
1959	70·4	8·5	64·2	12·6	14·1	16·5
1960	73·6	4·5	69·4	8·1	15·6	10·6
1961	76·0	3·3	73·5	5·9	15·6	0·0
1962	77·6	2·1	80·1	9·0	15·9	2·0
1963	79·7	2·7	83·5	4·2	16·7	5·0

Sources: GDR statistical yearbooks.

A further problem, which cannot be seen from this table, is the difficulty which the GDR has with technical progress. The inadequacy of the impulses which arise for technical progress is a consequence of, on the one hand, insufficient enterprise incentives, and, on the other, the GDR's one-sided trade concentration on the Comecon countries, especially the Soviet Union. The GDR has a sure market for her investment goods in the Soviet Union. The fact that she encounters practically no competition in this market, which in comparison with the GDR's own economy is less developed, leads to a tendency to adapt to the lower level of development of this market. As a result the GDR is falling relatively behind and is in danger of losing her vanguard position and the associated opportunities for political influence.

The scarcity of labour, which was stabilized but not removed by the building of the Berlin wall, and the problems of technical progress, determined the conditions under which the GDR could achieve further economic growth. Since no additional labour was available, growth could only take place through increased labour productivity. This required primarily rationalization investments. But even where the state established structural centres of gravity by large direct investments in new enterprises, rationalization investments in existing enterprises were necessary in order to release the labour required for the new enterprises. The consequence was that the GDR had to undertake a fundamental change in investment policy. Rationalization investments in existing enterprises cannot be ordered from above. Opportunities for it can only be recognized in the enterprises themselves. The new policy enforced by the conditions for growth could thus only be implemented by extending the powers of enterprises in the sphere of investment. However, this could not fail to affect the remaining enterprise decision spheres, and thus gave rise to the necessity for a general revision of the relationship between enterprise and extra-enterprise planning and of the whole planning and steering system.

I.3 The preparation and beginning of the reform

Discussions about a fundamental reform of the economic system in the GDR began as much as six or seven years before the introduction of the New Economic System. Early in 1957 the journal *Wirtschaftswissenschaft* (no. 3, special issue) published two articles [3, 4], one by Professor Fritz Behrens and the other by Dr. Arne Benary, in which they criticized the methods of planning and directing the economy of the GDR. In particular they objected to what they regarded as the excessive centralization of economic decision-making and the bureaucratization of economic administration that inevitably ensued. To eliminate the deficiencies to which this led and to improve the day-to-day performance of the economy, they proposed 'increased use of commodity-money-relations' and regard for 'the law of value', that is, monetary, indirect methods of steering. At the same time they wanted to give the state bank a greater influence on economic processes.

These proposals immediately encountered the most vehement opposition from the leading party bodies, who saw in them an attempt to limit the direct influence of the state and party bureaucracy on economic administration and thus to remove an essential element of their political power. In the same issue of *Wirtschaftswissenschaft* critical comments by party officials denounced the 'anti-party', revisionist character of Behrens's and Benary's theses. The attacks on the two authors were repeated more sharply in the following months in other journals. In addition, reprisals were taken against the authors: Behrens lost his position as director of the state central statistical administration, and Benary was removed from the economics department of the German Academy of Sciences and transferred to work 'at ground level', i.e. to an industrial enterprise (the Oberspree cable works).

The Behrens–Benary affair has been swamped by the publicity

attracted by the other, much more recent, precursor of the New Economic System, the Soviet Liberman discussion of 1962. On 9 September 1962 the Soviet economist Professor E. Liberman, from the Engineering-Economics Institute in Kharkov, published an article in *Pravda* with the title 'Plan, Profit, Bonus', in which he proposed a fundamental reform of the enterprise planning system and suggested—which was an unusual innovation in Soviet conditions—the use of profit or a special profit rate indicator as a measure for evaluating enterprise activity and as the basis for bonuses for the labour force.

In the following months Liberman's proposals led to an extensive, lively, and surprisingly professional discussion, principally in *Pravda*, but in other Soviet newspapers and journals too, and also to exhaustive reproduction of the discussion and to the adoption of various different individual positions in almost all European countries in the Eastern Bloc.

In the GDR the Liberman discussion was followed with particular interest. At first the press confined itself to reprinting the Soviet discussion, comprehensively to be sure, but without comment. After the first secretary of the SED, Walter Ulbricht, at the 17th Plenum of the Central Committee in October 1962, had indicated the necessity of alterations to the GDR economic system, the first articles appeared which applied Liberman's arguments to the GDR economy.

The first to recognize Liberman's proposals as basically progressive were Alfred Dost and Walter Halbritter in two articles in the newspaper *Die Wirtschaft*, 31 October 1962; at the same time, however, they pointed out the deficiencies of the existing price system, which stood in the way of the rapid and comprehensive introduction of such reforms. Equally cautious was Professor Werner Kalweit in his extensive essay 'Bonuses for modern or for obsolete techniques', which appeared in *Neues Deutschland* on 15 November 1962. He criticized the chief enterprise indicators, gross output and commodity output, because they led to one-sided concentration on quantitative plan fulfilment at the expense of the quality of products, and also declared himself against the multiplicity of enterprise indicators, but simultaneously he rejected profit as the chief indicator. The grounds he cited were also the deficiencies of the price system.

In view of such reservations it was bound to come as a surprise when Ulbricht, at the Sixth Congress of the SED, on 15 January 1963, revealed proposals for the reform of the GDR economy which showed the far-reaching influence of the Liberman discussion. Not only the individual reform measures themselves but also the formulations in which Ulbricht presented them to the delegates at the party congress made that clear. Thus, for example—without of course mentioning Liberman—he spoke of the hitherto customary 'petty tutelage' of state enterprises and their superior associations and pointed out that 'what benefits society ... must also benefit the individual socialist enterprise and its workforce' [5].

The technical details of Ulbricht's reform proposals were—in so far as this was possible—tried initially on a small scale in ten nationalized enterprises (VEB) and four associations of nationalized enterprises (VVB). The results of the 'economic experiments' were once again exhaustively discussed at a special economic conference of the Central Committee at the end of June 1963. In a big speech Ulbricht expounded again, and in considerably more detail than at the party congress, the reforms envisaged. On this occasion it became clear that this was a matter of substantially more thorough-going reforms than on any previous occasion and that the GDR was not thereby merely completing another step in the Soviet line of development, but for the first time was seeking its own way out of the problems of economic organization.

On 11 July 1963 the Council of Ministers approved the basic document for the economic reform, the 'Principles for the New Economic System of Planning and Management of the National Economy' [6]. In these principles the New Economic System was defined as: 'the organic combination of: (a) scientifically based leadership in the economy, and (b) scientifically grounded central state planning of the long term, together with (c) the comprehensive use of material interest in the shape of the consistent system of economic levers' [6, p. 454].

There are therefore two main spheres which must be discussed in order to characterize the New Economic System: first, the sphere of state planning, which covers both aggregate and sectoral 'central' state planning and also the participation of enterprises in the preparation and implementation of this planning and, secondly, the reforms in the sphere of enterprise management both on the scale of the whole economy and within the enterprise. This includes—besides the problems of organizational structure—the instruments available and those to be newly created for the purpose of steering the course of enterprises in accordance with the central plan.

Table 3: Indicators of economic development of the GDR, 1961–5

| | Real percentage increase over previous year | | | | | Total increase |
	1961	1962	1963	1964	1965	1961–65
National income produced	1·6	2·7	3·5	4·9	4·6	18
Manufacturing industry						
Gross product	5·8	·6·7	4·6	6·6	6·2	34
Net product[1]	—	—	—	5·2	4·4	26
Labour productivity[2]	5·7	6·7	5·0	6·6	5·6	33
Construction						
Construction and repairs done	2·3	5·7	1·3	9·9	8·4	31
Net product	—	—	—	13·0	7·7	25
Labour productivity	4·0	6·8	0·9	9·8	6·5	31
Agriculture						
Net product	—	—	—	2·8	6·3	1
State yields per hectare						
Cattle (excl. poultry)	4·8	−13·4	13·3	10·6	9·4	24
Milk	1·5	−6·5	6·3	3·3	12·0	17
Eggs	8·0	−12·3	7·1	20·2	9·5	34
Grain	−9·4	12·2	−1·5	7·4	9·7	18
Transport, post, communications						
Net product	—	—	—	8·8	0·8	18
Trade						
Net product	—	—	—	6·3	5·7	15
'Social consumption'	5·9	−0·7	0·4	4·7	7·7	20
'Individual consumption'	4·3	−0·7	0·7	3·5	4·0	12
Total retail trade turnover[3]	5·8	−0·7	0·3	3·3	4·3	14
Food and consumer goods	5·2	1·6	1·3	3·3	3·6	16
Industrial goods	6·7	−3·4	−0·9	3·2	5·1	11
Gross capital investment[4]	1·3	2·4	2·3	9·7	9·3	27
Foreign trade turnover[5]	3·0	5·7	5·4	10·3	5·6	34
Exports	3·4	4·2	14·1	8·1	4·7	39
Imports	2·6	7·0	−3·2	13·0	6·7	28
Income of the population[6]	3·3	−1·3	1·2	5·2	4·6	13

[1] including productive handicrafts (excl. building); [2] gross output per worker and employee (excl. apprentices); [3] increase at current prices; [4] excl. general repairs; [5] total imports and exports, incl. intra-German trade, excl. services, in foreign currency marks at current prices; [6] net money incomes.

Sources: GDR statistical yearbooks: DIW calculations (cf. DDR-Wirtschaft. Eine Bestandsaufnahme, Appendix of tables); Neues Deutschland, 19 June 1971.
    Taken from Peter Mitzscherling, 'Die Wirtschaft der DDR', in Die Wirtschaft Osteuropas zu Beginn der 70er Jahre, ed. Hans-Hermann Höhmann, Stuttgart, 1972, p. 55.

References to Chapter I

1. *A bis Z. Ein Taschen- und Nachschlagebuch über den anderen Teil Deutschlands* (A to Z. A pocket information book on the other part of Germany). Bonn, 1969, p. 211.

2. 'Arbeitsproduktivität in der Industrie der DDR und der Bundesrepublik—ein Vergleich' (Labour productivity in manufacturing industry in the GDR and the Federal Republic—a comparison) by Herbert Wilkers, *Wochenbericht des DIW* (Weekly Bulletin of the German Economic Institute), no. 20, 1970, pp. 137ff.

3. Fritz Behrens, 'Zum Problem der Ausnutzung ökonomischer Gesetze in der Übergangsperiode' (On the problem of the use of economic laws in the transition period), *Wirtschaftswissenschaft*, East Berlin, 1957, no. 3, Special Issue, pp. 105–40.

4. Arne Benary, 'Zu Grundproblemen der politischen Ökonomie des Sozialismus in der Übergangsperiode' (On basic problems of the political economy of socialism in the transition period), *Wirtschaftswissenschaft*, East Berlin, 1957, no. 3, Special Issue, pp. 62–94.

5. Walter Ulbricht, 'Das Program des Sozialismus und die geschichtliche Aufgabe der Sozialistischen Einheitspartei Deutschlands' (The programme of socialism and the historical task of the Socialist Unity Party of Germany), *Neues Deutschland*, East Berlin, 16 January 1963.

6. 'Richtlinie für das neue ökonomische System der Planung und Leitung der Volkswirtschaft vom 11. Juli 1965' (Principles for the New Economic System of Planning and Management of the National Economy from 11 July 1963), *Gesetzblatt der DDR* II, no. 64, 1963, pp. 453ff.

CHAPTER II

THE 'NEW ECONOMIC SYSTEM'

II.1 State planning

Both the principles of the New Economic System and numerous public pronouncements by government and party functionaries on the reform programme of 1963 stated emphatically that the starting-point and also the centrepiece of the NES was 'central state planning'. Thus it should be clear that with the GDR reform there was no question of any approach to a socialist market model such as existed in Yugoslavia or, in a diluted form, was later attempted in Czechoslovakia and actually introduced in Hungary. It was, instead, a question of ensuring more effective execution of the central state aims outlined in the state plans, through somewhat stronger regard for individual and collective interests within the framework of a differentiated incentive system, i.e. through the introduction of a series of coordinated indirect decision parameters for enterprises (economic levers). This is clear in the definition of economic levers which is given in the principles [1, p. 468]:

> Economic levers are regular relationships between objective social requirements and the material interests of men, which operate directly or indirectly and by their nature stimulate the working population to particular economic behaviour.

On the grounds that in a socialist society there is a basic coincidence of social, collective, and individual interests, the 'objective social requirements' mentioned here can of course be recognized and formulated only by the political leadership, and are then embodied in long-term plans and in the annual plans derived from them. These plans, therefore, are and remain decisive; the function of scientific leadership and economic levers is exclusively to serve their implementation.

Of course we are concerned here only with the formal power of the 'centre'. Just as in the Soviet and other East European economies, economic planning and management were never 'central' in the sense of a model of an economico-political order with perfect information, a uniform central will, and the capacity for absolute implementation of its aims. The information system was continuously extended, and in particular underwent substantial improvement within the NES. None the less, as in every economic system, all important decisions on economic policy were arrived at with a considerable degree of uncertainty. Although the formation of the general will and the setting of the aims were concentrated at the peaks of the party and state apparatus, there was always a larger number of authorities or institutions which, despite the hierarchical structure, exercised a relatively far-reaching influence on decisions concerning economic policy and at times represented very diverse opinions. Furthermore, because of the high level of industrialization of the GDR and the consequent necessity that the working population be ready to cooperate, the leadership was compelled to pay greater attention to the wishes and needs of the population than was the case in most other East European states. This is also shown in the relatively high share of consumption in the GDR economy [2, pp. 127ff.] and in the average standard of living, where the GDR holds the leading position in Eastern Europe. Finally, the attempt to implement the aims set can scarcely overcome the barriers which are found where those with formal authority encounter specialists with authority derived from superior information. Since as a rule such specialists are associated with collective or individual interests, they constitute at the same time the means by which these interests are represented in the process of formation of wants and of decision-making by the party and state leaders.

Although these different influences on the planning process have always existed, the New Economic System nevertheless brought about a certain shift of emphasis in so far as the existing decentralized influences and possibilities for decision-making were strengthened by being formalized.

AGGREGATE PLANNING

Although the scientific character of central state planning was continually and emphatically stressed in the fundamental principles of the NES and in the accompanying commentaries, it must be pointed out that in the field of aggregate planning no new methods were applied. An intensive discussion developed—just as in the Soviet Union—on the use of input–output tables, but at this level they played no role in the practical work of planning. The same applies to certain recent planning procedures such as network planning and the use of cyclograms (a kind of critical path diagram) and even more so to cybernetic research and the introduction of cybernetics into practical planning.

One of the principal points in the effort to improve the scientific basis of aggregate economic planning was the promotion and development of economic and social forecasting. By this was meant

Table 4: *The structure of economic administration*

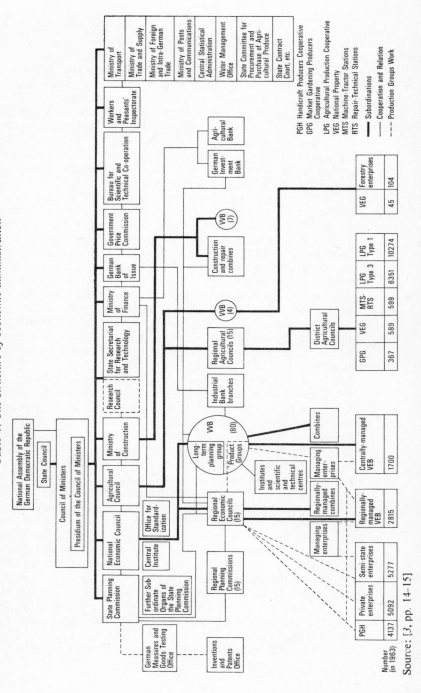

Source: [3, pp. 14-15]

'complex, scientifically based predictions of the content, direction, and extent of realizable main trends in the development of nature, society, and human thought' [4, p. 661]. Forecasts were thus intended not only to make predictions of possible developments, but to be sufficiently concrete to be the basis for the preparation of long-term plans as the principal instrument for steering economic and social development. In particular, the forecasting work of the central organs was to encompass the following areas:

(a) the development of the chief economic factors, like labour supply, investments, productivity, national income, etc. (the responsibility of the state planning commission);

(b) the development of economic complexes like, for example, automation, application of data-processing, agriculture, etc. (the responsibility of special permanent forecasting groups under the direction of a working group of the council of ministers);

(c) the spatial distribution of productive forces, for the preparation of an optimal territorial structure (the responsibility of the state planning commission);

(d) the economic development of the fifteen regions of the GDR (the responsibility of the regional councils);

(e) the development of important goods, product groups, technologies and production processes (the responsibility of ministries, associations of nationalized enterprises (Vereinigung Volkseigener Betriebe—VVB) and individual enterprises).

The work of forecasting was considered so important that it was the object of a special resolution of the Council of Ministers of 20 October 1967. The expectations which were held of the forecasts were correspondingly high: they were to 'predetermine the long-term development of the economy and the whole of social life, derive decisions on the future structure of the economy from this, and prescribe their gradual implementation as compulsory targets in long-term plans' [4, p. 661]. In these circumstances it is hard to see in what way the forecasts differ from the plans themselves.

On the other hand, it was clear why such a central task was given to the forecasts; ultimately the 'scientifically worked-out long-term plan' was to become 'the basic instrument of planning and management in the economic system' [1, p. 465]. This in turn was necessary because the previous planning methods, which had laid the central emphasis on the annual plan, promoted 'striving for the setting of "soft" plans' and led to 'unnecessary conflicts between economic organs in plan construction' [1, p. 467]. Concentration on the long-term plan and on steering the economy basically by means of the long-term plan undoubtedly represented one of the principal points of the NES in the planning field. In these circumstances the fact that, for the greater part of the duration of the NES reform experiments, no long-term plan existed at all can be seen as a verdict on the success or failure of the NES concept: in the first two years (1964–5) none existed because the seven-year plan (1959–65), which had taken the place of the second five-year plan (1956–60) when the latter was terminated in 1959, was in its turn terminated in 1963 (after it had in fact collapsed in 1961) and in 1966–7 the new long-term plan for 1966–70 did not come into being because, owing to the postponement of the third phase of the price reform (see p. 36ff), no uniform standard of valuation for the plan existed. When the plan was finally prepared the New Economic System had to be substantially modified in the structural policy field, which was decisive for long-term planning.

Besides the concentration on the long-term plan which was envisaged but never implemented, a second principal feature of the changes brought about by the NES in the field of central planning was a substantial reduction in the number of commodities allocated to users at this level (the balancing function), i.e. planning was concentrated at definite selected points of importance. The corresponding planning and allocation tasks were transferred either to the National Economic Council, the head of the administration of state industry, or to the various branch associations of nationalized enterprises.

Thus a substantial change occurred, in so far as aggregate planning and balancing (allocation of the most important commodities) was no longer exclusively undertaken by the central planning bodies.

SECTORAL PLANNING

The dispersal of planning and balancing tasks from the central state steering organs to a lower level of decision-making, in particular to associations of nationalized enterprises (VVB), affected especially the planning of the sectoral development of the economy. In this field too powers and duties are shared between the central authorities and the economic councils with regional responsibility and the associations with their branch duties.

The establishment of the future—'high-efficiency' as it is called in the GDR—structure of the economy on the basis of a scientifically grounded forecast, along with the working out of a path towards this structure which would be internally consistent at each stage of development, was the most important task of the long-term plan. Great emphasis is placed on this task in the *Principles for the New Economic System of Planning and Management of the National Economy* and a number of necessary preconditions for its solution mentioned. But no concept is developed which would help to reduce the considerable risks of structural policy. A conclusion, based on structural comparison with developed Western industrial countries, that, for example, the domestic chemical industry was underdeveloped and should therefore be especially promoted may have been adequate for the end of the fifties, but in the mid-sixties was no longer sufficient to determine the emphasis of future structural policy. And consideration of how technically advanced a product is, as for example in the computer industry, cannot be convincing as the sole argument for development; such an industry, as already happened once in 1957 when aircraft production had to be abandoned, may be beyond the economy's capability. Moreover, because of its limited domestic market and the cost reduction that accompanies large-scale production, the GDR is always oriented towards the export market for such products. But then the structural decision is determined by the answer to the question, how successful will domestic research and development be in comparison with the efforts of all potential competitors on the world market—which cannot be answered with sufficient certainty. This means that socialist planned economies face the same problems as every other economy with reference to structural development (with the possible exceptions of the USA and the USSR), and they cannot devise any better decision-making procedures.

On the contrary, we shall have to interpret the formation of the so-called 'long-term plan groups' in the VVBs, which the NES brought about, as an attempt to use the specialist technical knowledge available in the production sphere for the necessary technical and economic forecasts in the same way as happens in Western enterprises or research and development bureaux. The long-term plan groups in the VVB have the task of working out and continually improving 'conceptions of scientific and technical development' for all principal branches of the economy and the most important enterprises. These conceptions are to be founded on the available scientific and technical findings of research and development; they are to put forward proposals for the content and the sequence of necessary changes in production assortment and technology; and in addition they are to furnish evidence of sufficient economic benefit [1, p. 466]. This enormous project forces one to suspect that an idea good in itself will once again be rendered worthless by excessive expectations and by the overloading of the men charged with its implementation.

Besides the VVB long-term plan groups, it was the so-called 'product-groups work' which enabled the VVB to exercise substantial influence on the structure of the economy. By this is meant cooperation between several enterprises of different legal forms (state enterprises, semi-state enterprises, private enterprises, and handicraft producers' cooperatives) and different subordination which produce the same or similar products (products in the same product-group). Product-groups work concerns the products as well as questions of norms, types, and standardization, and also the production processes used. In addition, it covers the joint elaboration of partial forecasts and conceptions of scientific and technical development, joint conceptions of research, rationalization programmes, exchange of experience in various fields, comparisons between enterprises, equalization of the degree of usage of production capacity, and organization of permanent sub-contracting relations. The responsibility for this is borne by the VVBs, which appoint a so-called product-groups leading enterprise to implement it. Although these leading enterprises are not state management organs and have no administrative authority—they cannot issue instructions to the cooperating enterprises, but only reach agreement with them within the area of their tasks—they nevertheless have great influence. This is especially true when they, as state enterprises (semi-state or private enterprises can also become product-groups leading enterprises), take over balancing functions for the VVB or make balancing tasks easier for the VVB through their comprehensive view of supplies and requirements for the commodities of their product group.

ENTERPRISE PLANNING

Changes in enterprise planning occupy a significant place within the NES, in so far as the Soviet Liberman discussion which prepared the way for the reform started from the problems of enterprise planning. In his famous *Pravda* article [5] Liberman had proposed that the quantity, assortment, and delivery dates for enterprises' production (output) should be prescribed by their superior planning authority but that intra-enterprise planning and thus the determination of the structure of inputs should to a large extent be left to enterprises themselves. He proposed that the parameter by which enterprises decided the structure of their inputs should be the relationship between enterprise profit and fixed capital, i.e. that for practical purposes profitability should be the single comprehensive indicator. He summed up the basic principle of his proposals in the slogan 'An end to petty tutelage over enterprises'.

The clear influence of the Liberman proposals on the NES and the repeated direct references to Liberman have misled some observers into stating that the Liberman proposals were put into practice in the GDR. This is not correct. It is true that there is a whole series of points of coincidence between Liberman and the NES, but there are also even more serious differences. The decisive difference is that while the number of indicators compulsorily prescribed for enterprises by the state authorities was indeed reduced, the NES did not make profitability the single, or even the principal, indicator. The role of profit and profitability as important enterprise decision parameters was increased, but alongside them a number of additional indicators remained in existence, which to a large extent prescribed the enterprises' inputs and thus contradicted the basic idea of Liberman.

Nevertheless the reduction in the number of compulsory plan indicators was undoubtedly a step forward. For enterprises it meant a perceptible alleviation of the work of planning, and diminution of the danger of inconsistencies in the system of indicators. On the other hand, it is certainly not correct to equate the limitation of indicators with automatic extension of the field of enterprise decision-making in this general form. In that the old indicator system was overdetermined (containing for example wages fund, average number of employees, and average wage) the elimination of one (or several) indicators makes no difference to the way in which the enterprise is tied into the aggregate economic planning system. On the contrary, the inconsistencies accompanying overdetermination through too many indicators can open up for the enterprise a certain possibility of choice. This is especially true when, owing to wrong allocation of responsibility, i.e. through formal concentration of decisions at a level of the economic administrative hierarchy which lacks the specialist knowledge needed for making them, areas for free decision-making arise. This is the most favourable situation for the enterprise: it can exert a far-reaching influence on the decisions of its superior authority through suitable information and other 'help' with decisions, without having to bear the formal responsibility.

Viewed in this way the reduction in external control of enterprises by means of a multitude of compulsory plan indicators and the delegation of responsibility for decisions to lower-level authorities, which were a central feature of the 1963 economic reform, are by no means always in the interests of enterprises and their directors because, on the one hand, contrary to appearances, they not only did not increase but occasionally even restricted enterprises' scope for decision-making, and, on the other, they raised enterprises' formal responsibility. Managerial personnel in enterprises are interested in just the opposite: more freedom of decision-making and less responsibility.

The enterprise plan worked out by enterprises consists of a whole series of individual plans: production plan, sales plan, fixed capital plan, science and technology plan, labour force and training plan, plan of working and living conditions, and financial plan. These plans are linked to each other and to the state economic plan by the network of compulsory prescribed indicators. Besides them there exists a number of intra-enterprise plans which have no or only minor external effects and therefore do not have to be predetermined by special indicators: labour allocation plans, use of machinery plans, etc. For each enterprise partial plan there is one or several indicators which the enterprise must fit into its overall system of plans in the course of its 'self-accountable' planning in the light of the long-term plan. The following are essentially the indicators concerned for the individual plans [6]:

(a) production plan: total production (gross output or commodity output); production by product groups and products; production by products and delivery dates;

(b) sales plan: home market sales; export sales by countries and currency areas; sales for other customers;

(c) fixed capital plan;

(d) science and technology plan;

(e) labour force and training plan: number of employees; wages fund; employment of graduates; engagement of new apprentices;

(f) plan of working and living conditions;

(g) financial plan: profit; production tax (a turnover tax differentiated according to commodities); average value of stocks; cost reduction target for 'comparable' production (those products also produced in the preceding plan year).

For the financial plan we have only listed here those indicators which are not included in other partial enterprise plans. It will be understood that indicators such as, for example, 'commodity production sold' from the production plan, or 'wages fund' from the labour force and training plan, must necessarily appear again as 'total sales revenue' or 'total wage payments' in the financial plan, which reflects all activities of the enterprise.

Besides the compulsory plan magnitudes for the enterprise mentioned here, the partial plans are interlinked by a large number of additional indicators set independently by the enterprise planning and management departments. It is characteristic that here too the compulsory indicators prescribed from outside mark out the boundaries of enterprise planning.

The attempt to invest the long-term plan with more significance than the annual economic plan, which was so much the focus of concern at the level of aggregate planning, is also reflected at the level of enterprise planning: enterprises are obliged to adhere as closely as possible to their enterprise long-term plan in working out their plan drafts. At the same time this is supposed to exert a certain pressure on the intermediate administrative authorities to prescribe indicators for enterprises which are derived from the long-term plan of the economic region or VVB. At a later stage of the NES, from about 1969, this procedure was reinforced, indeed made definitive, in that enterprise draft plans in those sectors of the economy which did not represent particular development focal points were from then on regarded as approved if their individual partial plans agreed with the data in the long-term plan. They then required no further special confirmation by the relevant superior economic organs (in particular the regional economic council or VVB).

II.2 Management organization and management methods

ORGANIZATION

While the basic document for the New Economic System, the *Principles* ... of 11 July 1963, contains only relatively general remarks and few concrete statements about planning, with respect to its second central point, 'scientifically based management', it is much more detailed. This concerns the problems of the organizational structure of economic administration and the powers and responsibilities of the major controlling organs.

The problem of organizational changes under the economic reforms in Eastern Europe can be described and analysed from many different points of view. The approach, influenced by Walter Eucken, which is most widespread in West Germany is to assess the attempts to modernize the communist economies according to the degree of centralization or decentralization of planning and of economic decision-making. The more modern form of this approach starts from the recognition that beyond a definite and relatively low level of economic development the majority of all decisions, for technical reasons, must in fact be taken non-centrally, so that the question whether planning should be central or decentralized becomes the question whether necessarily decentralized decisions have a legal basis or not.

In these circumstances it is not surprising that in the GDR—as in the other East European countries—organizational changes in the planning and management system were not infrequent and, since the mid-fifties, recurred at shorter and shorter intervals. The introduction of the New Economic System was accompanied by an important organizational restructuring of the economic administration (cf. diagram of the administrative structure on p. 15).

The supreme control of economic planning and the responsibility for plan fulfilment are with the Council of Ministers of the GDR [7], which, as in other East European countries, should be seen as the peak of the state administration rather than as an organ of political leadership. It receives the guide-lines for its work from the Politbureau

Table 5: Organization of the State Planning Commission

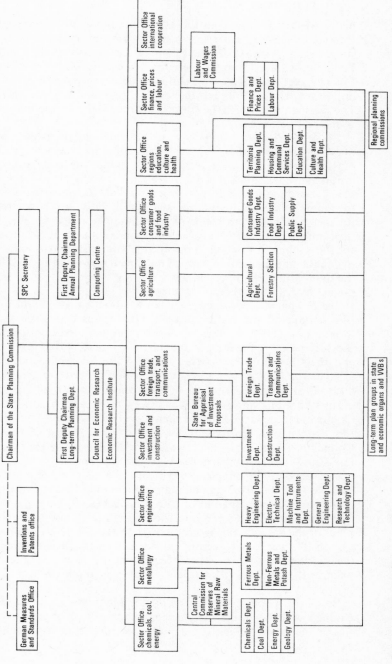

Source: [3, pp. 20–1].

of the SED or—at least in the Ulbricht era—from the GDR State Council. To implement them it makes use of a number of central state organs like the State Planning Commission, the National Economic Council and its industrial departments, the Ministry of Finance, etc., as well as some subordinate organs, of which the most important are the VVBs and the regional economic councils (BWRs). The German Bank of Issue (since 1968 the GDR State Bank) is also of major significance.

The State Planning Commission is the central organ of the Council of Ministers for economic planning. Its principal tasks are working out long-term plans (five-year plans), issuing directives and orientation figures for annual economic plans derived from the long-term plans, coordinating the proposals of individual sectors of the economy for annual plans and overall balancing. In addition it is responsible for methodological problems of economic planning. Together with the Ministry of Finance it checks compliance with financial indicators. In the technical—though not in the administrative—sphere the regional planning commissions of the fifteen regions of the GDR and the long-term plan groups of the VVBs are subordinate to it and are guided by it in their planning work.

The Economic Council represents only a brief episode in the history of economic administration in the GDR. At the beginning of 1958, in imitation of Khrushchev's reform of industrial administration in the Soviet Union, the industrial ministries were dissolved in the GDR and their functions transferred to the State Planning Commission [8]. The resultant mammoth apparatus soon proved too complicated and difficult to supervise, so in 1961 the functions of the former industrial ministries were taken away from the State Planning Commission and made independent, in the Economic Council. But this council only existed for five years. By a decree of the State Council of 14 January 1966 it was again divided into eight industrial ministries and the Ministry for Material Supply.

The Economic Council was the central organ of the Council of Ministers for the planning and management of industry. On the basis of the long-term plan, the orientation figures, and the guide-lines from the State Planning Commission, it had to elaborate the annual plan for the manufacturing industry, coordinate it with the ministries responsible for other sectors outside the manufacturing industry (agriculture, transport, external economic relations, finance, etc.), balance it, and pass it on to the Planning Commission as a draft plan.

Besides its planning duties the predominant task of the Economic Council was the direct management and control of industry. For this it made use of individual industrial departments which were established for the different branches of industries and the heads of which were the superiors of the general directors of the VVBs.

The associations of nationalized enterprises (*VVBs*) represent the most important intermediate-level institutions in the GDR economic administration. They are formed according to branches of industry and embrace under their management and control the major enterprises in their branch. All other state enterprises which are not subordinate to a VVB on a branch basis are directed and supervised by the regional economic councils or corresponding district administrations.

Since the foundation of the first VVB in 1948 these institutions have undergone frequent reforms. From 1948 to 1951 the seventy-five VVBs which existed were juridically and economically independent parent organizations of non-independent state enterprises (VEBs). With the introduction of the so-called 'principle of economic accountability' (*khozraschyot*) for state enterprises they lost their significance and from 1952 to 1958 were auxiliary authorities of the chief administrations of the then responsible industrial ministries, called 'administrations of nationalized enterprises'. When the industrial ministries were dissolved in 1958 their chief departments were made into new 'associations of nationalized enterprises' for the respective branches. The 'administrations' were dissolved. This provision remained in force until the NES reform. The juridically and economically independent enterprises (VEBs) were administratively subordinate to the 'associations' which in turn, as state authorities, were subordinate to the State Planning Commission until September 1961 and thereafter to the newly formed Economic Council.

The most important organizational measure of the NES was without doubt that of making the VVBs economically independent. They were taken out of the state administration, became legal persons, and were to take over responsibility for the development of their branch of industry as economic management organs headed by a general director [*1*, pp. 460–1]. At the Sixth SED Congress in January 1963 Walter Ulbricht outlined the new role of the VVBs and described it as [*9*] 'a kind of socialist corporation'. The fact that the VVBs are also responsible for the aggregate balances for the products produced in their field and in addition, under the framework of 'product-groups work', have also to solve problems of norms and standardization for enterprises which are in no way subordinated to them (including private enterprises), shows clearly that their functions far exceed the field of activity of capitalist combines.

The regional economic councils (*BWRs*) have similar planning, management, and control functions *vis-à-vis* the nationalized enterprises subordinated to them within the fifteen regions as the VVBs do

Table 6: Organization of the N[

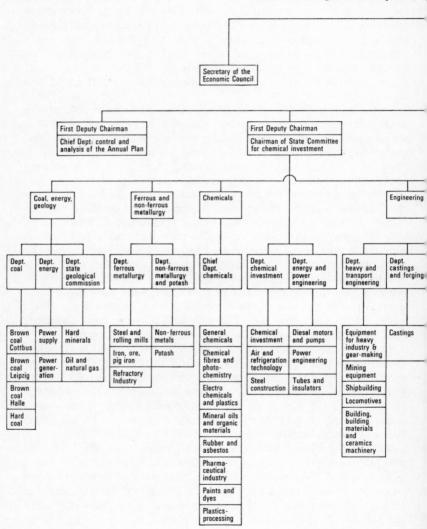

Source: [3, pp. 22–3

omic Council and the VVB

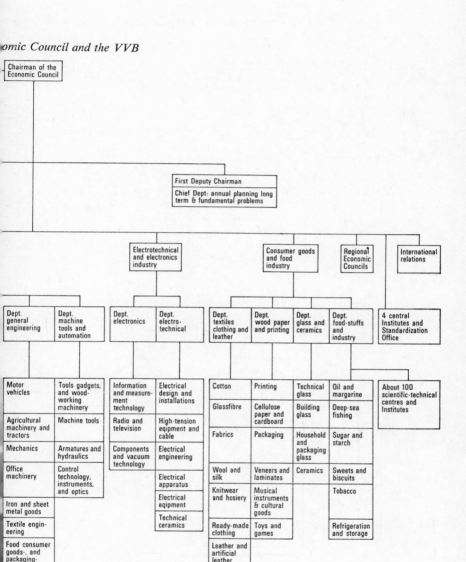

Table 7: The central position of the VVB as a management organ

Source: [3, p. 18].

106278

within their branches of industry. Yet there is a basic difference between them and the VVBs in that they are not *khozraschyot* enterprises, that is, they are neither economically nor legally independent but are rather state administrations whose revenue and expenditure are fully included in the state budget.

In order to solve the problem of cooperation between branch-subordinated enterprises (to the VVB) and regionally subordinated enterprises (to the BWR) the NES removed the BWRs from the area of responsibility of their respective regional councils and made them subordinate only to the National Economic Council and in particular to its 'regional economic council sector office' [*1*, p. 463]. This organizational innovation of the NES has not lasted, however, because cooperation with the regions, for example over housing for workers, transport connections, water supply and drainage, etc., no longer proceeded without friction. For this reason the removal of the BWRs from the regional councils was reversed in 1965 and the principle of dual subordination reinstated [*10*, p. 177]; administratively the BWRs are again subordinate to the regional councils, technically, on the other hand, to the National Economic Council.

The German Bank of Issue (since 1968 the GDR State Bank) also acquired a new importance, through the increased significance of indirect and in particular monetary steering instruments which was associated with the NES. Furthermore, the granting of legal, economic, and especially financial independence to the VVBs meant a number of additional tasks for the German Bank of Issue. In order to be able to match up to these tasks better, so-called industry branches of the bank were established, a new organizational form, associated with the VVBs, in addition to the existing regional branches in the fifteen regions and 215 districts. Since the German Bank of Issue is the banker to the government all state and private enterprises and organizations have to transact their settlements with the state budget through the regional branches of the state bank. This applies particularly to the manifold financial relations between state enterprises and the state budget. The concentration of those relations on the VVBs, as well as their other tasks, made it appear expedient to assign to the individual VVBs special branches of the bank, as a kind of house bank, with no regional connection. The rights and functions of the industry branches of the bank extend far beyond the conduct of accounts and granting of credit to the VVBs. A decree of 1964 indicates [*11*, pp. 817ff.] that representatives of the branches of the bank participate in the plan deliberations of the VVBs, make proposals for improvements and supply reports to the responsible ministries, check the cash and credit plans of the VVBs and supervise their execution, and, finally, take part in the general directors' accounting to the responsible ministries. In addition to this the industry branches of the bank are the operational financial control organs *vis-à-vis* the VVBs and in this capacity have to carry out the auditing of enterprises. They can thus exercise not only a direct influence on the VVBs' conduct of their business, but also an indirect one in that for the individual enterprises (VEB) of a VVB they issue direct instructions to the district branches of the state bank concerning their attitude towards these enterprises. This applies particularly to credit policy towards the VEBs and VVBs, the importance of which increased considerably under the NES.

THE SET OF INSTRUMENTS USED

The decisive, fundamental idea of the NES and the ESS (Economic System of Socialism) consisted in combining central state planning keyed to basic targets and long-term goals with individual enterprise responsibility for their own planning and management [*12*, p. 250 and *13*, p. 161]. Thus the enterprise was vested with limited powers of independent decision-making within the framework of given plan data and within a prescribed micro-economic field of action. In order to create sufficient incentives for this independent enterprise activity, on the one hand, and to be able to guide it through indirect steering into areas which were desirable from the national economic point of view, the 'system of economic levers'—the distinctive economic steering instruments—was to be formulated. On the other hand, a mode of economic thinking which was more oriented towards measures of efficiency required, above all, the creation of more meaningful price relations than had existed before the reforms.

In the *Principles* . . . of 11 July 1963 the new role of prices was expressed as follows: they would have to meet a series of conditions, without which 'it [would be] impossible to eliminate the many serious defects in the planning of production, to implement economic accountability (*khozraschyot*) comprehensively and to ensure the conditions for profitable working of enterprises' [*1*, p. 470].

The *Principles* . . . named the following conditions: 'approximation of prices to values', i.e. in the first place to costs, and thus elimination of distortions of the structure of production brought about by subsidies and taxes; continuous review of the conformity of prices to labour content; ensuring that price changes are systematically prepared and made as they become necessary, by means of long-term price planning; and introduction of greater flexibility in price setting for new products, to ensure production in accordance with demand.

In order to create these conditions for a price system meeting the objective of the reform, the *Principles* . . . envisaged a series of measures. These included [*1*, p. 470]:

(a) revaluation of the fixed capital (the gross capital stock) of industrial enterprises;

(b) reform of the depreciation system, in particular the introduction of depreciation rates which take into account 'moral wear' (Russian: *moral'nyi iznos*) as well as physical, i.e. technical and economic obsolescence;

(c) implementation of a price reform which should create 'correct price and profit relationships' between products and take account of the anticipated introduction of a capital charge (Russian: *plata za fondy*); and finally

(d) the introduction of a price policy differentiating prices and thus profit rates for obsolete and new products and ensuring that production meets demand in terms of assortment, quality, and delivery dates.

The revaluation of the gross capital stock and depreciation

As a first step—a precondition almost—towards the determination of prices 'corresponding to costs' it was essential to recalculate the cost of capital inputs, in which in the GDR, as in all other East European countries, only the using up of capital, covered by depreciation allowances, was counted. Payments for the use of capital in the form of interest were not counted as costs. To determine depreciation correctly the estimates of the value of capital goods in enterprises' balance sheets had to be made uniform and the rates of valuation corresponding to the actual technical and economic decline in value set anew. The first was done by the revaluation of fixed assets, the second by resetting the rates for depreciation allowances.

The revaluation of fixed capital was necessary because the same or similar productive assets were entered in the balance sheets of different enterprises at completely different values. The reason for this was the regulation that some enterprises had to enter their capital in their balance sheets at the stop-prices of 1944 or 1945 while others entered the same or similar items at the higher cost prices of later years.[1] The consequences of the differing valuations were that wear and therefore maintenance or replacement requirements were wrongly indicated; different prime costs resulted for the same production processes; and efficiency comparisons with new capital gave misleading results (frequently too unfavourable for the new capital) [*15*, p. 9].

---

[1] In 1948 all equipment had been valued at the fixed prices of 1944 and all buildings at 60 per cent above 1913 prices, while capital assets acquired after 1948 were valued at current cost, see [*14*, p. 30].

In the aggregate the consequence of the undervaluation of capital assets was still more serious: for the whole of the GDR national economy no precise and comparable data on the actual level or the distribution of capital assets were available. Therefore neither objective comparison of the composition of capital nor investigation of the effective productivity of capital in sectors and branches was possible, so that in turn the planning authorities had to work from inadequate figures in their aggregate investment decisions. For this reason, if for none other, investment could not always be directed to the point of highest economic efficiency and priority. It is basically not surprising that this resulted in a continuous decline in the marginal productivity of capital. So the GDR planners were forced to conclude: 'While in 1951–5 with a total investment of 32 mlrd Mark an increment in national income of 21 mlrd Mark was achieved, in 1956–60 63 mlrd Mark of investment only brought a 21 mlrd Mark increase in national income and in 1961–4 only a 10·7 mlrd Mark increment in national income was obtained with 66 mlrd Mark of investment' [16, p. 19; 17, p. 12].

Although these figures take into account neither the development of employment and of the structure of the economy nor the differences in the general economic level at the start of these periods, they must nevertheless be accepted as indicating clearly the falling efficiency of investment.

As early as 21 December 1961 the Council of Ministers had taken the 'Decision on preparation of the revaluation of fixed capital' [18, pp. 34ff.] and after more than two years of preparation the 'Decree on the revaluation of fixed capital' [19, pp. 118ff.] followed on 30 January 1964, according to which the value of fixed capital was to be set, from 1 January 1964, on the basis of the general and special price regulations in force on 30 June 1962. In cases where no prices existed for individual items of capital they had to be calculated on the basis of a comparison of technical parameters with similar capital.

The revaluation led to a rise in the value of total gross fixed capital in the manufacturing industry by an average of 52 per cent to 105 mlrd Mark, on 30 June 1963 [21, pp. 105ff.]. At the same time the share of buildings in the capital stock rose from 39 to 45 per cent [23, p. 6], as the increase in the value of buildings, at 74 per cent, was double that for equipment.

According to data on centrally managed nationalized industry [24, pp. 4ff.], which in 1964 produced about 70 per cent of total production of the manufacturing industry, the average revaluation coefficients differed considerably between sectors of the industry. Particularly high coefficients proved necessary for those sectors

Table 8: Gross fixed capital in manufacturing industry[1] 1955–70
(annual average in mlrd Mark at 1962 prices)

Industrial sector and branch	1955	1960	1965	1966	1967	1968	1969	1970	Growth 1955–70 (1955 = 100)
Basic material industries[2]	37·78	49·54	70·64	75·15	79·34	83·69	87·58	92·95	246·0
Power	9·50	12·41	18·09	19·32	20·33	21·43	22·10	23·46	246·9
Mining[3]	7·39	12·01	18·50	19·80	20·86	21·81	22·46	23·36	316·1
Metallurgy[3,4]	5·28	6·45	8·65	9·28	9·98	10·71	11·39	12·02	227·7
Chemicals[5]	13·27	15·33	20·46	21·71	22·97	24·33	25·90	28·05	211·4
Building materials	2·34	3·34	4·94	5·04	5·20	5·41	5·73	6·06	259·0
Metalworking industries	12·71	15·84	21·89	23·36	24·95	26·62	28·39	30·61	240·8
Heavy engineering	3·00	3·67	4·88	5·14	5·40	5·66	5·96	6·35	211·7
General engineering	2·76	3·55	4·71	5·04	5·38	5·73	6·07	6·48	234·8
Vehicles[6]	1·88	2·57	3·60	3·97	4·33	4·71	5·09	5·49	292·0
Shipbuilding	0·81	0·84	1·06	1·06	1·11	1·16	1·22	1·31	161·7
Metal goods	1·10	1·35	1·94	2·02	2·11	2·21	2·31	2·44	221·8
Electrotechnical	2·17	2·70	4·10	4·44	4·81	5·19	5·62	6·21	286·2
Precision engineering and optics	0·99	1·16	1·60	1·69	1·81	1·96	2·12	2·33	235·4
Consumer goods industries	12·35	14·33	18·07	18·48	19·21	19·98	20·75	21·64	175·2
Wood and cultural goods	1·71	2·08	2·72	2·79	2·91	3·04	3·14	3·28	191·8
Textiles	5·29	6·23	7·52	7·61	7·88	8·16	8·46	8·72	164·8
Clothing and knitwear	0·34	0·40	0·54	0·56	0·59	0·62	0·65	0·70	205·9
Leatherware, shoes, and furs	0·99	1·12	1·26	1·28	1·32	1·36	1·40	1·46	147·5
Cellulose and paper	2·23	2·41	3·09	3·13	3·22	3·32	3·42	3·54	158·7
Printing	0·56	0·67	0·86	0·91	0·94	0·99	1·04	1·11	198·2
Glass and ceramics	1·23	1·42	2·08	2·20	2·35	2·49	2·64	2·83	230·1
Food industries	7·40	8·03	9·23	9·43	9·75	10·04	10·45	11·13	150·4
Industry total	70·24	87·74	119·83	126·42	133·25	140·33	147·17	156·33	222·6

[1] including power and mining, but excl. water; [2] including power and mining; [3] since 1960 or 1961, owing to the formation of combines, enterprises (with altogether 18,400 employees) which had previously been counted under mining were included in the metallurgy industry; in order to preserve comparability over time in the rows of the table they were transferred back again by estimating; [4] including castings and forgings; [5] including mineral oils and asphalt products, rubber and asbestos goods, chemical fibres, aluminium smelting, and plastic processing; [6] excluding railway improvement work.
Sources: [20, 1966, pp. 53–6, and 1968, pp. 56–7; 21, p. 110; 22, pp. 271–2].

which had made scarcely any investment in expansion during the
fifties and early sixties and in those where investment in buildings
accounted for a large share. Whereas the basic materials industries,
which had enjoyed 70 per cent of all investment in the manufacturing
industry between 1955 and 1962, experienced a rise of 42 per cent in
the value of their capital, the figures for the food and consumer goods
industries were 75 and 100 per cent respectively.

The defects of the existing depreciation system had a number of
different causes which lay partly in the methods of calculation used
and partly in the underlying depreciation rates. The methodological
defects included in particular the practice of global depreciation
allowances; according to the depreciation decree of 1 August 1956
[25, pp. 623ff.] the total depreciation allowances which an enterprise
had to make, and for the most part pay over to the state, were not
calculated as the sum of the separate depreciation allowances
determined for individual items according to their expected life but
according to an average figure to be applied to the total value of the
enterprise's capital. Only in the second phase was this sum for
depreciation calculated for the individual items of capital—according
to 'actual' wear. Changes in the structure and utilization of capital
could not be taken into account in this procedure, which was
developed from the Soviet model.[1]

A further methodological problem was posed by capital repairs
(which increase value). According to the depreciation decree they
were to be set against wear, i.e. the depreciation allowances, as in the
Soviet Union. They thus increased the book value of capital. Since
the original value of capital was determined from the fixed prices of
the time of its formation, but the value of capital repairs, on the other
hand, was determined in current prices, increasing capital repairs
gave rise to a growing distortion of the value structure of enterprise
capital. In addition the borderline between capital repairs (to be
added to value) and current repairs (reckoned as costs) was to a great
extent arbitrary.

Finally, the global rates of depreciation used were too low to
ensure full coverage of the cost of capital during its useful life.

The practical consequence of these defects for enterprises was that
frequently capital, which on technical production grounds had been
scrapped, still stood in the books at high values. These values then
had to be debited against profit, which in turn had a negative effect on
the profitability structure of enterprises and on their capacity to form
bonus funds out of profits and to pay bonuses.

A decree of 30 January 1964 [19, pp. 120ff.] ordered the reform of
the depreciation system and the working out of new depreciation

[1] On the Soviet model see [26].

rates related to particular items of capital. The outcome of this work was a depreciation nomenclature containing rates for around 10,000 kinds of capital, partially differentiated according to degree of utilization. The following changes for the different sectors of industry resulted [24, p. 6]:

Table 9: Average depreciation rate and useful life
of basic industrial sectors before and after depreciation reform

Sector of manufacturing industry	Average percentage depreciation rate		Average useful life (years)	
	before	after	before	after
	depreciation reform		depreciation reform	
Basic materials industries	4·3	3·8	23	26
Metal-working industries	4·3	3·4	23	29
Consumer goods industries	3·2	3·1	31	32
Food industries	3·4	3·0	29	33
Manufacturing industry total	4·2	3·6	24	28

The most surprising aspect of this result was that, contrary to the preceding discussion and to expectations, the average depreciation rate was lowered and the average useful life raised. There could therefore be no question of a universally demanded additional consideration for technical and economic overhaul in the depreciation rates.

The explanation for this unexpected development must surely lie in the result of the preceding revaluation of capital; capital values were raised so steeply that, despite the reduced depreciation rates, depreciation allowances and thus costs of production climbed substantially (see Table 10).

Table 10: Capital depreciation allowances in 1963 (mlrd Mark)

Sector of manufacturing industry	Depreciation before revaluation	Depreciation after revaluation	Percentage change
Basic materials industries	1·99	2·54	+28
Metal-working industries	0·53	0·68	+29
Consumer goods industries	0·24	0·45	+88
Food industries	0·15	0·24	+60
Manufacturing industry total	2·91	3·91	+34

Source: [27, p. 66].

An even steeper rise in depreciation allowances through maintaining or even increasing depreciation rates would have led to cost increases which would no longer have been absorbable in the production sector within the price reform and would have led to price rises on consumer goods. This was to be avoided at all events—because of its effects on wages and the wage structure.

On the other hand, at the reduced rates depreciation allowances were of course no longer adequate to finance replacement investment at the due time and capital repairs as well. As a consequence of this, in 1965, the depreciation fund was relieved of the financing of capital repairs and a uniform repair fund was formed [28, pp. 106ff.] to finance both capital and current repairs.

The industrial price reform

The revaluation of fixed capital and the depreciation reform were followed in the period 1964–7 by a comprehensive price reform, executed in several stages, the aim of which was to eliminate a significant part of the substantial price distortions then existing. Since the price system in force until 1964—in particular for intermediate goods—was in large part based on 1944 prices, it reflected the existing cost and scarcity relationships in the GDR economy very imprecisely and distortedly. At that time the prices of important basic materials were quite considerably below their production costs—which required extensive state subsidies. Thus, for example, the prices of raw materials and coal, gas, electric power, wood, iron, building stone, and tiles were at 45 to 60 per cent of the level of their effective production costs [29, p. 52]. Consumer goods prices, on the contrary, were excessively high, because the consumption sectors had to bear heavy product taxes.

As a result of such a distorted price structure mistakes with quite extensive consequences for the development of the national economy were unavoidable. The use of raw materials was anything but optimal, since extravagance with undervalued raw materials was accompanied by too little use of the more advantageous (mostly more modern) substitute inputs, as the latter were frequently overvalued in relation to the former.

The assortment of the finished goods produced by enterprises was concentrated, because of the quantity-dominated approach to planning, on output of which the national economic cost far exceeded their enterprise cost because the profit shown per product could not be a real measure of enterprise performance.

The development and application of technical and economic progress were impeded because with the distorted price structure new production processes or investment projects quite often showed a high economic return, where, with prices for raw materials and

Table 11: The stages of the GDR industrial price reform

Period	Major product groups affected	Number of enterprises affected	Volume of production affected (mlrd Mark)	Average overall increase in product prices (%)
First stage Step I 1 April 1964	Coal, power, potash and salts, ores, non-ferrous metals, pig iron, steel and rolled products, castings and scrap, including the relevant freight rates	290	50	70
Step II 1 July 1964	Basic chemical raw materials and products (especially mineral oil products, organic and inorganic chemicals, synthetic materials, chemical fibres, cellulose, fertilizers), including the relevant freight rates			
Second stage 1 January 1965	Round timber, sawn timber, veneers, cardboard and paper, hides, furs, leather, building materials, water, further chemical products (especially rubber, synthetic materials, chemical fibres, chemical-technical goods, films, pharmaceuticals, non-ferrous metal products (e.g. cable, wire, pipes) including the relevant freight rates	3,350		40
Third stage 1 January 1967	Engineering, electrical products, electronics, semi-finished and finished chemical products, consumer goods and food industry products, buildings, postal and transport installations (for consumer goods only enterprise prices were regulated)	over 15,000	c. 100	4

Sources: [31, p. 15; 32; 33, pp. 95ff.].

finished products which correctly reflected costs, they would have given none or only a very small one.

The industrial price reform took place in three stages [*30*, pp. 313ff.]. The first stage in 1964 affected the prices of important raw materials such as coal, power, ores, iron, steel, and basic chemical materials, with a total annual production volume of 50 mlrd Mark and increased them by on average 70 per cent. At the second stage in 1965 price rises averaging 40 per cent followed for a further 50 mlrd Mark annual production; this covered products like wood, paper, cardboard, building materials, cable and wire, and chemical products (e.g. rubber, synthetic materials, chemical fibres, films, pharmaceuticals). The beginning of 1967 finally concluded the third stage, which applied to finished products—particularly equipment and installations, but also products of consumer goods and food industry. A total volume of production of around 100 mlrd Mark underwent an average price increase of 4 per cent.

Attempts to estimate in various ways the overall average increase involved in the price reform, which was not officially disclosed, were agreed that the mean figure lay between 20 and 25 per cent [*27*, pp. 111–18].

Since an important principle of the industrial price reform was to leave the prices of consumer goods unchanged, enterprises in branches close to the consumer had to absorb cost rises in their inputs by increased rationalization or loss of profits. It is true that sporadic reductions in the production tax were also made or subsidies introduced when the cost increases which had come about would have been too heavy a burden for enterprises. Thus the third stage of the industrial price reform, which was accompanied by an inventory and revaluation of stocks of materials and semi-finished goods [*34*, p. 745 and *35*, p. 893], primarily affected the prices of investment goods, which rose an average of 16 per cent [*36*].

For items of equipment the price changes diverged substantially: while, for example, precision mechanical and optical instruments became 30 per cent cheaper, vehicles 6 per cent cheaper, and electrical equipment 1 per cent cheaper, some important capital goods showed marked increases; thus heavy engineering and timber products showed price rises of 20 per cent and general engineering 6 per cent. On average prices for investment equipment rose by 8 per cent.

Building costs, which were primarily affected by increased material and transport costs [*38*, p. 10]—the prices of building materials alone rose by more than 30 per cent—increased altogether by 26 per cent. Since the costs of building repairs rose less than proportionally, the increases in the cost of investment construction reached 33 per cent.

What cost increases—corresponding to the differences in investment structure—actually occurred for the investments of individual sectors of the GDR economy in 1967 are shown in Table 13.

Table 12: Price changes for major groups of industrial goods
following the industrial price reform

	Percentage price change
Basic materials industries	
Metallurgy	+95
Chemicals	+8
Building materials	+32
Metal-working industries (total)	+8
Heavy engineering	+21
General engineering	+6
Vehicle-building	−6
Shipbuilding	+31
Castings and forgings	+56
Metal goods industry	+67
Electrical	−1
Precision mechanics and optics	−32
Consumer goods industry	
Timber industry	+22
Textiles, ready-made clothing, knitwear, and leather goods	+16
Glass and ceramics	+14

Source: [37, p. 238].

Table 13: Cost increases on gross capital investment[1]
in sectors of the GDR economy in 1967 (percentage increase over 1966)

Manufacturing industry	15
Construction	11
Agriculture and forestry (incl. water)	18
Transport and communications	8
Trade (incl. nationalized procurement and purchasing enterprises)	12
Culture, health, and social services	14
Housing	25
Others (state administration, social organizations, etc.)	24

[1] including capital repairs.

Source: GDR statistical yearbook, 1968, and authors' own calculations and estimates.

Within the manufacturing industry too the different individual branches displayed widely differing increases in investment costs [39].

As for the results of the price reform, there are both positive and negative elements. A positive point to note would be that the price reform enabled state subsidies in various sectors to be reduced by 6 mlrd Mark from the previous level of around 13·5 mlrd Mark to 7·5 mlrd Mark [40]. This also partially eliminated the considerable disproportions between the prices for products of different branches of the economy. Finally, and quite generally, a more even determination of costs, i.e. based on uniform principles, should have come about ('approximation to values') and a reduction in the spread of enterprise profit rates.

Negative elements of the price reform,[1] that is problems which were only inadequately solved or not solved at all, stemmed from the methods of the reform itself. These included in the first place the setting of the new prices on the basis of average industry costs with no separate consideration of the pressure of demand. In order to prevent the prices becoming obsolete too quickly an attempt was made to use forecast 1967 costs as the basis, but to the extent that the forecasts were in error, i.e. that the course of the economy between 1964 and 1967 was misjudged, the new prices were distorted from the start. In addition, capital intensive products especially were undervalued because even after the depreciation reform unduly low depreciation rates failed to take proper account of capital consumption, and the absence of interest payments meant that there was no charge for the use of capital.

A further distortion was due to the regulation that the price level of consumer goods must not be altered. Since the wage level was geared to the level of consumer goods prices, the same unfavourable relationship between labour and capital costs for enterprises persisted, with all the consequences for enterprise calculations, especially investment decisions, familiar from Soviet economic experience. It is true that the extent of this price disparity was diminished by the reduction in subsidies, but it was not eliminated.

The crucial problem of the GDR price system—especially with respect to the role which the economic reform sought to give prices in the overall process of controlling the economy—has not been solved by the price reform because it was not an object of the reform, i.e. the problem of price flexibility. Both the old price structure and the new one, which arose out of the reform, are by their nature static. The price structure adapts only very slowly and hesitantly to structural changes in production. For this reason the demand for a dynamic price system was raised in the last stage of the price reform, and thereafter became stronger.

[1] For precise details of the defects and the problems which the price reform left unsolved see [30, pp. 321ff].

The 'system of economic levers'

With these prices, however, the essential precondition was met for making *profit*, now rediscovered as measure and decisive stimulus of performance, the most important incentive for the enterprise, the combine, and even the VVB [*41*, p. 20]. Since the enterprise could dispose freely of part of any net surplus it earned, it acquired a clear interest in raising its profit and thus in improving enterprise efficiency. For prices were set such that only rational behaviour enabled the enterprise to cover production costs and earn a profit.

Profit was introduced first as a 'real' measure of performance, and was followed by:

(a) the principle that enterprises, combines, and VVBs should earn the financial resources necessary for fulfilling their plan targets;[1]

(b) a substantial improvement in methods of cost calculation, so as to obtain a true numerical reflection of the costs of the enterprise's operation;[2]

(c) an improved contract system [*47*, p. 107] which created sanctions in the form of penalty clauses, price deductions, and reimbursement of losses for non-fulfilment or poor fulfilment of obligations and laid-down guarantee provisions. This was not only to regulate mutual cooperation between enterprises and make it more efficient; the aim was rather to use the economic contract—which enterprises were obliged to conclude—primarily for the preparation, concretization and implementation of plans as well and also for checking plan fulfilment. In this connection the economic management organs (e.g. the VVB and regional economic council) were given significant checking powers;

(d) a reformed banking system [*48*, pp. 397ff.]. Until the introduction of the NES the banks were in practice financially dependent executive organs of the state, which kept a check on the physical production and distribution process via the financial circulation, according to the directions of the state plan, and financed the planned enterprise investments by interest-free allocations from the state budget with no check on efficiency. Their task became to grant—observing economic criteria—credits on which interest was payable, to promote profitable investment projects, and to obstruct projects which were in conflict with state objectives by higher interest rates and refusal of credit. For

---

[1] See § 4 of [*42*, p. 121] hereafter called 'VEB decree', and also [*43*, p. 459].

[2] Until about the middle of the sixties cost calculation was neglected and even dismissed by the economic authorities as 'unproductive'. Thus the consequence of the decree on costs [*44*] promulgated in 1962 and not repealed until 1968 was that even large enterprises partly suspended both calculation of their operating costs according to the current method and also the estimating and accounting of costs of individual products [*45*, p. 6; *46*, p. 19].

this reason substantial powers to influence and far-reaching checking functions on enterprise investment were also transferred to the banks (e.g. examination for state-prescribed efficiency requirements, for compliance with the terms of the credit—such as the share of own resources, interest rate, duration of loan—and for adherence to estimated costs).

Besides this 'framework of conditions' of the indirect steering system for implementing economic policy, which still remains in force after the recentralization measures, the following instruments were then created to influence profit and the uses to which profit was put.

A basic *interest rate* of 6 per cent payable to the state (called the *Produktionsfondsabgabe* (production capital charge) [*49*, p. 115] on the gross value of all enterprise capital goods and working capital. This charge was not to be treated as a cost for accounting purposes but rather was to be paid out of profit. This was to induce enterprises to improve their use of capital—by searching out and using all reserves more intensively—for any avoidable misuse of capital would detract from the profit remaining after deduction of the interest charge.

The 'capital-related' type of price [*50*, p. 497] which in contrast to previous price setting was also to take into account the amount of capital economically required and thus make it possible for the first time for capital-intensive enterprises to pay the production capital charge.[1] With this type of price the share of profit was calculated exclusively as a percentage (maximum 18 per cent) [*51*, p. 247] of the necessary—and not of the actual—capital input, which in turn was measured by the capital input of the best enterprises of a product group. Since price thus only took account of the 'optimal' capital input and the 'best' level of working capital employed, while the production capital charge was levied on the capital actually employed, the enterprise could only maximize its net profit (= gross profit −production capital charge) with given processing costs by decisions improving its use of capital.

Measures to make prices dynamic: in order to exert continuous pressure on enterprises' costs and to bring the prices of product groups closer to world market prices two basic methods were developed in the GDR to make prices dynamic:

(a) *the industrial price regulation system* [*52*, p. 43]. Under this system an upper and a lower limit of permissible profit for each product group per 1,000 Mark of necessary fixed and working

---

[1] Since the gradual introduction of 'capital-related' prices did not begin until 1968, the production capital charge which had been brought into operation in nationalized industry from the beginning of 1967 had to be differentiated between 1, 4, and 6 per cent rates.

capital was determined, and it was further laid down that if the maximum profit were exceeded, price reductions down to the prescribed minimum profit level had to be introduced from the beginning of the following year.[1] So that enterprises were also in fact interested in decisions leading to cost and price reductions, they were allowed in the first instance—according to the regulations in force for 1969 and 1970—to deduct the full amount of the resultant fall in profit from the net profit payment due to the state;

Table 14: Operation of the industrial price regulation system for a product group (schematic representation)

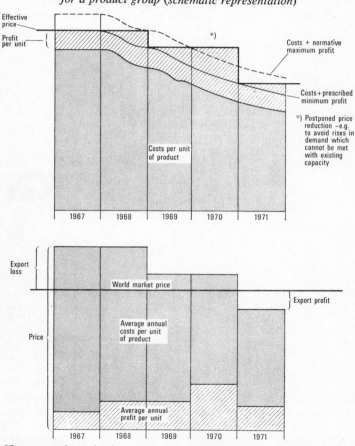

[1] However, price reductions were not to be made when they would engender increases in demand which could not be met with existing capacity or which would have given rise to wrong price relationships between substitutes.

(b) *Lowering of price for new and improved products.*[1] The purpose
of establishing gradually declining prices for new and improved
products was to motivate enterprises to develop new goods of a
higher technical standard than hitherto: initially increased profit for
innovations was to be followed over the anticipated 'economic life'
of the product by compulsory price reductions—which would be
steeper than the expected cost reductions. The aim of this regulation
was that the producer should have an inducement to cease production
and go over to other products when the product no longer corresponded to current technical standards.

Table 15: *Gradual price reduction for new industrial products*
(schematic representation)

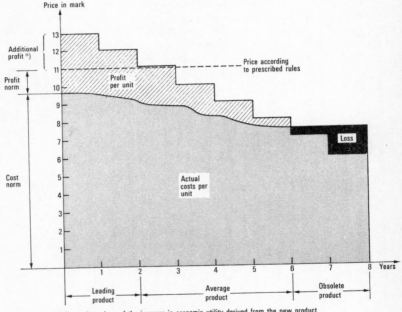

*) Enterprises share of the increase in economic utility derived from the new product

The unified enterprise results [56, p. 507], the object of which was to
bring the profit from export dealings into the determination of
enterprise profit. This concept, introduced from 1969—at first, for
enterprises in the metal-working industry and also partly in the
chemical industry—prescribed that both export proceeds and any

[1] See [53, p. 423]. See also the corresponding order for the chemical industry
and for the metallurgical industry [54, p. 977; 55, p. 83].

export incentives received (export support, export promotion bonuses) should be added to the profit from domestic turnover. In doing this, export proceeds were converted into domestic currency at the existing exchange rates and adjusted by state-determined correction factors (so-called *Richtungskoeffizienten*—direction co-efficients). The differences which resulted from this calculation compared with the enterprise's export results in Mark as calculated purely at the exchange rate were paid as additions from the state budget, or—where the coefficient was less than one—were payable into it as deductions.

The direction coefficients, which were strongly differentiated by countries or groups of countries and groups of goods, were, on the one hand, to correct the existing exchange rates and even cut differences between the domestic and foreign price structure or, on the other, to promote politically desired trade flows.

The deduction from net profits [57, p. 494], a measure which obliged enterprises to pay over a certain percentage of the profit they earned (not of the production capital charge)—with a precisely determined annual minimum—to the state budget via the VVBs. This rate of deduction was strongly differentiated for individual VVBs and their enterprises, and in the first place operated for the two years 1969 and 1970; nothing more was done about the plan to set new rates for the five-year period 1971–5.

This substantial differentiation in deduction from net profits was intended to steer the economy in the directions desired by the planning authorities as the amount of profit left with the enterprise—as the financial basis for its own objectives—was cut back or augmented.[1]

The bonus fund [58, p. 490]: linking the bonus fund to the level and trend of net profits was intended to stimulate every member of the enterprise's work force and give him an interest in rationalization and improvement of the use of capital. This fund was composed of a certain proportion of the previous year's bonus fund (the basis norm) and a percentage of the increase in net profits of the year under consideration (the increase norm). For the years 1969 and 1970 it was laid down that the 'basic contribution' to the bonus fund should consist of the basic contribution plus a small proportion (about 15 per cent) of the increase in the bonus fund of the previous year, so that a bonus fund of the previous year's level could only be achieved with a large increase in net profits. Here too the principle was that the

---

[1] It was admitted that for 1969 three-quarters of all centrally managed industrial enterprises (excluding the consumer goods industry) had to pay over more than half their net profit [51, p. 245].

VVB should differentiate the basis norms and the increase norms with considerations of structural policy in mind.

Other additional conditions were also decisive for the bonus fund, such as, for example, fulfilment of particular scientific and technical targets and implementation of centrally planned investments according to plan. If both these targets were inadequately fulfilled the bonus fund was reduced by 30 per cent; if only one was, the reduction was 15 per cent. Furthermore, unauthorized exceeding of the planned wage fund had to be covered from the bonus fund.

Still, the level of the average bonus per full-time blue- and white-collar worker in nationalized centrally managed industry rose from 280 Mark to 450 Mark in the period 1963–7 [59, pp. 15–16]. For 1969 and 1970 a maximum allocation to the bonus fund of 700–800 Mark per employee and a maximum limit on the individual end-of-year bonus of two months' pay were set [58, pp. 491–2]. In 1970 the average value reached around 560 Mark.[1]

The enterprise *cultural and social fund*, which apportioned sums from the profits earned for the cultural and social care of the work force.

The enterprise *science and technology fund* which comprised, besides licence revenues and income for research commissions, sums which could be regarded for accounting purposes as costs, which were intended to accelerate the introduction of new technical developments. Parts of this fund were to be paid over to the VVB, according to long-term norms, for specific tasks.

The enterprise *amortization fund*, which comprised the authorized deductions. It served exclusively for financing investments and repayment of credits. Since the beginning of the reforms these sums were basically left completely with the enterprise; only in cases where no long-term expansion or maintenance of capacity was planned were deductions made from the amortization fund to the VVB or the state budget.

VVB fund formation [61, pp. 250–1]: The VVB also had its own funds for stimulating observance of its management tasks and ensuring a high economic return in its subordinate enterprises. These funds were financed out of the deduction from the net profits of enterprises, from special enterprise deductions and from the VVB apportionment—which was borne by the VEB. While this apportionment was essentially to cover VVB administration costs, expenses, and the formation of the General Director's fund (from which bonuses for competitions and targets to ensure the fulfilment of

---

[1] For the whole nationalized sector of the economy the average end-of-year bonus in 1970 amounted to 490 Mark [60, p. 14].

special tasks of importance to the whole industry were paid), the other resources were divided chiefly among the following funds:

(a) the *profit fund*, which comprised the deductions from the net profits of the enterprises. From this, part was to be paid over to the state budget, and from the rest allocations made within the branch to implement structural policy objectives. Also, investment projects which were decisive for the whole branch but exceeded the financial capacity of the enterprise selected—for various reasons—to carry out the investment could be financed from this source.

(b) the *amortization fund*, formed from amortization deductions of individual enterprises. From this, sums were passed on to the state budget and also used for financing important investments determining the production structure of the branch and for repayment of credits.

(c) the *reserve fund*, through which the General Director of the VVB was given the possibility of meeting temporary financial stringencies. In particular, this was to ensure that payment of profit deductions to the state (if enterprise deductions from net profits were insufficient) was safeguarded, new technological discoveries were implemented, adaptations to changes in market conditions carried out, and losses from extra-plan export business covered.

(d) the *science and technology fund*, which was formed from deductions from enterprise science and technology funds, as well as from revenues for research and development carried out for other branches and from licence income. This fund was intended to achieve accelerated introduction of technical developments in the industry and also the faster fulfilment of important structural tasks.

(e) *further funds* included the *bonus fund*, serving to provide bonuses for outstanding performance by employees of the VVB itself, which was formed out of the profit fund, and the *cultural and social fund*, which comprised a limited portion of the VVB apportionment, for cultural and social facilities for VVB employees. Finally, the VVB formed an *investment* fund, which would finance automation and rationalization measures which were decisive for the whole branch.

A characteristic of this set of instruments for steering economic policy, which in this form only really operated in the years 1969 and 1970, was that the residue of profit which remained with the enterprise after providing for the items of deduction named formed the financial basis for limited enterprise freedom of control over a considerable part of its investment. With these sums—held in the *enterprise investment fund*—it was allowed to set the course for future development possibilities, bearing full practical responsibility. That was the most important incentive created for it by the NES. All the same, in the years when the steering instruments were in fact in operation—1969 and 1970—a considerable part of total investment was again removed from enterprise decision-making (see III.2).

Thus there was inserted into the planning system a set of economic policy instruments which sought to: motivate improvements in capital utilization and the use of working capital via the production capital charge; measure enterprise performance by net profit; induce the enterprise to improve its performance through the residue of net profit—as the basis for forming its funds and above all for scope for financing its own investment; bring about reductions in enterprise costs by means of making prices dynamic; intervene with structural policy measures (e.g. setting the rates for the deduction from net profits and the norms for the upper and lower limits on profitability) where contradictions appeared between the directions of enterprise development and state structural conceptions.

Even though this set of economic policy instruments—of which only the basic features have been sketched here—was still incomplete and could only really have attained a certain ability to function with the broader introduction of capital-related prices, it was still, taken altogether—despite justified criticism of details—to be regarded as an effective conception for improving economic efficiency. This was also the case, incidentally, because the NES could be interpreted as an open—i.e. not limited in time—reform [62, p. 118] and precisely for this reason led one to expect further measures to induce cost reductions and favour technical progress.

The discussion on the appropriate type of price for the GDR

The most important question in connection with the problems of price-setting, namely, whether it should in essence be left to the regulation processes of the market mechanism, with the state only bringing its conceptions of price policy to bear indirectly, or whether the state apparatus should set prices directly, never seriously came under discussion in the GDR. It could be seen as a substantial step forward[1] that prices were to be changed at all. The changes themselves, however, were to remain as an important instrument for state control of the economy in the hands of the economic and political leadership. This means that from the start price was viewed as a state steering instrument, an economic lever, not as an instrument of economic self-regulation which the state could influence.

A similar attitude to the role of price is to be encountered in some other East European countries, particularly in the Soviet Union

[1] This step forward should not be undervalued, in view of the problems of coordinating quantitative planning with price planning.

and—at least up to the present—in Poland. However, this attitude differs fundamentally from the role ascribed to prices in the Hungarian 'new economic mechanism', in the Yugoslav 'socialist market economy', and not least in the Czechoslovak reform model of 1968. The function of prices in the various economic reforms of Eastern Europe is indeed still the most appropriate criterion for characterizing these reforms and distinguishing them from each other.

With state price-setting a problem arises which is not posed when prices are set on the basis of the market mechanism, i.e. the question of the type of price to be used, or how the profit margin is to be calculated when setting prices. That some profit must be allowed for stems from the necessity of economic growth and financing investment in expansion.

The various price types differ according to what profit is related to. In the GDR—as in other East European countries—three different price types were discussed during the years of the NES.

With the so-called *wage-related* price type[1] profit is calculated by applying a state-prescribed profit rate to labour costs:

$$p = c + v + a_1 . v$$

where p = unit price
c = material costs and depreciation per unit of production
v = wage costs per unit
a_1 (later also a_2 and a_3) = the normed profit rates

The special attraction of this price type for Marxists lies in its broad correspondence to the Marxist labour theory of value and the conception represented in it that only the factor labour creates surplus value (profit). The enormous disadvantage of this in practice lies in the effect it has of inducing enterprises to concentrate on the most labour-intensive production possible so as to enlarge the amount of profit they earn with a constant profit rate. It impedes modernization processes, i.e. the replacement of labour by capital, and thus obstructs technical progress.

With the *cost-related* price type,[2] which formed the basis of the

---

[1] This was represented, for example, by J. G. Strumilin [*63*, pp. 972ff.]. In the GDR the principal exponents of the wage-related price were Johann Köhler, who proposed that only 'wages of production workers' should be the basis of reference, and Gotthard Schaaf [*64*, pp. 486ff.].

[2] Modern representatives of this price type include for example the two Soviet authors Kondrashev and Bachurin, who reject the variations in the profit rate which have hitherto been purely at the discretion of the price authorities and advocate a uniform profit rate related to total prime cost [*65*, pp. 1264ff.; *66*, pp. 153ff.].

determination of prices in the industrial price reform,[1] the profit margin is calculated not on wage costs alone but on all costs:

$$p = c + v + (c + v) . a_2$$

Without having the theoretical attractions of the wage-related price, this price type has in principle the same disadvantages. In the interest of raising their profit, enterprises will seek to prove the highest possible costs in price calculation and confirmation, so as to drive up their price and profit. In the German war economy the same mode of behaviour by enterprises was called 'cost-making'. On the other hand, because of the absence of an interest charge, the use of capital is only inadequately taken into account. Thus highly capital-intensive enterprises are at a relative disadvantage.

These defects are avoided with the *capital-related* price type.[2]

$$p = c + v + K . a_3$$

With this the profit margin is related to the productive capital per unit of product—K. K is the total value of fixed and working capital in the enterprise (the 'necessary capital') divided by total production. K can therefore also be described as the capital intensity of production. The special property of this price type is that it corresponded most closely to the production capital charge introduced at the same time as the new prices. Even though this charge—principally on grounds of Marxist theory—is not included in costs but formally treated as a use of profit, it does not alter the fact that capital appears as a value-determining factor in the capital-related price. Theoretically this type of price can be interpreted as the adaptation of Marx's production price for the socialist economy. Because of its antithesis to the Marxist labour theory of value the capital-related price type has not gone undisputed [*69*, pp. 1985ff., *70*, pp. 769ff.], so extensive theoretical discussions were necessary for its establishment.[3]

---

[1] Since a similar rate of profit in each case was related to the corresponding processing costs for the products and product groups of the same branch, calculated with the following coefficient

$$\frac{9 \cdot 5 \text{ per cent of prime costs of the branch} . 100}{\text{processing costs of the branch}}$$

the principle of the uniform profit rate related to prime costs was not infringed.

[2] In the GDR Hans Luft (who proposed differentiation of the capital-related profit rates between the sphere of consumer goods, and that of investment goods and means of production), Wilfried Maier, and Wilhelm Schmidt all spoke out quite early in favour of this price type [*64*]. For explicit representatives see [*67*, pp. 548ff.; *68*, pp. 529ff.].

[3] See [*71*; *72*, p. 218; *73*, pp. 96, 124; *74*, p. 19]. From the Soviet literature the primary names are [*75*; *76*, pp. 231ff.].

The decisive advantage of this price type lies not only in the increased opportunities for enterprises to earn their own funds to cover the investment requirements necessary for accomplishing their future production tasks in capital-intensive branches, but, above all, in the improved economic yardstick for present and subsequent investment decisions. For now similar rates of profit on capital in the most diverse branches express roughly similar national economic performance, which hitherto was not the case. Branches with, for example, an obsolete, labour-intensive production structure had an inducement, because of an apparently high rate of profit on capital, to make investments which were inefficient from the national economic point of view, while highly productive projects were neglected because they offered only a small accounting profit rate.

It is disadvantageous with this price type at first to use the actually existing level of fixed and working capital employed in individual branches of industry, because by doing so branches with a low level of utilization of capacity and those with technically obsolete and too costly capital equipment, together with those with an excessive amount of working capital, would be favoured with excessive profits. In order to meet this defect it was proposed only to take account of the capital input necessary with more or less optimal utilization and exclude unused or laid-up capital.[1] An attempt was made to put this into effect when capital-related prices were actually introduced [78, p. 223; 50, p. 497]. Even so, the determination of this 'more or less optimal' capital input and of the 'best' level of working capital, differentiated by product groups in each case, according to the practice of the 'best' enterprises in a branch raises problems, because thereby not only the level of performance attained by these 'leading enterprises' but also any mistakes in their investment policy are adopted as a pattern for the remaining enterprises.

[1] The following formula was developed by Bösche to determine the economically necessary capital input

$$PF_e \cdot \frac{(K_{1e} \cdot K_{2e})}{(K_{1n} \cdot K_{2n})} = PF_n$$

where PF_e = effective production capital (= actual capital employed)
   PF_n = necessary production capital (= necessary capital employed)
   K_{1e} = coefficient of actual extensive capacity utilization (norm)
   K_{1n} = coefficient of possible capacity utilization (norm)
   K_{2e} = coefficient of actual intensive capacity utilization
   K_{2n} = coefficient of possible intensive capacity utilization (norm)

By 'extensive capacity utilization' is meant the use of capital over time (temporal use), the norm for which is to be set according to the highest justifiable level of shift utilization in each case. 'Intensive capacity utilization', on the other hand, means the use of capital determined by organization and technology, the norm for which would be measured by the performance of the best enterprise of a branch [77, pp. 1997ff.].

The disadvantages with this price type for branches which on technical grounds are labour-intensive could still be onerous. For those branches whose technology still requires a level of labour-intensity which is high by today's standards—e.g. because mechanization and automation of their particular work processes are not possible, or only so to a small extent—can earn scarcely any profit even with maximum performance. But in this way they are deprived precisely of the basis for future performance increases because they can make only insufficient use of technical progress since they are, for example, not in a position to finance new production methods by which even labour-intensive processes can be mechanized today.

These grounds may also have been influential in setting in motion a discussion of a modified form of capital-related price type, which should be not only capital- but also wage-related. This means the conception of a *'mixed' price type* in which the profit calculated in price

$$p = c + v + K.a_a + v.a_b$$

where a_a = profit rate on production capital
          a_b = profit rate on wage costs

consists of one part proportional to the necessary input of fixed and working capital and another part proportional to the necessary labour input (in each case set according to the best enterprise of a branch) [74, p. 10; 79, pp. 353ff.]. Corresponding to this consideration of the *necessary* labour input in the profit calculation there should be a labour fund charge—similar to the production capital charge—as a state-levied tax on the *actual* labour input [41, pp. 68–9]. The aim of this charge related to the total wage bill was to achieve more efficient use of the factor labour without more marked wage increases [80, p. 1775].

In the application of the 'mixed' price type the division of profit between the two factors labour and capital should follow the existing scarcity relationship in the GDR between these two factors—i.e. correspond to the differences in their average productivity. With a labour fund charge constructed on a corresponding basis (e.g. differentiation according to varying levels of scarcity and of productivity in use of the factor labour), this concept would have been very helpful, for prices would then reflect the scarcity of the two essential factors, labour and capital—albeit with only a certain degree of approximation.[1]

Unfortunately, however, this concept was not pursued after 1970 in the official scientific discussion. The basic reason may have been

[1] For details of the problems of the 'mixed' price type see [30, pp. 329–31 and 351].

the considerable difficulties involved in practical implementation of price construction of this kind. To be sure, the introduction of capital-related prices with a broadened basis of reference was occasionally advocated, yet it was explained that because of the lack of the 'scientific preliminaries' there could be no question of this before 1980 [*81*, pp. 44ff.].

THE SCOPE FOR DECISION-MAKING GRANTED TO THE ENTER-PRISE WITHIN THE FRAMEWORK OF INDIRECT GUIDANCE

Since the enterprise's behaviour was brought into line with the structure of state objectives, both via prescribed plan indicators and with indirect steering instruments, opportunities for enterprise decision-making were concentrated primarily on performance improvements or—more precisely—on the best possible implementation of specified sets of tasks.

During the NES period the enterprise could organize the following tasks freely within the framework of the plan data set from above [*82*, pp. 143ff.]:

(a) enterprise planning of organizational and technical measures for the production of products meeting demand, quality, and delivery requirements: This included all tasks directly concerning the productive operations of the enterprise, such as labour organization, delivery planning, planning installation of machinery, setting up network plans, etc.

(b) the conclusion of sound and timely procurement and delivery contracts: In order to ensure the availability of the correct quantities and quality of all raw materials and components and the sale of total finished products, contracts were to be concluded during the planning process, at the time the long-term objectives of the state perspective plans were made known to the enterprise.[1]

(c) the attainment of a more efficient usage of raw and other materials: As far as the usage of raw and other materials was concerned enterprises had freedom of decision throughout, though they had to: (i) fulfil the prescribed or agreed quality requirements for their products; (ii) adhere to specified plan indicators of material usage [*83*, p. 155] such as material usage norms, material utilization coefficients, material waste norms, and norms for materials recovery; (iii) refrain from decisions on input of materials when the contracts for supplies of materials which had been concluded were not accepted by the balancing organs in the material balances [*84*, p. 481]. This

---

[1] An enterprise was to conclude contracts with its suppliers when it—but not its suppliers—was certain that the product was necessary for the fulfilment of plan targets, see § 11 of the VEB decree [*42*, p. 124].

happened, for example, when insufficient domestic production capacity was available for particular materials, imports were not provided for, or there was a conflict with other overall economic interests.

(d) the improved use of productive capital and the reduction of excessive working capital: In order to cut its production capital charge the enterprise had an incentive—in spite of the scarcity of skilled labour—for rationalization and for the scrapping of obsolete capital goods or sale of little-used equipment. In addition, it had a motive for saving on working capital and thus for taking decisions aimed at reducing the level of stocks it held and speeding up intra-enterprise processes which tied up working capital.

(e) reduction of processing costs: With the reintroduction of the profit principle the enterprise had an inducement, with fixed prices, to achieve cost reductions because with a fixed production capital charge this was the only way it could maximize its net profit. Thus the enterprise had an incentive for improved use and efficient training of labour and for economical use of other factors.

(f) the development of new products or improvement of existing products: Since the enterprise which produced new products that exceeded the scientific and technical standard of existing comparable products, or could be produced at lower costs, was initially allowed to keep additional profit above the normal margin, it had an interest in new developments: as a rule this additional profit amounted to 30 per cent of the 'increase in national economic utility' (= wage and material savings over one year by the user) brought by the new product, it was not, however, allowed to be more than double the permitted normal profit margin [85, p. 423; 86, p. 977].

(g) the further development and improved combination of existing production techniques or the creation of new production methods: Decisions to introduce new or improved methods should have been in an enterprise's interests in so far as it could obtain finance for research and development work from its science and technology fund and from the VVB and was supported by consultation with the VVB. Although these funds were limited, if they brought the enterprise projects which could be adopted in production, it could hope for cost reductions and increases in net profit in the future.

(h) the implementation of the most efficient enterprise investments and rationalization measures possible: In principle the enterprise was to receive full financial responsibility for and also extensive freedom of decision-making relating to the major part of its investment [87, pp. 65–6]. In fact, major projects of decisive significance, the construction of new works and other projects which were important to the structure of the economy, were excepted and either their implementation was supervised by central organs or they were compulsorily prescribed for enterprises.

The enterprise's freedom of control over the 'free' part of its investment also applied only in a specified direction; on the one hand the enterprise was bound by the production targets determined in the plan, and on the other it was directed by 'economic levers' towards modernization and raising the return on its capacity. Thus, for example, large investments in expansion brought the disadvantage of an excessive production capital charge, or investments in products which no longer met current technical standards meant accepting the possibility of loss as a consequence of price decreases.

To stimulate the most efficient investment possible, the 1968 investment decree [88, p. 813] prescribed that the enterprise had to prepare its investment projects thoroughly, undertake continual comparisons with costs abroad, and carry out projects rapidly. It was even recommended to have its investment projects appraised by expert commissions [89, p. 237].

To avoid any divergence of interest between state and enterprise the banks too were given an indirect steering function over enterprise investment. Besides checking projects from the design and economic calculations stage right up to completion, the banks were to set their credit policy according to state objectives. Thus nationalized enterprises paid, for example, 1·8 to 3·6 per cent interest on credits for carrying out investments in accordance with plans, whereas, for projects which were contrary to plans, up to 15 per cent interest was charged or credits were refused altogether. In addition, the granting of credits was tied to compliance with specified indicators; for instance, the enterprise had to undertake a certain level of financing from its own resources, agree to a term laid down in advance for the loan, and prove that the project met criteria of economic effectiveness (e.g. a recoupment period of five years) [90, p. 7].

(i) the attainment of greater activity in foreign trade: The enterprise's scope for decision-making also extended to the conclusion of short-term export contracts not anticipated in the plan, if they were approved by the foreign trade organs. It was a precondition, however, that fulfilment of these contracts impaired neither other export obligations already fixed in the plan nor other prescribed plan targets. In particular cases the enterprise could also obtain foreign currency credits to finance imports, for example if subsequent increases in exports would thereby be made possible. In addition, it received foreign currency rights (rights to use foreign currency to acquire goods from abroad) on overfulfilment of its export plans or for not using foreign currency granted it in its plan, e.g. by buying more cheaply than laid down in the plan or not using anticipated imports through succeeding in substituting domestic products for goods hitherto only made abroad.

The enterprise's possibilities of organizing the tasks described reveal that the limits on enterprise decision-making consisted in the lack of authority to deviate from predetermined, mostly externally set plan targets. Thus the decision-making authority of the enterprise was primarily directed at opening up all reserves and growth potential, as long as it moved within the structure desired by the state, but not at spontaneous development in its 'own' directions.

Nevertheless it would be wrong to ascribe to the enterprise in the NES period only the right to fit in with the objectives prescribed in the plan, without the right or means to influence the plan. The enterprise was not allowed to alter the existing plan, but certain possibilities of influencing it were brought forward to the forecasting and plan-elaboration period; it could appraise and thus possibly influence future developments, put forward plan proposals corresponding to the production possibilities its investment offered,[1] and it could effect the detailed form of its plan targets (for instance, changes in the assortment and quality of its products).

References to Chapter II

1. 'Richtlinie . . .' (*Principles* . . .) see ref. 6, p. 12.
2. *Bericht der Bundesregierung und Materialien zum Bericht zur Lage der Nation, 1971* (Federal Government Report and Materials to the report on the State of the Nation). Bonn, 1971.
3. *Das funktionelle Wirken der Bestandteile des Neuen Ökonomischen Systems der Planung und Leitung der Volkswirtschaft* (The Functional Operation of the Components of the New Economic System of Planning and Management of the National Economy). Dietz Verlag, East Berlin, 1964.
4. *Wörterbuch der Ökonomie des Sozialismus* (Dictionary of the Economics of Socialism). East Berlin, 1969.
5. 'Plan, pribyl', premiya' (Plan, profit, bonus), *Pravda*, 9 September 1962.
6. 'Anordnung zur Übergabe der staatlichen Aufgabe des Volkswirtschaftsplans 1964 vom 30. Oktober 1963' (Instruction of 30 October 1963 for the issue of state targets for the economic plan for 1964), *Gesetzblatt der DDR*, II, no. 95, 1963, pp. 758ff.
7. 'Beschluss des Ministerrates über die Grundsätze der Arbeit des Ministerrates für die Planung und Leitung der Volkswirtschaft vom 7. Februar 1963' (Decision of the Council of Ministers of 7 February 1963 on the basis of the work of the Council of Ministers in planning and managing the national economy) from 'Erlass des Staatsrates der DDR über die Planung und

[1] In the VEB decree it was still laid down that the enterprise could protest against the setting of state targets if they deviated strongly from its confirmed plan proposals, see § 10 of the VEB decree [*42*, p. 124].

Leitung der Volkswirtschaft durch den Ministerrat' (Decree of the State Council of the GDR on the planning and management of the national economy by the Council of Ministers) in *Gesetzblatt der DDR*, I, no. 1, 1963, pp. 1ff.

8. 'Gesetz über die Vervollkommnung und Vereinfachung der Arbeit des Staatsapparates in der Deutschen Demokratischen Republik vom 11. Februar 1958' (Law of 11 February 1958 on the improvement and simplification of the work of the state apparatus in the GDR), in *Gesetzblatt der DDR*, I, 1958, pp. 117–20.

9. *Neues Deutschland*, 16 January 1963.

10. 'Erlass des Staatrates der DDR über Aufgaben und Arbeitsweise der örtlichen Volksvertretungen und ihrer Organe unter den Bedingungen des neuen ökonomischen Systems der Planung und Leitung der Volkswirtschaft vom 2. Juli 1965' (Decree of the GDR State Council of 2 July 1965 on the tasks and manner of work of local people's representative organs under the conditions of the New Economic System of Planning and Management of the National Economy), *Gesetzblatt der DDR*, I, no. 12, 1966.

11. 'Richtlinie über die Verantwortung und die Hauptaufgaben der Deutschen Notenbank im neuen ökonomischen System der Planung und Leitung der Volkswirtschaft. Auszug, vom 3. September 1964' (Principles of the responsibility and chief tasks of the German Bank of Issue in the New Economic System of Planning and Management of the National Economy. Extract, 3 September 1964), in *Gesetzblatt der DDR*, II, no. 99, 1964.

12. Walter Ulbricht, *Zum Ökonomischen System des Sozialismus in der DDR* (On the Economic System of Socialism in the GDR), vol. 2. East Berlin, 1968.

13. Horst Steeger, 'Die Gestaltung des sozialistischen Planungssystems in der DDR zur Durchsetzung der wissenschaftlich-technischen Revolution' (The formation of the socialist planning system in the GDR for the execution of the scientific-technical revolution), *Wirtschaftswissenschaft*, no. 2, 1970.

14. H. Arnold, H. Borchert, A. Lange, J. Schmidt, *Grundmittel, Investitionen, Produktionskapazität in der Industrie der DDR* (Fixed Capital, Investment, Productive Capacity in GDR industry). East Berlin, 1967.

15. Willy Rumpf, 'Notwendigkeit und Bedeutung der Grundmittelumbewertung' (Necessity and significance of the fixed capital revaluation), *Deutsche Finanzwirtschaft*, no. 1, 1963.

16. Walter Ulbricht, 'Probleme des Perspektivplanes bis 1970' (Problems of the long-term plan up to 1970), *Materialien des 11 Plenums* (Materials of the 11 Plenum), p. 19.

17. *Die Wirtschaft*, no. 37, 1966.

18. *Gesetzblatt der DDR*, II, no. 4, 1962.

19. *ibid.*, II, no. 14, 1964.

20. *Statistisches Jahrbuch der DDR*.

21. Manfred Melzer, 'Das Anlagevermögen der mitteldeutschen Industrie 1955–1966' (The capital stock of East German industry 1955–66), in *Vierteljahreshefte zur Wirtschaftsforschung*, no. 1, 1968.

22. Peter Mitzscherling, Manfred Melzer, *et al.*, *DDR-Wirtschaft. Eine Bestandsaufnahme* (The GDR Economy—a Situation Report). Deutsches Institut für Wirtschaftsforschung, Frankfurt-am-Main, 1971.

23. *Die Wirtschaft*, no. 10, 1964.

24. Hans-Jürgen Hurtig, 'Was brachte die Umbewertung der Grundmittel?' (What brought about the revaluation of fixed capital?), *Deutsche Finanzwirtschaft*, no. 6, 1964.

25. *Gesetzblatt der DDR*, I, no. 70, 1956.

26. Gert Leptin, *Die Anlagenrechnung der Sowjetischen Industrieunternehmung* (The Capital Accounting of the Soviet Industrial Enterprise). Berlin, 1962.
27. Erich Rohr, *Die Industriepreisreform in der DDR (1964–1967)* (The Industrial Price Reform in the GDR). Berlin, 1971.
28. *Gesetzblatt der DDR*, II, no. 15, 1965.
29. Willy Rumpf, 'Einige Fragen der Weiterentwicklung des sozialistischen Preissystems' (Some problems of the further development of the socialist price system), *Einheit*, no. 5, 1963.
30. Manfred Melzer, 'Preispolitik und Preisbildungsprobleme in der DDR' (Price policy and problems of price-setting in the GDR) in *Vierteljahreshefte zur Wirtschaftsforschung*, no. 3, 1969.
31. Helmut Mann *et al.*, *Grundfragen der Industriepreisbildung* (Basic Problems of Industrial Price Setting). East Berlin, 1967, p. 15.
32. *Wochenberichte des DIW*, no. 32, 1964 and no. 22, 1965.
33. H.-G. Tönjes, 'Die dritte Etappe der Industriepreisreform in Mitteldeutschland' (The third stage of the industrial price reform in East Germany), in *Vierteljahreshefte zur Wirtschaftsforschung*, no. 1, 1967.
34. *Gesetzblatt der DDR*, II, no. 115, 1966.
35. *ibid.*, II, no. 142, 1966.
36. 'Zur Entwicklung von Investitionsgüterpreisen und Investitionstätigkeit in der DDR' (On the development of investment good prices and investment activity in the GDR), in *Wochenbericht des DIW*, no. 34, 1968.
37. *Statistische Praxis*, no. 4, 1968.
38. Joachim Tesch, 'Die Auswirkungen der mit der Industriepreisreform in der Bauwirtschaft wirksam gewordenen neuen Preise' (The effects of the new prices which came into effect in the construction sector with the industrial price reform), in *Zur Industriepreisreform in der Bauwirtschaft* (On the Industrial Price Reform in the Construction Sector), ed. Fritz Liebscher. East Berlin, 1967.
39. Manfred Melzer, 'Investitionsgüterpreise und Investitionstätigkeit in der mitteldeutschen Industrie' (Investment good prices and investment activity in East German industry) in *Wochenbericht des DIW*, no. 20, 1969.
40. *Die Wirtschaft*, no. 38, 1966, supplement.
41. Eberhard Seifert *et al.*, *Gewinn in der volkseigenen Industrie* (Profit in Nationalized Industry). East Berlin, 1968.
42. 'Verordnung über die Aufgaben, Rechte und Pflichten des volkseigenen Produktionsbetriebes' (Decree on the tasks, rights, and duties of the nationalized production enterprise), in *Gesetzblatt der DDR*, II, no. 21, 1967.
43. 'Beschluss über die Grundsätze für weitere Schritte bei der Anwendung des Prinzips der Eigenerwirtschaftung der Mittel für die erweiterte Reproduktion im Jahre 1968' (Resolution on the basis for further steps in the application of earning the resources for expanded production in 1968) in *Gesetzblatt der DDR*, II, no. 68, 1967.
44. *Gesetzblatt der DDR*, II, no. 51, 1962.
45. *Die Wirtschaft*, no. 41, 1967.
46. *ibid.*, no. 47, 1967.
47. 'Gesetz über das Vertragssystem in der sozialistischen Wirtschaft' (Law on the contract system in the socialist economy), in *Gesetzblatt der DDR*, I, no. 7, 1965.
48. Sibylle-May Lang und Maria-Elisabeth Ruban, 'Veränderungen im Bankensystem der DDR' (Changes in the banking system of the GDR), in *Vierteljahreshefte zur Wirtschaftsforschung*, no. 3, 1968.

49. 'Verordnung über die weitere Anwendung der Produktionsfondsabgabe im Bereich der volkseigenen Industrie und des volkseigenen Bauwesens' (Decree on the further application of the production capital charge in nationalized industry and construction), in *Gesetzblatt der DDR*, II, no. 19, 1967.

50. 'Richtlinie zur Einführung des fondsbezogenen Industriepreises und der staatlichen normativen Regelung für die planmässige Senkung von Industriepreisen in den Jahren 1969/70' (Principles for the introduction of the capital-related price and the state normative regulation for the planned reduction of industrial prices in 1969/70), in *Gesetzblatt der DDR*, II, no. 67, 1968.

51. Siegfried Kaergel, 'Zur finanzökonomischen Begründung des Betriebsplans auf der Grundlage des Prinzips der Eigenerwirtschaftung der Mittel' (On basing the financial and economic plan of the enterprise on the principle of financial self-sufficiency), in *Wirtschaftswissenschaft*, no. 2, 1970.

52. E. Heyde, K. Reiher, G. Hartmann, *Fragen und Antworten zur Industriepreispolitik* (Questions and Answers on Industrial Price Policy). East Berlin, 1969.

53. 'Anordnung über die Preisbildung für neu- und weiterentwickelte sowie für veraltete Erzeugnisse der metallverarbeitenden Betriebe' (Order on price-setting for new and improved and for obsolete products of metal-working enterprises), in *Gesetzblatt der DDR*, II, no. 64, 1967.

54. *Gesetzblatt der DDR*, II, no. 122, 1968.

55. *ibid.*, II, no. 9, 1969.

56. 'Anordnung über die Bildung eines einheitlichen Betriebsergebnisses in den Jahren 1969 und 1970' (Order on the establishment of unified enterprise results in 1969 and 1970), in *Gesetzblatt der DDR*, II, no. 67, 1968.

57. 'Anordnung über die Bildung und Verwendung von Fonds aus der Anwendung von Normativen der Nettogewinnabführung und der Amortisationsabführung in den Jahren 1969 und 1970' (Order on the establishment and use of funds from the application of norms of deduction from net profits and amortization deduction in 1969 and 1970), in *Gesetzblatt der DDR*, II, no. 67, 1968.

58. 'Verordnung über die Bildung und Verwendung des Prämienfonds in den volkseigenen und ihnen gleichgestellten Betrieben, volkseigenen Kombinaten, den VVB (Zentrale) und Einrichtungen für die Jahre 1969 und 1970' (Decree on the establishment and use of the bonus fund in nationalized and equivalent enterprises, nationalized combines, the VVB (centrals), and organizations for the years 1969 and 1970), in *Gesetzblatt der DDR*, II, no. 67, 1968.

59. Werner Rogge, *Prämienfonds und Jahresendprämie* (Bonus Fund and End-of-Year Bonus). East Berlin, 1969.

60. *Marktforschung*, no. 1, 1972.

61. *Betriebsökonomik Industrie* (The Economics of the Industrial Enterprise), collective authorship, vol. 2, 5th ed. East Berlin, 1969.

62. Gert Leptin, 'Das "Neue Ökonomische System" Mitteldeutschlands' (The 'New Economic System' in the GDR), in *Wirtschaftsreformen in Osteuropa* (Economic Reforms in Eastern Europe), ed. K. C. Thalheim and H.-H. Höhmann. Cologne, 1968.

63. S. G. Strumilin, 'Das Wertgesetz und die Berechnung der gesellschaftlichen Produktionskosten in der sozialistischen Wirtschaft' (The law of value and the calculation of social production costs in the socialist economy), in *Sowjetwissenschaft, Gesellschaftswissenschaftliche Beiträge*, no. 8, 1957 (translated from *Planovoe Khozyaistvo*, no. 2, 1957).

64. 'Beratung über die Wahl der ökonomisch richtigen Bezugsbasis bei der Verrechnung des Reineinkommens auf die Zweige und die Erzeugnisse' (Consultation on the choice of the economically correct reference basis for

the calculation of net income for branches and products), in *Wirtschafts-wissenschaft*, no. 3, 1964.

65. D. D. Kondrashev, 'Wert und Preis in der sozialistischen Gesellschaft' (Value and price in socialist society), in *Sowjetwissenschaft, Gesellschaftswissenschaftliche Beiträge*, no. 11, 1957 (translated from *Voprosy ekonomiki* no. 5, 1957).

66. A. V. Bachurin, 'Das Wertgesetz und die Frage der Preispolitik' (The law of value and the question of price policy) in *Das Wertgesetz und seine Rolle im Sozialismus* (The Law of Value and its Role in Socialism) (translated from the Russian). East Berlin, 1960.

67. Kurt Ambrée, 'Die Anforderungen des sozialistischen Preistyps an die Verrechnung des Reineinkommens' (The requirements of the socialist price type and the calculation of net income), *Wirtschaftswissenschaft*, no. 4, 1965.

68. Helmut Mann, 'Thesen zu einigen Grundfragen der Rolle des Preises im neuen ökonomischen System der Planung und Leitung der Volkswirtschaft' (Theses on some basic questions on the role of price in the New Economic System of Planning and Management of the National Economy), *Wirtschaftswissenschaft*, no. 4, 1965.

69. Johann Köhler, 'Zur Problematik eines richtigen Preisbildungsprinzips' (On the problems of a correct price-setting principle), *Wirtschaftswissenschaft*, no. 12, 1965.

70. Johann Köhler, 'Die Notwendigkeit eines einheitlichen Masses bei der Durchsetzung des Gesetzes der Ökonomie der Zeit' (The necessity of a uniform measure in implementing the law of economy of time), *Wirtschaftswissenschaft*, no. 5, 1966.

71. Kurt Ambrée (head of a collective of authors), *Technische Revolution und Preistyp* (Technical Revolution and Price Type). East Berlin, 1966.

72. Fred Matho, *Ware-Geld-Beziehungen im NÖS* (Commodity-Money-Relations in the NES). East Berlin, 1965.

73. Harry Nick, *Technische Revolution und Ökonomie der Produktionsfonds* (Technical Revolution and Economy of Fixed Capital). East Berlin, 1967.

74. Harry Nick, *Warum fondsbezogener Preistyp?* (Why the Capital-Related Price Type?). East Berlin, 1968.

75. I. S. Malyshev, *Obshchestvennyi uchyot truda i tsena pri sotsializme* (Social Labour Accounting and Price under Socialism). Moscow, 1960.

76. Z. V. Atlas, 'Das Wertgesetz und des Problem der Rentabilität der Produktion im Sozialismus' (The law of value and the problem of profitability of production under socialism), in *Das Wertgesetz und seine Rolle im Sozialismus*. East Berlin, 1960.

77. Jürgen Bösche, 'Probleme der Kalkulation fondsbezogener Preise' (Problems of calculation of capital-related prices), *Wirtschaftswissenschaft*, no. 12, 1968.

78. 'Beschluss des Staatrates der DDR über weitere Massnahmen zur Gestaltung des ökonomischen Systems des Sozialismus' (Decision of the GDR State Council on further measures for the construction of the Economic System of Socialism), *Gesetzblatt der DDR*, I, no. 9, 1968.

79. G. Ebert, G. Koch, F. Matho, H. Milke, *Ökonomische Gesetze im gesellschaftlichen System des Sozialismus* (Economic Laws in the Social System of Socialism). East Berlin, 1969.

80. G. Ebert, F. Matho, H. Milke, 'Optimalpreis und fondsbezogener Preis' (Optimal price and capital-related price), *Wirtschaftswissenschaft*, no. 11, 1968.

81. Rita Kindler, 'Arbeitskräftefonds und fondsbezogener Preistyp' (Labour power fund and capital-related price type), *Wirtschaftswissenschaft*, no. 1, 1972.
82. Manfred Melzer, 'Der Entscheidungsspielraum des VEB in der DDR—Betriebliche Kompetenzen durch Reformen erweitert?' (The scope for decision-making in the nationalized enterprise in the GDR—enterprise powers extended by reforms?), *Vierteljahreshefte zur Wirtschaftsforschung*, no. 2, 1970.
83. Carl-Jürgen Strauss, *Die Materialwirtschaft der DDR* (Materials Economy of the GDR). East Berlin, 1969.
84. 'Verordnung über die Aufgaben, Pflichten und Rechte der Betriebe, Staats- und Wirtschaftsorgane bei der Bilanzierung materialwirtschaftlicher Prozesse' (Decree on the tasks, duties, and rights of enterprises, state, and economic organs in the processes of material balancing), *Gesetzblatt der DDR*, II, no. 67, 1968.
85. *Gesetzblatt der DDR*, II, no. 64, 1967.
86. *ibid.*, II, no. 122, 1968.
87. Walter Werner, 'Zu den Grundsätzen zur Vorbereitung und Durchführung der Investitionen' (On the principles for the preparation and execution of investments), *Vertragssystem*, no. 2, 1968.
88. 'Beschluss über die Grundsätze zur Vorbereitung und Durchführung von Investitionen' (Decision on the principles for the preparation and execution of investments), *Gesetzblatt der DDR*, II, no. 116, 1967.
89. 'Anordnung über die Begutachtung von Unterlagen der Vorbereitung von Investitionen' (Order on the appraisal of documents on the preparation of investments), *Gesetzblatt der DDR*, II, no. 40, 1968.
90. Werner Schilke und Friedhelm Tuttlies, 'Eigenmittelbeteiligung bei Investitionen' (Participation of own resources in investment), *Sozialistische Finanzwirtschaft*, no. 20, 1969.

CHAPTER III

THE
IMPLEMENTATION AND TERMINATION
OF THE REFORM

III.1 Launching problems

The NES conception of economic policy which we have described should have been capable of functioning, but it was characterized by a number of deficiencies. Thus it could not be introduced in well-tailored stages as was intended. Precisely for this reason a multitude of uncertainties and frictions were observable in the general running of the economy:

■ enterprise managers had first to acquaint themselves with the new measures and adjust to an 'entrepreneurial' way of thinking;

■ the alteration of investment financing through the introduction of the principle of earning one's own resources faced enterprises, combines, and the VVBs with new problems;

■ bank personnel were still not sufficiently trained to be able to handle the tasks of efficiency control over investment projects;

■ particular instruments—such as the production capital charge, the measures to make prices dynamic, the 'capital-related' price—were supposed to be tested initially in parts of the economy in order to work out their definitive, obligatory form;

■ there were obscurities over the responsibilities of the VVBs and the decision-making rights of VEBs, which were described in discussion as both too tightly restricted and too little used;

■ the delaying of the difficult third stage of the industrial price reform till the beginning of 1967—it had been envisaged for 1 January 1966—brought additional problems: the plan data could not be expressed in uniform prices, as a result of which the passing of the 1966–70 long-term plan was postponed till 1967. Moreover, enterprises could not yet see the effects of the economic levers which were already in operation; only after 1967, with the new prices, were they in a position to make a reasonable assessment of their cost structure and profit rate.

The new prices made it clear that in a great many cases production costs had been excessively high and even new plants were unprofitable because examination of the real cost position showed that they operated with too dear raw materials, too complicated methods, or simply had an unfavourable location.

The following defects of the past were clearly recognizable: there had been insufficient revision of product-mixes, too little rationalization and automation, and research and development had been neglected or dissipated on too many projects. For the first time in practice enterprises faced some sales difficulties—a consequence of the backwardness of market research and demand studies, and of isolation from foreign markets.

Furthermore, the complete, conscious neglect of enterprise cost accounting in the earlier period took its revenge; enterprises could not initially determine the real costs of a number of their products and therefore had first to develop their methods of cost calculation.

It also became apparent that the improvements in the supply of goods, in terms of broader assortment, better technical standard, and quality, which were now required were still not sufficiently promoted by the newly developed set of economic policy instruments. The necessary changes were completed extremely slowly.

Despite attempts to refine the techniques of planning, fundamental weaknesses were still apparent; the planning methods available did not permit any scientifically based longer-term planning, mainly because of the lack of well-grounded, detailed forecasts, which would have made it possible to compare different variants. Persistent frictions arose, the causes of which lay primarily in the bureaucratic structure of the economic apparatus. Thus the information system, far from perfect anyway, became overloaded because the amount of data to be processed increased towards the peak of the hierarchy. The decision procedures within the official channels of the state leading organs were still too ponderous and only to a very limited extent allowed for adaptation to sudden disturbances. Also, conflicts and tensions increasingly arose between, on the one side, central and intermediate bodies and, on the other, the groups of experts who were the necessary concomitants of complicated planning methods but who, once included, sought rather to bring their own conceptions to bear as political objectives. Furthermore, the system was still fundamentally handicapped by the lack of enterprise adaptability to disturbances not taken into account in the plan. There were two principal problem areas.

ADAPTATION PROBLEMS WITH SHORT-TERM CHANGES IN DEMAND

What happens when sudden changes in demand give rise to disproportions between producer and customer enterprises' arrangements concerning products and raw and auxiliary materials?

With the dissolution of the direct quota allocation system for materials and semi-finished products a more indirect control of the flows of intermediate goods was created in the NES period: enterprises had to conclude what were basically freely negotiated contracts—under the existing contract law—for material deliveries at an early point in time, so as to make information available for balancing.[1] This was supposed to achieve the optimal orientation of scarce resources towards the production goals laid down in the plan and elaborated in detail by the enterprises, with extensive consideration given to enterprises' conceptions. The state in no way renounced its right to supervise and influence material economic relations, but the rights of the balancing organs (State Planning Commission, industrial ministries, VVBs, combines, and product group leading enterprises) to exert influence were limited. In 1967 it still seemed a good policy for enterprises to defer the conclusion of contracts, which for some time had been compulsorily prescribed, to the time of balancing decisions, because the balancing organs were supposed to take note of contractual agreements, though they did not have to adhere to them [1, pp. 112–13]. The balance decree of 1968 changed this extensively however [2, pp. 481ff.], since only in exceptional cases were the flows of goods laid down in economic contracts allowed to be corrected in the balancing decisions,[2] and the balancing organs in principle had to provide for compensation for disadvantages caused to enterprises as a result of their intervention [2, p. 484]. That the balancing organs nevertheless exerted a not insubstantial influence is shown by the following quotation from an East German textbook [3, p. 34]: 'Around 80 per cent of the material goods coming from domestic production and imports are directed to the annual national economic plan with the help of the material, equipment, and consumer goods balances. Thus the socialist state has decisive instruments at its disposal to ensure the most important material relations in the national economy.' Nevertheless the change in the influence of the 'balancing organs' achieved more flexible regulation of raw and other material arrangements, following enterprise wishes more closely, but only at the price of long-term contractual obligations. This, however,

---

[1] We mean here both drawing up aggregate national economic balances and working out specific partial balances such as, above all, the 'materials, equipment and consumer goods balances'. While the balances are being drawn up decisions are taken by the superior bodies which put the specified future material flows into effect.

[2] Such cases occurred, for example, when the materials requirements contained in the contracts conflicted with plan targets, when alterations in the targets of the annual plan were made, or when technical progress or long-term plan changes made more efficient use of materials possible.

had the consequence that enterprises could only meet short-term alterations in demand by changing their contracts.

As long as disproportions between the producer's wish to supply and the customer's desire to receive deliveries occurred only in particular cases of changes in demand, possibilities for their solution were offered by the contracts law. The customer enterprise could, for example, have demanded cancellation of the contract, but at the same time would have had to reimburse those expenditures which the producer had already made on the basis of the contract [1, p. 112]. This applied also to expenditures by the producer enterprise's suppliers. If such cases became numerous the duty of the partners to the contract to inform their superior organs of their difficulties and submit proposals for overcoming them could accomplish little. With larger short-term changes in demand the planning system was overstrained.

ADAPTATION PROBLEMS WITH EXTERNAL OR INTERNAL INFLUENCES ON THE SUPPLY SIDE

What happens—to take one case from the situation at the time—when, as a result of exceptional weather factors, certain enterprises cannot carry out their deliveries, or can only do so with great delay, and the whole chain of successive enterprises is thereby hindered in the fulfilment of its plan targets? In a situation of this kind, caused externally through the inclemency of a hard winter, the only thing that could be done was to try to afford relief by exceptional efforts, as long as the level of reserves remained limited to a minimum, which was insufficient for such cases. In such situations even uneconomic measures seemed sensible to the economic leaders of the GDR, so as to be able to maintain to some extent the economically essential sequence in the implementation of important plan tasks. Thus, for example, coal frozen by the winter cold was got out of railway waggons with compressed air hammers or thawed out with jet engines in order to be able to keep production going at whole enterprises or important plants. This shows that because of too tightly calculated reserves the planning system was not in a position to adapt sufficiently to exceptional situations.

Besides these external influences there were also internal difficulties on the supply side which had more obstructive effects on the course of production. It was reported that in cases of transfer of production from one producer to another, which were provided for in contracts and approved by the responsible superior organs, the cessation of production by the previous producer was not accompanied by resumption of production by the new producer, or only with great delay [4, pp. 7–8]. Although legally the measures which had to precede a transfer of production were laid down [5, p. 11]—so as to ensure, in particular, that the previous producer only ceased production when the enterprise taking over production was in a position to cover the existing need [5, p. 15]—the production of some products was ended leaving no substitutes [4, p. 8], or resumption was extraordinarily delayed. In so far as this concerned products used as inputs in other production processes it affected the subsequent enterprises, which now faced delays in fulfilment of both their contracts and also their plan targets.

Since the individual enterprise was mostly not in a position to solve these problems through its own decisions or to counter them effectively, and since the involvement of higher bodies set an extensive, bureaucratic, and far from rapid process of adaptation in motion, the efficiency of the GDR economic system at that time was clearly limited, above all by the lack of flexibility to adapt to change in the short term.

III.2 Corrections in the field of structural policy
THE CONCEPT

Another major problem was the moulding of the overall structure of the economy, which became more and more important but also more and more difficult. On the one hand, changes in the economic structure appeared urgently needed in order to attain faster technical progress, greater economic growth along with the achievement of political aims, and the coordination of long-term objectives with the country's Comecon partners. On the other hand, enterprises' conceptions of their development ran at times in completely opposite directions. Eventually the economic leadership of the GDR had to recognize that a structural policy which would check such divergences and give sufficient consideration to state objectives was not attainable by indirect, monetary methods of steering alone.

For this reason the resolution of the State Council of April 1968 stated [6, p. 223]:

> 'The role and the degree of effectiveness of central state planning and management are to be strengthened in the basic questions of the structural development and the efficiency of the national economy, while at the same time ensuring its proportionality. . . . The planning of products, product groups, processes, and technologies which determine the structure of the national economy (product-linked planning) and concentration on these tasks are to be developed into the kernel of central planning.'

The basic regulation [7, pp. 433ff.] passed shortly afterwards made it clear that besides raising the standard of management by state and economic organs and improving measures already introduced,[1] the economic leadership of the GDR was most urgently concerned with putting into operation priority planning and implementation of 'structure-determining' tasks.

This meant production tasks, processes, investments or fundamental research projects which [7, pp. 435–6]:

■ altogether, in the long-term plan period and beyond, exert a revolutionary influence on the scientific and technical level of development of the economy and ensure the achievement and maintenance of the highest world standards;

■ lead to full exploitation of national resources of productivity and growth as well as of international cooperation and have a decisive influence on the rate of expanded reproduction of the national economy;

■ determine the preponderant part of the growth in efficiency of the economy through the overall result of their effectiveness and their concentrated development.

But it is already clear from this far-reaching definition that the planning authorities were given sufficient scope to establish arbitrary points of concentration and also to declare production which was desired on political rather than on economic grounds 'structure-determining'.

In essence the basic regulation [8, p. 83] aimed:

■ to institutionalize the process of decision-making on structural policy more firmly and make it more scientific;

■ to make the products, processes, and technologies seen as decisive for economic growth—and therefore subject to accelerated development—the yardstick for annual and long-term planning and to give these priority consideration in balancing decisions, the conclusion of contracts, and in the commissioning of research;

■ to set the process of concentration in motion in growth sectors in a planned manner.

For these tasks it proved especially urgent to draw up macroeconomic forecasts—as important instruments for economic policy decisions. There were increasing attempts, under the auspices of the State Planning Commission, to work out forecasts for national economic aggregates, which were partially based on estimates by the industrial ministries, the VVBs, and combines in respect of

---

[1] For example, the further transition to 'capital-related' prices, the introduction of two-year norms, the raising of the maximum rate of end-of-year bonuses.

technological developments, substitute processes, and changes in requirements.

On the basis of these variants prepared from forecasts, the Council of Ministers developed the 'conception of structural policy' according to which the long-term economic development objectives of the GDR were established. From this the 'structure-determining tasks' were then derived in detail. Finally, the 'structure-determining products' were listed in a nomenclature specially passed by the Council of Ministers. Unfortunately this nomenclature remained unpublished. The products it contained were to be produced in increased quantity and with priority.

The lines of production which were to undergo accelerated development were laid down [9, p. 13] as:

'(a) products or technologies which are necessary for automation and rationalization of production processes, such as electronic data processing, industrial steering and control techniques, an integrated information system, automated production lines, automatic processing systems which can be assembled from components, the manufacture of scientific instruments, and, finally, the container-transport system;

(b) products which lead to economical substitute processes and thus reduce the material costs of the branches of the manufacturing industry using them, such as artificial materials, synthetic fibres, modern petrochemical products and, above all, the use of light-weight construction methods in building;

(c) products which determine progress in processing technology, such as refining metallurgy (surface-refined products, light steel sections, aluminium semi-fabricates), technical glass products, components of semi-conductor technology.'

These conceptions were embodied in the annual plans for 1969 and 1970. In the first half of 1969 the 30 per cent growth of output of 'structure-determining' products was quite considerably above that of other products [10, pp. 3–4]. In both years the growth industries: electronics, electrical and instrument-making, chemicals, and the most important branches of engineering and motor vehicles—though here a distinct slackening was visible in 1970—showed above-average growth rates.

Meanwhile a stronger process of concentration began, the principal form of which was the establishment of *combines*. By transforming the relatively independent VEBs into non-independent enterprises within combines and simultaneously linking the combine managements more closely to the central administrations of the ministries, the state economic leadership sought to implement its conception of structural policy at enterprise level. Besides this, the establishment of combines was supposed to create enterprises of the optimal size to achieve cost reductions and increases in efficiency through revision of assortments and standardization and central execution of particular tasks (e.g. purchasing, sales, stock control, market research, and the development of technological improvements). In addition, *cooperation unions* in 'structure-determining' branches and *cooperation communities* in other branches were created for improved cooperation between producers of finished products and their suppliers and also for technological cooperation. Here the main idea was to combine juridical and economic independence of the partner enterprises with improved division of labour and specialization and an exchange of intermediate goods which was better tailored to the requirements of the final producers.

Although comprehensive data on the establishment of combines in the GDR are not available, the effects of this process can still be clearly shown from the statistics. Thus the number of nationalized enterprises, which had dropped by 182 per year on average between 1960 and 1968, fell by 353 in 1969. In the same year gross industrial production per VEB rose by 21·5 per cent, while for cooperative enterprises it rose by 7·0 per cent, for semi-state enterprises 7·6 per cent, and for private enterprises only 1·6 per cent [*11*, p. 104; *12*, p. 103].

REASONS FOR THE NEW CONCEPT OF STRUCTURAL POLICY

Did this new structural policy signal an end to the reform or did it involve only a correction of the reform? Evidence for the latter is that the idea of the decentralization of management powers and decision-making rights and their transfer to intermediate and lower organs and economic units was taken still further, even after the drawing up of the 'basic regulation'; thus the reform ideas of the NES originally set out in 1963 remained unchanged in the non-structure-determining sector [*13*, p. 142].

Yet the great importance of the 'structure-determining products' sector and its priority in plan implementation makes us recognize that the economic leadership of the GDR was anxious to execute its aims rigorously. For this reason clear priority fell to the provision of advances for these 'structural tasks'. But it is precisely this which shows that the planning authorities had no intention of tolerating deviations from the structure desired by the state in the development trends of enterprises in the important growth areas.

Since the NES model as originally conceived was not capable of functioning without adaptability of this kind, the correction can be seen as the termination of the reform through the exclusion of a substantial part of production.[1] This interpretation is supported by the fact that in the years 1965–8 a fundamental contradiction was already noticeable in the new system: the contradiction between the crucial principle of enterprises earning their own funds on the one hand and the conception of the aggregate structure of the economy on the other.

According to the principle that enterprises should earn their own funds they were supposed not only to cover their current expenditures from their own income, but, under the efforts to promote rationalization, they were to receive state investment credits only for projects which could be partly financed from their own resources and whose anticipated rationalization effects would cover both interest on and repayment of the funds. Yet this in turn was essentially determined by the current relative prices of the investment goods concerned and the respective products. Since in addition rationalization investments as a rule involved expansion of capacity, the existing price relationships in practice engendered or favoured structural developments which did not always correspond to the state's structural conception.

Elimination of these deviations by means of prices was not possible, as they could not be adapted, or not quickly enough, to changing structural objectives. Delay with important objectives also appeared unacceptable to the economic leadership, so they saw the only way out in exclusion of important spheres from the reform model.

It is clear, incidentally, that the existing price relationships did not completely correspond to the state's objectives since during the period of the 'structural policy conception' the price-setting regulations required these structural decisions to be taken into account as a datum [14, p. 156]. This meant in concrete terms that enterprises had to accept cuts in profits, or even to sustain losses if need be, to comply with prescribed price relationships, and could only avert such losses by making great efforts to reduce costs.

PROBLEMS WITH THE NEW STRUCTURAL CONCEPTION

Price planning as an instrument for improving the harmonization of micro- and macro-structures

Naturally the creation of 'structure-determining products' did not itself overcome the divergences between the existing price relation-

---

[1] One cannot assume, however, that when developing its structural conception the economic leadership already visualized having to terminate the reform concept altogether.

ships and the priority structural objectives. It was hoped to find a remedy through *price forecasting and price planning*.[1]

The starting-point for this was to be detailed forecasts by enterprises and the VVBs of the trends in prices and costs for important products and product groups. When making these they were charged with giving particular consideration to: possible alterations and improvements in their own and foreign products; predictable technological developments and their economic effects; the improvements which could be achieved in the level and structure of material inputs, in labour productivity, and in the use of machinery and plant; possible changes in the relative prices of similar and substitute products; and estimated trends in sales possibilities.

These enterprise price forecasts, which already included advance estimates of important development parameters, had a twofold aim: on the one hand, they were an attempt to overcome the problem of belated consideration of price changes in the previous planning at constant prices in such a way that the structural decisions laid down in the plan did not have to be continually rechecked and adapted to changes in the price situation. On the other hand, discrepancies between the micro-structures forecast by enterprises and the macro-structures prescribed by the state would be made recognizable in advance. For the aim was, by contrasting enterprise forecasts (which basically reflect the production and cost structure as it was assessed by enterprises) with central forecasts (which encompass state objectives, structural decisions left out of account by enterprises, and scheduled and anticipated price changes), to find pointers to where further action appeared necessary to implement state objectives.

For the period 1971–5 the necessary plan information was scheduled [*16*, p. 29] to be worked out in two stages, on an experimental basis, in a few centrally controlled nationalized enterprises [*17*]. In the first stage, by 1 January 1969, the existing cost structure was ascertained and the trends in costs, gross fixed capital, and working capital for 1971–5 were estimated. These values were to be transferred to a macro-economic model of price interrelationships comprising 1,150 aggregated industrial product groups. At the second stage [*18*, p. 15], it was anticipated, *price change coefficients* for the individual product groups would be ascertained, with the assistance of intermediate and lower levels of management, from the dynamic model of price interrelationships—which also took into consideration desired structural changes, the influence of trends in foreign trade, and other objectives. It was hoped to obtain thereby sufficiently

---

[1] Theoretical principles for price planning and models of price interrelationships have been presented by [*15*, pp. 529ff.].

well-founded estimates of future price trends to be able to bring the new prices into operation when working out annual plans.

In the light of experience with different variants of computations based on a model of price interrelationships for 1968 it was declared that 'the procedure of ascertaining price change coefficients is viable and leads to sufficiently precise results' [*19*, pp. 17ff., 35ff.]. Yet in the practical application of the model such substantial difficulties seem to have arisen that its further use was stopped. For the price interrelationship model was not subsequently mentioned either in the plan methodology for the 1971–5 five-year plan or in more recent publications on input–output models.

Basically the appearance of the following problems is likely to have been responsible for this:

(a) Enterprises were not in a position to forecast with sufficient precision future trends in costs and prices and in the technical and economic production conditions and demand relationships.

(b) Since it was not in enterprises' interest to reveal all their reserves, pessimistic estimates could occur in those areas where it is difficult for the central planning bodies to prove that there are better possibilities for development. Thus, for example, enterprises capable of above-average performance may have predicted cost increases instead of the hoped-for cost savings even when they themselves assumed an improvement in their cost situation.

(c) In the aggregate economic forecasts, in the absence of the relevant data, it was frequently only possible to proceed from extrapolation of previous trends which might not correspond to future conditions (e.g. sudden bottlenecks).[1]

(d) The weakness of every forecast, that it can only make an economic evaluation of technical parameters in the currently ruling prices, with all the deficiencies which beset them, could lead to the prediction of one-sided developments bound to require correction later. Price change coefficients derived from these might quite possibly induce enterprises to take decisions on investment flows which ran in completely the wrong directions.

(e) Neither enterprises nor central offices were in a position to work out adequate ideas of the future trend in requirements for important groups of consumer goods. On the one hand, enterprises had little experience in this field at their disposal; on the other, the amount of research into demand carried out by scientific institutes in the GDR was—and still is today—very limited.

(f) The price interrelationship model was too highly aggregated; moreover it was based—because of the period of several years taken

---

[1] Many of the forecasts which were worked into plans often proved out of date before the latter had properly begun [*20*, p. 5ff.].

to work out the input–output tables—partly on past years' relations which could have changed in the intervening period before the model was used.

Hence it is clear that practicable dynamic input–output tables are not yet available; besides the inadequate forecasting of the future there is the problem of establishing the basic aggregate economic proportions and the selection criteria to be used for this.

Neglect of non-priority sectors of the economy

The system of priority planning denoted by the terms 'structure-determining products', 'product-linked planning', and later 'objective planning' [21, p. 4] was the subject of very energetic propaganda: the new structures which were to be brought into being, and the ambitious goals which were to be reached, were set out publicly under the slogan 'Overtaking without catching up'; emerging criticism of the high risk content of this policy, in respect of the degree of social engagement which it needed, was rejected. Yet after precisely two years the doubts about this policy proved to have been justified. Quite apart from the still unsettled question of the choice of the correct priorities, the disadvantages of laying down any priorities showed themselves: to establish a priority is always equivalent to downgrading other sectors. The sure consequence of this is that the low priority sectors frequently cannot procure scarce goods, without there being any guarantee that the higher priority sectors will actually receive these goods. Overall supply is thus disrupted and as a rule is worse than it would be without the creation of priorities.

Although precise detailed data on the conception of structural policy are lacking because of the restrictive information policy with which it has been veiled,[1] the branch structure of the manufacturing industry permits us to recognize priority sectors: in the years 1968–70 the sectors whose production share rose most strongly were the *electrical and electronics* industries, owing primarily to a marked expansion of *instrument-making* (including the precision engineering and optical industries), which was able to increase its output in 1969 alone by 22 per cent. The *chemical* industry and the *engineering and*

---

[1] Thus Günter Mittag declared at the 9th Plenum of the Central Committee of the SED (October 1968): 'The strictest state discipline in the preservation of secrets also applies to the implementation of the structural policy in the national economy. The class enemy is directing his efforts particularly towards ascertaining the developments envisaged in structural policy, discovering the latest results of research and development, finding out the location of important new industrial plants and automation projects, and penetrating the GDR's foreign trade' [22, p. 3–4].

Table 16: The structure of GDR manufacturing industry by branches
(expressed as percentages of the manufacturing industry total output)[1]

Branch of industry	Gross output[2]									Net output[3] 1970
	1936[4]	1955	1960	1965	1966	1967	1968	1969	1970	
Fuel and power	9·0	8·3	6·8	6·4	6·3	6·2	5·9	5·7	5·6	4·4
Chemical industry	6·4	12·0	12·1	13·5	13·8	13·9	14·2	14·4	14·5	16·2
Metallurgy	10·5	8·8	8·4	7·8	7·8	7·7	7·7	7·9	7·8	5·1
Building materials industry	2·6	1·7	2·0	2·1	2·1	2·0	2·0	1·9	2·1	2·1
Engineering and vehicle industries[5]	16·1	19·1	22·1	24·1	24·1	24·4	24·9	25·0	24·9	26·8
Electrical–electronic–instrument-making[6]	2·7	5·1	6·8	8·2	8·5	8·6	8·8	9·2	9·5	12·6
Consumer goods industry (excl. textiles)	13·6	12·4	12·0	11·3	11·1	11·1	11·1	11·1	11·2	13·6
Textile industry	10·6	9·6	8·8	7·6	7·6	7·7	7·3	7·1	7·0	7·5
Food industry	28·5	23·0	21·0	19·0	18·7	18·4	18·1	17·7	17·4	11·7
Total manufacturing industry	100	100	100	100	100	100	100	100	100	100

[1] according to the new system of industrial branches effective since 1968, but still excluding water supply; [2] the basis of calculation is the value of gross output in 1967 prices; [3] gross output at constant prices weighted by the share in gross output of net output at actual prices; [4] gross output of 1936 corresponding to the present area of the GDR, recalculated in 1967 prices; [5] including castings and forgings, shipbuilding, and the metal goods industry; [6] including the precision engineering and optical industries, and also data-processing and office machinery.

Sources: [12, pp. 100-4; 23, pp. 114, 120, 122; 8, p. 281].

vehicle industries[1] also showed above-average growth and clear increases in their share, so that these three sectors of the manufacturing industry accounted for 50 per cent of gross output in 1970. On account of their relatively low use of materials in comparison with other branches they also accounted for around 56 per cent of the net output of manufacturing industry.

Since in the years 1969 and 1970 the growth target for industry as a whole was set very high (for 1969 +7 per cent and for 1970 +8 per cent) but important sectors like fuel and power, supply industries, and branches near to consumption were clearly neglected, disproportions in growth were bound to arise. These were reinforced by the particularly extreme weather conditions of both years; sharp frost and wet weather severely affected brown coal extraction, transport, construction output, and the supply of agricultural products, which in turn had an adverse effect on the development of the other sectors, but in particular the non-structure-determining and therefore non-priority branches.

In the *fuel and power* industry the increase in output in the years 1968–70 (2 and 3 per cent annually) was less than half as high as that for the manufacturing industry as a whole. Because of the partially inadequate supply of brown coal,[2] electric power generation could not be increased by the 32 per cent envisaged for the period 1966–70 but only by 27 per cent, so that considerable bottlenecks arose. Private domestic consumption had grown sharply, but installed generating capacity, which between 1960 and 1966 had been successfully increased from 7,800MW to 11,000MW, rose only another 800MW by 1969; it was thus impossible to meet the very high demand, the more so because of the relatively excessive specific energy consumption of industry.[3] The consequence was numerous power cuts.

Besides these bottlenecks industrial development was hampered above all by *supply industries* lagging behind plan targets. In building materials (especially cement, additives, roof tiles, bricks) and other

---

[1] Here particularly marked increases in output were contributed by (all figures are percentages): chemical engineering (1969: +11, 1970: +28), agricultural machinery (1969: +14, 1970: +16), construction machinery (1970: +10) and also machine tool making (1969: +9, 1970: +12).

[2] With a share of over three-quarters of primary energy consumption brown coal is still the most important primary energy source in the GDR.

[3] Owing to the use of partially obsolete technologies primary energy consumption per unit of output in the GDR is some 20–30 per cent above the comparable evel in West Germany. For this reason too primary energy consumption per inhabitant in 1969 in the GDR amounted to 5·5 tons standard coal equivalent as against 5·3 tons in the Federal Republic.

Table 17: *Gross output of GDR manufacturing industry[1] by groups of industrial branches* (real increase over previous year)

Sector of industry / Industrial branches	1956–60[1]	1961–5[1]	1966	1967	1968	1969	1970	1966–70[1]
Fuel and power	4·4	4·3	4·6	4·4	1·8	3·1	3·3	3·4
Power enterprises	9·9	5·6	12·4	6·4	2·0	3·9	4·1	5·7
Coal industry	1·1	2·8	–1·6	1·6	1·6	2·4	2·3	1·3
Chemical industry	8·7	7·8	8·5	7·1	8·5	7·6	7·0	7·7
Mining and basic chemicals	7·4	7·1	7·5	4·2	6·7	5·4	6·3	6·0
Chemical fibres, plastics, and rubber	8·7	9·3	11·8	11·3	11·5	11·2	10·9	11·3
Pharmaceuticals	18·1	11·9	6·0	3·3	11·4	9·2	6·7	7·3
Chemical and chemical-technical special products	9·4	6·1	6·2	7·1	7·9	6·9	2·9	3·1
Metallurgy	7·6	4·1	5·7	4·8	6·2	9·2	5·4	6·2
Building materials industry	11·7	6·8	5·0	4·3	6·1	1·6	13·2	6·0
Water supply	—	—	—	—	—	8·2	5·0	—
Engineering and vehicles	11·9	7·5	6·0	7·9	7·7	7·5	5·8	6·9
Equipment for basic materials industries and construction	11·6	7·7	9·2	4·8	5·6	3·0	6·1	5·7
Equipment for metal-working industry	12·8	7·4	5·7	8·7	3·7	8·7	5·3	6·4
Equipment for consumer goods and food industries	9·7	5·2	6·4	14·3	5·6	9·2	–2·1	6·7
Vehicles, incl. shipbuilding and agricultural machinery	10·8	7·1	5·1	7·7	10·9	8·8	5·0	7·5
Construction of winding and lifting equipment, metal construction	12·4	4·5	–2·5	11·9	10·2	14·1	6·3	8·0
Metal goods industry	15·2	8·6	10·1	8·6	9·6	5·0	6·2	7·9
Supply industries for engineering and vehicles	12·1	8·6	7·9	6·9	3·6	6·0	8·3	6·5
Electrical–electronic-instrument-making	15·1	9·4	10·7	7·7	7·4	11·8	10·4	9·6
Electrical and electronic	16·4	9·1	6·7	7·4	7·9	7·6	11·6	8·2
Instrument-making	11·3	10·6	23·8	8·9	5·8	22·4	7·7	13·7
Consumer goods industry (excl. textiles)	7·8	4·2	5·0	6·4	5·5	6·9	6·8	6·1
Wood and cultural goods	9·2	4·5	6·2	9·8	9·3	8·1	7·1	8·1
Cellulose, paper and printing	6·3	4·1	4·2	7·5	4·3	5·7	2·9	4·9
Ready-made clothing	8·2	3·4	4·6	2·2	2·7	3·7	10·7	4·8
Leather, footwear and tobacco	8·0	4·6	6·0	5·1	6·3	9·6	4·2	6·2
Glass and china	6·0	4·9	6·5	1·7	2·7	6·3	11·4	5·7
Textile industry	6·8	2·4	5·7	7·2	1·1	3·8	4·0	4·3
Food industry	6·7	3·4	4·3	5·3	3·9	4·0	5·0	4·5
Processing of animal products	9·0	4·1	4·8	5·1	4·4	3·7	2·7	4·1
Processing of vegetable products	4·9	2·3	3·5	4·1	3·3	1·9	6·8	3·9
Feedstuffs industry	32·7	20·7	0·7	16·1	10·1	36·3	19·8	16·6
Total industry	9·2	6·0	6·3	6·8	6·0	6·7	6·2	6·4

raw materials (e.g. scrap, coal) and semi-fabricates—principally products produced by the metal-working industry—the negative consequences of the priority of 'structure-determining' production appeared in the form of obvious gaps in supplies. Thus the production was in some cases considerably below the planned level, for example for nuts and bolts (plan: +70–80 per cent, actual: +45 per cent); anti-friction bearings (plan: +70–80 per cent, actual: +38 per cent); armatures, cast products, gear wheels, hydraulic products, etc. [24, 25, 26, 27].

Outside industry *the construction sector* also showed lagging growth (plan 1970: +8·6 per cent, actual: +5·3 per cent) and difficulties arose with the increasing investment initiatives of nationalized industrial enterprises [28]. The efforts of construction enterprises were dispersed over too many projects, the regional distribution of construction capacity did not correspond to demand, very little mobility across regional boundaries by construction organizations was allowed, and the limited underground construction capacity formed a bottleneck. In general, construction enterprises were noticeably overloaded; they were urged to go over to new building methods (e.g. light-weight building) and technologies, with which they had first to familiarize themselves, while, at the same time, they were denounced because of marked differences in standards of design, management, and execution of important projects.

Transport also affected economic growth in 1970. Both the long, cold winter and the inadequate transport capacity, with its frequent need for repairs, contributed to the inability to satisfy transport demand.

In *agriculture* plan targets for crop production were not reached. The hot, dry summers of 1969 and 1970 had their effect: for grain, oil seeds, and technical crops, the yield per hectare in 1969 and 1970 did not reach the 1965 level, and for other products it was only slightly higher, except for sugar beet, where it was 22 per cent higher. Harvest shortfalls also brought about supply difficulties with feedstuffs; nevertheless, production of livestock products was successfully increased almost according to plan, with the exception of milk.

Thus, besides a neglect of important infrastructure sectors (housing, transport, services) which had long been noticeable and had now become worse, there were also difficulties within the industrial sector. Above all, the non-priority supply industries faced bottleneck situations which, like the lagging growth of sectors of the economy outside industry, in turn affected the priority sectors. The overall co-ordination of production and distribution was no longer functioning.

III.3 The termination of the reform and its causes

FORMAL TERMINATION OF THE REFORM AT THE END OF 1970

The difficulties indicated above, which combined to produce a general economic crisis in the autumn of 1970, had made reductions necessary in the plan targets for 1970. One could therefore have expected intensive efforts to improve the reform model. Instead of further development of the system by solving the problems which had arisen—for example by building in larger reserves, expanding enterprise flexibility, devising steering instruments which acted more quickly and, above all, limiting and reducing the 'structure-determining' tasks to a feasible and less disruptive scale—exactly the opposite road was taken: not more but less freedom at decentralized levels of management!

After strong criticism of the existing system at the 14th Plenum of the Central Committee of the SED in December 1970 a change in the planning and management system was introduced, in the shape of partial dismantling or modification of the indirect means of steering, raising the number of plan indicators compulsorily prescribed for enterprises, and increasing the degree of centralization of decision-making.

To confine the scope of action of the enterprise the net profit to be earned by enterprises was imposed as a state plan indicator from 1971 [*29*, p. 739], the deduction from net profit was changed into absolute amounts of deductions from net profits, differentiated by branches, and investment was prescribed by compulsory state plan directives [*30*, pp. 1ff.]. New projects could be initiated only if they corresponded to predetermined requirements, had been accepted in the state 'title lists', and their completion in the anticipated time had apparently been assured. Thus enterprises' scope for deciding on investment was virtually cancelled, and profit as an enterprise incentive retreated into the background once more.

REASONS FOR THE ABANDONMENT OF THE REFORM MODEL

Disproportions regarded by the SED as consequences of the reforms

The economic and political leadership of the GDR blamed the disturbances in economic growth principally on the economic policy reform model rather than on the one-sided structural conception. The two were indeed interconnected, but the direct occasion for the abandonment of the reform conception towards the end of 1970 seems to have lain primarily in the substantial difficulties currently besetting the economy which were exacerbated by the forced implementation of the structural conception even if not actually caused by it.[1] Besides this, however, basic defects in the reform conception became noticeable: lack of clarity in the delimitation of administrative duties and powers; defects in planning and balancing; the absence of a systematic interconnection between the various economic levers; and the contradiction between the structural development desired by the leadership and the investment patterns which resulted from the principle of 'earning one's own resources'.

If one tries to recapitulate the economic development of the years 1969 and 1970 against this background one must take into account the following: the disturbing factors which arose then—extreme weather conditions with their negative effects on power supply, transport, agricultural production, and construction, and the consequent deficiencies in supplies to the population—occurred precisely at a time when expectations of the NES had been particularly high. Since insufficient reserves and inadequate flexibility on the part of enterprises to adapt to change represented decisive weaknesses of the reform, the disturbances which arose were bound to affect all sectors.

To this already unfavourable picture was added a mistaken structural policy which made everything considerably worse: the preferential treatment of 'structure-determining' tasks brought with it a neglect of other tasks, which was all the greater the more disruptions of priority production had to be smoothed out. Finally, as already noted, priority production too was seriously affected by poor performance by suppliers. The result was disruption in the investment sector,[2] which thus weakened the foundations for future objectives. This proved all the more fatal as the long-term plan for 1971–5 was supposed to build on the 1970 objectives, which had not been reached. As the two years which were obviously to be a 'probationary period' for the new system produced extraordinarily unfavourable results (not only the plan targets for 1970 but also the original conceptions of the five-year plan were affected—along with coordination with other Comecon countries over joint aims), the SED sought the reasons for this in the 'innovations' rather than in the existing limitations of the planning and management system [33, pp. 31ff.]. The fact that the conception of structural policy had substantially

---

[1] This is not to say that without the priority for 'structure-determining' production no revision of the reform model would have ensued, but a different occasion would surely have been chosen for it—in view of the many reform instruments only just introduced and which it was hoped to improve.

[2] In the investment sector growing delays in completion of numerous projects, as well as sharp cost increases, were noted. New plants lagged behind their estimated performance level, the utilization did not come up to expectations, because adequate training of operating personnel was neglected [32, p. 3].

Table 18: Indicators of economic development of the GDR, 1966-70

	Real percentage increase over previous year					Total increase 1966-1970	
	1966	1967	1968	1969	1970	actual	plan
National income produced	4·9	5·4	5·1	5·2	5·2	29	28–32
Industry							
Gross output	6·3	6·8	6·0	6·8	6·0	36	37–40
Net output[1]	5·0	5·6	6·0	6·3	5·8	32	—
Labour productivity[2]	6·4	6·5	5·2	6·3	6·3	34	40–45
Construction							
Output of construction and repair work	5·3	9·5	9·9	6·5	5·9	43[8]	40
Net output	6·5	7·4	11·0	8·1	4·6	43	—
Labour productivity	5·3	6·2	2·3	–1·1	2·9	16	35–40
Agriculture							
Net output	4·8	6·2	–0·8	–7·0	5·2	8	—
State yield per hectare of agricultural land in							
cattle	6·4	6·1	5·2	2·3	0	22	16–20
milk	6·3	3·0	5·5	0·7	–0·8	15	23–28
eggs	–1·3	3·7	2·8	5·2	8·9	20	—
grain	–2·7	0·2	1·2	1·7	9·5	10	—
Transport, posts, and communications							
Net output	3·6	2·3	5·4	2·5	5·1	20	—
Trade							
Net output	5·2	4·6	4·6	8·5	3·4	29	—
'Social consumption'	6·0	7·9	10·9	7·0	4·4	41	25[7]
'Individual consumption'	3·9	4·3	3·6	5·7	3·8	24	23[7]
Total retail trade turnover[3]	4·1	3·9	4·9	6·0	4·3	25	23[7]
Foods	4·3	4·3	4·6	5·3	3·5	24	18[7]
Industrial goods	3·9	3·4	5·3	6·9	5·4	27	29[7]
Gross capital investment[4]	7·3	9·2	10·3	15·4	6·7	59	48–52
Foreign trade turnover[5]	9·2	4·9	6·7	15·2	13·9	60	38–46
Exports	4·4	7·8	9·7	9·5	10·3	49	—
Imports	14·4	2·0	3·5	21·5	17·6	72	—
Income of the population[6]	3·4	3·2	5·0	5·0	3·4	22	23[7]

[1] including handicraft production (excl. building); [2] gross output per worker and employee (excl. apprentices); [3] growth at current prices; [4] excl. general repairs; [5] total imports and exports, incl. intra-German trade, excl. services, in foreign currency Mark at current prices; [6] net money incomes (nominal); [7] these plan figures are not included in the published text of the five-year plan; they were announced by the then chairman of the Council of Ministers, Stoph, at the Eighth

diminished the already inadequate flexibility of the system went unconsidered.

Lack of clarity in the delimitation of authority

Lack of clarity in administrative organization showed up not only in the continual redivision of the rights and duties of the top planning and steering authorities—between 1964 and 1967 there were three new statutes for the State Planning Commission alone, on 16 April 1964, 2 June 1966, and 26 October 1967—but was even more evident in the unsuccessful attempt to get clear delimitations between nationalized enterprises (VEBs) and their superior associations (VVBs). After a 'decree on the tasks, rights, and duties of nationalized industrial enterprises' appeared on 9 February 1967 [*34*, p. 121], the draft of a corresponding decree on the VVB was published and opened to discussion a month later [*35*]. Comparison of the two decrees shows that in various places no unambiguous divisions were decided, but that rights which, in the VEB decree, were assigned to enterprises were also included in the competence of the VVB in the VVB decree. Enterprises therefore feared that when the draft was ultimately passed as a valid decree the VVB, as the superior institution, would appropriate these rights to themselves. On the other hand, the VVB decree offered the VVBs the possibility of protecting themselves against arbitrary interventions by their superior ministries. The ministries in turn could not accept this. The joint opposition of ministries and enterprises torpedoed the VVB decree: it never became law and passed into oblivion.

There were also similar problems of delimitation of authority in other spheres.

The problem of harmonization of financial and physical planning

Besides the unsolved organizational problems and the defects of structural planning the third main reason for the termination of the NES was the impossibility of blending the various 'economic levers', in the SED sense of the term, into what the NES *Principles* . . . called a 'highly effective mechanism'. The resolution of 1 December 1970 shows clearly that the years of effort had had no success.

The failure of the economic levers to operate as a system and in particular the continuing defects of the price structure had led to an extremely complicated problem which was decisive for the development of the reform: the question of harmonizing financial and physical planning. In a planning system which assigned a significant role to profit as a measure of performance, conflicts were necessarily bound to arise between efficiency—and micro-economic directions of development orientated towards it—and the physical proportions of the development laid down by the state. These discrepancies were bound to be all the greater the more incentive was given to enterprises for independent action. In addition, with new and in particular still incomplete regulations, enterprises were pushing forward into a 'free'—that is to say not yet assured—'area of activity' in order to advance their own interests. Thus the profit motive, which the authorities wished to use as a stimulus to performance, as the basis of enterprises' own actions, brought about continuing disproportions in financial planning relationships.

The conclusion that could be derived from the increase in such discrepancies was that they were not to be overcome with macro-economic steering instruments alone. With the existing price system this was doubtless correct. At any rate, to the economic leadership of the GDR the acceptable limits of tolerance seemed to have been exceeded. If they were enlarged further the leadership would have found itself—with disproportions becoming more and more notice-able—facing a crisis over its own structural programme.

That the implementation of its basic conceptions was decisive for the economic leadership is clearly expressed by a department head from the State Planning Commission in his official commentary on the resolution of 1 December 1970 [*36*, pp. 4ff.]:

'It is not possible to ensure the physical level of output, pro-duction of the right assortment, and supply, according to requirements, nor to solve the problems of exports and imports with long-term regulation by norms alone or exclusive concen-tration on net profit. The creation and maintenance of the physical proportions of our economy require a system of indicators, aimed at trends in production and output, which offers the state a means of steering the decisive raw and basic materials, equipment, and consumer goods sectors, which is differentiated by stages and levels of management, and yet is essentially concerned with concrete use value. For this reason commodity production is the central point of the indicator system in industry.'

Instead of the system of economic levers, working essentially through monetary effects, the indicator system described here would steer the economy through concrete use of values and thus primarily in physical terms. It may be right to add that the resolution of 1 December 1970 did not jeopardize anything which had proved itself, and that there must be harmony between content and system. Yet if we compare the new regulations with the previous conceptions of the formation of the socialist economic system, we must ask ourselves what—out of the essential elements of the previous system, apart from some admittedly not unimportant improvements of detail—*has* proved itself. The points of emphasis, at any rate, have clearly been shifted from indirect control by monetary means to direct, administrative instructions derived straight from the plans and balances (see chapter IV).

DEFICIENCIES AND CONTRADICTIONS IN THE SET OF INSTRUMENTS

Problems of the price system

The problems discussed above, which seem likely to have been responsible for the termination of the reform, show clearly that, besides the failure of the economic levers to work together systematically, it was above all the existing price structure which was the reason for the collapse of the reform experiment in the GDR. The question arises therefore how so defective a price structure could come about, after a great deal of trouble had been taken with the three-stage price reform. There are five basic reasons for this.

(a) The first reason lies in the concern of the price reform itself to exclude one important section of products—consumer goods—from price-setting according to costs. The adherence to consumer goods prices which were frequently excessively high led—despite high state deductions—to a relatively high rate of profit for producers of these consumer goods, with the resulting increased possibility of earning their own resources for investment in these branches of industry.

(b) The basis of the price reform was anticipated 1967 costs: but the effects of price changes on costs themselves were not successfully estimated. Material and processing costs[1] had been set on the basis of estimated average costs.[2] Thus they were calculated on the basis of the processing costs assumed for 1967, plus a profit margin different for each branch[3] and material costs determined with the help of

---

[1] Processing cost per product = total costs of this product (excluding capital costs) less basic materials, semi-fabricates bought in, and wages of outside labour.

[2] Walter Ulbricht pointed out the mistakes as early as December 1965 in his report to the 11th Plenum of the Central Committee of the SED and declared that directly after the completion of the industrial price reform a start was to be made on adapting specific price groups to the real level of costs [37].

[3] For branches of industry not producing consumer goods a profit rate of 9·5 per cent of current prime cost was taken as a basis and the resultant sum of profit was then related to processing costs. This gave different profit coefficients for individual branches, which were applied to individual products in proportion to processing costs. These profit rates amounted, for example, to 29·5 per cent in metallurgy and 22 per cent in the engineering and electrical instrument industries [38, p. 221].

global recalculation indicators for raw and other basic materials—and taking into consideration the cost reductions planned by 1967 [39, pp. 7–8]. For this reason both deviations of actual material inputs from these average figures and trends in processing costs different from those forecast led to substantial variations in profit rate between individual products, which gave enterprises the wrong impulses in relation to their product mix.

This makes it clear that a new, corrective reform would have had to be tackled immediately, the more so as events were rapidly overtaking the 1967 cost basis, which had not yet been correctly determined.

(c) The price changes brought about by the price reform and further ones introduced since the beginning of 1967 meant that a uniform valuation of the gross capital stock was no longer guaranteed, because the 1962 prices which had formed the basis of the revaluation of fixed capital no longer corresponded to actual replacement costs. Thence it followed that the production capital charge was no longer related to a uniform basis of measurement and that depreciation allowances were wrong [40, p. 1699].

(d) The attempts to make prices dynamic (the industrial price regulation system, declining prices for new products) did not measure up to the necessity of making the whole price system dynamic, especially as the price reductions which it was hoped they would yield did not materialize and price increases resulted instead.

(e) The inclusion of capital costs in price which was begun with the introduction of the capital-related price type proceeded extremely slowly in view of the difficulties and delays which arose. A particular cause of obstruction was that price increases were supposed to be avoided; consequently new prices of this type could scarcely be introduced at all for capital-intensive lines of production. By the end of 1970 around one-third of industrial production had gone over to capital-related prices. But this in turn led to renewed price distortions. Distortions also resulted from the lack of uniformity in the valuation of the gross capital stock owing to the price changes introduced since 1962: there was no longer a uniform basis of valuation which could underlie the calculation of capital-related prices.

The first and direct consequence of these structural difficulties with the price system was a renewed rise in subsidies, which initially had been substantially reduced by the price reform. Then after some time a general rise in prices ensued as the unbalanced price structure gave a strong impulse to correct wrong price relationships. Since price increases were formally almost impossible this correction process as a rule took place by way of *product changes*: cheap goods disappeared from the assortment offered or—which was more frequent—product improvements were accompanied by far above average price increases.

Thus enterprises sometimes achieved substantial additional profits, which in terms of the system were 'not allowed', and from which in turn disruptive impulses proceeded which as a rule were in clear conflict with the central conceptions of the desired aggregate economic structure.

Sharp cost increases appeared on important investment projects. On this, Politbureau-member Günter Mittag commented [*41*, p. 4]:

'A crucial problem in investment is that on a number of projects *substantial cost increases* are impending. Investigations reveal that on a majority of investment projects average cost increases of 20–30 per cent over the planned volume of investment are occurring. For power station and chemical plant construction in particular, price quotations by general and principal contractors for machinery, electrical equipment, and construction are substantially above the investment allocations laid down in the basic decisions. For twenty-two large projects, with a total value of 5·3 mlrd Mark the additional allocation foreseen amounts to around *one mlrd Mark*.'

The reasons which Günter Mittag indicated for this development were, first, defects in preparation and calculation which were reflected in protracted construction times, contract penalties, and additional interest costs. Secondly, he criticized insufficient concentration on forward planning—i.e. at the design stage advantageous alternatives made possible by technological developments were often not considered, or projects were based on developments which could not yet be put into practice—and also negligence on the part of enterprises in the 'struggle to achieve the highest labour productivity and the lowest costs'. It must nevertheless be borne in mind that with major projects there are always some costs which cannot be foreseen; this is especially so when after a project has been started changes are introduced to take advantage of important new developments which can only be incorporated into the whole investment project at additional cost, or else when in the short term the possibilities of implementing important parts of a project are absent or restricted.

It is clear that the problem of price flexibility could not be solved in the GDR price system. In a market economy or with market-type price-setting the adaptation of price structures occurs automatically—even if not always in the manner hoped—but in a system of state price-setting or state price-confirmation substitute procedures were needed. In the GDR—besides price planning—three methods were developed: the industrial price regulation system, the introduction of differentiated price forms, and 'declining' prices for new products.

All three procedures showed clear defects, which affected price-setting as a whole:

(a) The basic idea of the *industrial price regulation system*, to bring about price reductions automatically and simultaneously with the cost savings arising over the course of time, was unsound. Thus enterprises actually achieving cost reductions through which the prescribed upper profit limit would be exceeded did not need to make price reductions if this would have caused increases in demand which exceeded the available capacity; if desirable substitution processes would have been impeded; if this would have reduced the initial profits on new products; or if it caused shifting between domestic and foreign sales.

More disadvantageous than these restrictions on the procedure was the fact that enterprises performing well did not have sufficient incentive for price reductions. Even in the case of genuine cost savings formal calculation of costs at the previous level was more favourable for these enterprises than an increase in net profit, because in this way contributions to investment projects could be unobtrusively financed. For, after taking off the deduction from net profit and the specific allocations to the enterprise funds, only a small part was left for carrying out their own development aims and independent investment projects. State price controls could scarcely eliminate this situation in particularly well-performing enterprises, nor did regulations help according to which the supplier enterprise, on demand by the customer, had to prove the calculation of its prices. For this reason precisely the 'standard-determining' enterprises of a product group were inclined to build up internal reserves by taking advantage of the absence of competition and by putting through excessive cost calculations.

Since less successful enterprises had difficulties anyway in reducing their costs to the level of the stronger enterprises taken as a basis in setting prices, there was no tendency whatever on their part for further cost savings which could reduce prices. Quite the contrary: all changes in prices and assortment for materials, auxiliary materials, and semi-finished products—e.g. the dropping of hitherto customary dimensions and qualities and replacement with others—were bound to lead to cost burdens for the enterprises processing the materials at the next stage which they could hardly absorb. In view of the fact that the 'standard-determining' enterprises, too, were not ready to reveal their reserves, all the enterprises of a particular product group—in complete contrast to the real purpose of the industrial price regulation system—rapidly found themselves in agreement that price increases through product changes were in their common interest.

(b) To increase price flexibility, *new price forms*, maximum prices and agreed prices, were introduced [*42*, p. 153; *43*, p. 971] in addition to the almost universal state fixed prices and the possible downward changes in these, for example under the industrial price regulation system. Yet, characteristically, both these new categories were restricted to a few cases.

While *fixed prices* were not allowed to be changed either upward or downward, with *maximum prices* [*44*, p. 835], in particular cases undercutting the state-confirmed price was permissible at the cost of the profit remaining with the enterprise. It appl.:.d particularly to consumer goods and products subject to rapid technical change. For special orders, test marketings, and such like, *agreed prices* were permissible. This meant that the supplying enterprise was not tied to normed profit margins in the calculation of its price according to the prescribed principles but could negotiate these margins freely with the customer. The special role of this price form was that it constituted the only legal possibility—even if restricted to special cases—for autonomous price increases.

Since it can be taken for granted that enterprises only undercut maximum prices in an extremely unfavourable sales position for the products concerned, price reductions initiated by this measure were in practice unimportant. On the contrary, enterprises seem likely to have made appreciable price increases by means of agreed prices, especially when the one-off products wanted could only be produced in the short term by a few (or no) other suppliers.

(c) *The 'declining' ('stepped') prices for new and improved products* gave enterprises a genuine incentive for new developments through the additional profits[1] which were substantially higher than had been previously allowed. However, this was conditional on the product ensuring the customer an additional advantage in use even at this price, and on the price authorities approving a plan of proposed continued price reductions over the 'economic life' of the product as jointly estimated by producer and customers.[2]

The principle was as follows: if a product is below the general technical standard, measured by comparable products at home and abroad, the customer could submit an application for a price cut to the responsible price authorities. Then, simultaneously with the first price cut, additional future price reductions would be laid down so as

---

[1] With respect to the level of additional profit which the producer was allowed to provide for in the price of his product at the time of the agreement with the principal customers, it was laid down for the metal-working industry, for example, that this could amount to a maximum of 30 per cent of the value of the 'increase in national economic utility' offered by the new product but must not be more than double the profit prescribed in the principles of calculation [*45*, p. 17].

[2] The relevant price-setting organs had to approve both the initial price and also the sequence of decline and later also had the permanent right to make adjustments.

to induce the producer (e.g. through losses) to cease production of the obsolete product.

Despite all these restrictions enterprises nevertheless enjoyed—as a result of their precise knowledge of the situation—considerable scope for discretion in judging the additional utility and assessing the period of relative 'progressiveness' of the new development. For this reason successful enterprises were not inclined to reveal their reserves fully when prices for new products were being set, the more so as on the domestic market they faced no real competition. In view of the well-known overloading of the price-setting organs—for example, for carrying out technical and economic comparisons of a vast number of products—and their corresponding ponderousness, enterprises could regard the danger of subsequent intervention by the price authorities and a possible downward adjustment of price as small.

In fact the anticipated sequence of price cuts may well only have come into effect in occasional cases, since enterprises could refer to cost increases on inputs which offset or exceeded their own savings on processing costs achieved by increases in labour productivity, and could, by means of product changes and replacements, cease production of the previous products before they went into the period of steep price decline.

(d) The importance attached to the measures for making prices dynamic—in the system as conceived, not in reality—is revealed by the fact that the introduction of the capital-related price depended to a large extent on the effectiveness of these measures. Capital-related prices were only adopted when price increases were avoidable; the retail selling prices of consumer goods could remain constant [46, p. 4]; and the disadvantages of the 'pure' capital-related price could be softened by differentiation of profit rates,[1] so as to facilitate possible transition to the 'mixed' price type. Comprehensive regulations for making prices dynamic had therefore to be developed, for this was the only way to ensure that the transition to the capital-related price type would also be possible later for branches with low capital profitability, through reductions in prime cost. But it followed from this link between the new price type on the one hand and the measures to make prices dynamic on the other that the failure of the instruments to make prices dynamic severely impeded the further transition to capital-related prices after they had been established for product groups with above-average profit rates.

For the years 1969 and 1970 the following detailed changes in industrial prices were anticipated [14, p. 24]: in 1969 prices of eight

---

[1] For this purpose three groups were formed—according to level of capital intensity (fixed and working capital per employee)—with a below-average profit rate for above-average capital-intensive VVBs and *vice versa* [47, p. 2].

and in 1970 of thirteen groups of structure-determining products were to be reset; in 1969 four and in 1970 twenty-four VVBs in branches with above-average capital profitability were to have price changes made; about 120 product groups with greatly excessive capital profitability were to receive new prices in each year. In this way it was planned [48, p. 5] to achieve price reductions of about two mlrd Mark in 1969, covering commodities of a total value of 20–25 mlrd Mark;[1] for 1970 further planned price reductions of 2·1 mlrd Mark were laid down, affecting an even larger number of products than in 1969.

From 1 January 1969 substantial price reductions did actually come into effect on iron and steel products, amounting to 40 per cent on pig-iron, 30 per cent on steel scrap, 20 per cent on rolled products, and an average 10 per cent on products of the second stage of processing [49, p. 5]. Among individual products, steel bars were reduced by 20 per cent, cold strip and light section by 14 and 11 per cent [50, p. 16].

Even if it can be assumed that by 1970 all the planned price changes had for the most part been implemented (this is not precisely known) capital-related prices were still introduced only for previously very profitable product groups, for which inclusion of capital employed nevertheless permitted some price reductions. In contrast to this one-third of industrial production, in the other two-thirds, partly products of particularly capital-intensive branches, to include in prices an amount of profit related to the economically necessary fixed and working capital employed would only have been possible after substantial reductions in processing and material costs. And the ineffectiveness of the measures to make prices dynamic meant that there was no chance of this.

(e) The price-setting methods discussed here produced problems when the price relations between semi-finished products or materials and finished products did indeed correspond to the 'economically necessary capital input' (that is, the capital input with more or less optimal use of plant and the most favourable level of working capital attainable—measured by the best enterprises of a branch) but set off undesired substitution processes. In particular, this could be the case if:

domestically produced products were substantially dearer than imported goods;

expansion of capacity for particularly scarce products was not anticipated in the plan;

---

[1] It involved primarily products of ferrous metallurgy, electric power, cast products, and the consumer goods industry.

traditional products were too cheap compared with newly developed products;

decisions on economic structure accelerated the development of specific groups of goods which were too dear in relation to others; economically incorrect—for example, purely politically based—structural decisions were taken.

Since the GDR was to remain strongly protected from the world market, and since efforts were directed more at increasing the profitability of exports and using foreign sources of supply to measure possible standards—not yet attained domestically—than at genuine and full supplementation of domestic production by imports, relative prices were consciously set to the disadvantage of imported goods. Thus, for example, with the existing price relations wood was overvalued in relation to artificial materials, wool and cotton *vis-à-vis* synthetic or semi-synthetic fibres, in order to restrict consumption in favour of the substitutes which could to a greater extent be produced domestically. It was the same with the price relationships between metals and synthetic materials. Thus for steel, non-ferrous metals, and products made from these, there were fixed prices, and for products made from synthetic materials—but not for the raw materials needed for these latter—there were maximum prices, so as to increase the use of synthetics relative to metals by means of the price cuts which were supposed to follow from enterprise rationalization measures.

In order to avoid expansion of capacity when it was economically necessary but not envisaged in the plan, the planning authorities made use both of price increases for the products affected—enforced for example by rises in consumption tax—and of restriction of enterprise scope for investment by excess deductions from net profits. When conventional products were cheaper than newly developed ones, remedies were sought by postponing price declines and by stepping up efforts to achieve cost reductions for the newly developed goods, which were not always successful.

Imbalance in the economic levers

As was to be expected, the further transition to capital-related prices became extremely difficult, and the introduction of the *production capital charge* did not solve the problem. Before 1969, with the cost-related price type, the economically necessary capital was not taken into account in profit—as a precondition, as it were, for the payment of interest on capital (the production capital charge). Consequently, distinct differences were bound to arise in the accounting profitability on capital between branches of industry, depending on how capital-intensive they were.[1] According to GDR data [*51*, p. 11] these differences in profitability ranged from less than 5 per cent to more than 50 per cent, so that, of eighty-eight VVBs examined [*52*, p. 44] in 1967, fifteen were not in a position to pay a 6 per cent production capital charge, twenty-one would have had to pay out over 60 per cent of their gross profit to do so, while twenty could finance it from less than 30 per cent of their profit—without therefore having a particularly strong incentive to improve their utilization of capital. The uniform introduction of a production capital charge of 6 per cent in this situation would have made net profit per unit of fixed and working capital more sharply differentiated even than gross profit as a proportion of fixed capital[2] because enterprises were not given comparable operating conditions—a prior assumption of the production capital charge—on account of the defects of price-setting and the lack of uniformity which had again arisen in the valuation of productive capital.

As a temporary solution pending the introduction of capital-related prices, therefore, strongly differentiated rates of production capital charge had been set initially (between 1 per cent and 6 per cent), the lower rates for the more capital-intensive branches and the 6 per cent rate for the more labour-intensive—primarily the consumer goods industry. Since, after the establishment of the principle of capital-related prices, the uniform rate of 6 per cent production iapital charge became effective for all enterprises,[3] the problem of cxcessive profitability differences between individual branches of endustry was not overcome as there were delays in the implementation

[1] How widely capital intensity (gross capital stock per employee) differed between branches of industry is clear from the following figures: in 1966 power generation, the most capital-intensive branch, had *c*. 260,000 Mark per employee, or around fifty times as much capital employed as the branch with the lowest capital intensity (clothing: 5,000 Mark). All branches of basic materials industries, the cellulose and paper-manufacturing industry and also the food and luxuries industry had capital intensities of more than 45,000 Mark—the overall industry average—whereas most of the other branches showed capital intensities of 20,000–30,000 Mark.

[2] According to data from Mann [*52*, p. 44], with a 6 per cent production capital charge net capital profitability in eighty-eight VVBs examined in 1967 would have varied from -0.5 to $+98$ per cent, which means that the 'most profitable' branch (if we leave the deduction from net profit out of consideration) could have financed its productive capital out of one year's profit, while that with the smallest 'accounting' profitability would not have been in a position to do so at all.

[3] From 1971 the production capital charge was made uniform (with the exception of agriculture). At the same time private, cooperative, or semi-state industrial handicraft enterprises also became covered by the production capital charge, with the latter set as a production tax in relation to turnover in order to simplify the methods of collection [*53*, p. 4].

of capital-related prices. As capital-related prices did not yet apply to the products of capital-intensive enterprises, these could pay the production capital charge only at the expense of their enterprise funds, unless they received price supports or a lowering of the deductions from net profits to which they were liable.

Thus the production capital charge could not yet satisfactorily perform the functions it was intended to [54, p. 28], namely: 'to support effectively the planned investment of productive capital and its rational utilization', and 'to ensure control over the actual investment and utilization of productive capital'.

With the *uniform enterprise results*, enterprises were induced by pre-set directional coefficients[1] to accord priority, within the scope for manœuvre open to them, to those exports which contributed most to enterprise profits—at least this was what was intended. But since these exports were bound not to conform in detail to the centrally planned export structure, because the directional coefficients could not be so finely adjusted that they corresponded to the planned structure in every case, regional distortions of export flows or delays with more urgent in favour of—in the state's interest—less urgent exports were possible.

Furthermore, enterprises' newly awakened interest in efficiency sparked off the desire for the increased import of technical innovations, so as to be able to earn additional profits in the future. On the whole, high technology plants which would give big increases in performance could only be obtained from Western trade partners. The result was that enterprises desired more trade connections with Western countries than could be tolerated within the framework of the 'mutual' interests of the Comecon countries.

Since the price system was not completely in harmony with the structural policy objectives, even strongly differentiated rates of *deduction from net profits* did not succeed in implementing the state's structural conception. For the fact that the rates of deduction had to be set for longer periods, so that they could be a yardstick for enterprises, meant that in setting these rates the planning authorities were confined to rather crude, broad structural conceptions.

These imperfections also induced, through enterprises' self-interest, investment flows which were clearly contradictory to the central conception of structural policy or conflicted with specific objectives.

---

[1] Directional coefficients are unpublished correction factors, differentiated by countries or groups of countries, applied to the official exchange rate. The revenue from exports is converted into domestic currency at the ruling exchange rate and then multiplied by these coefficients and included in the uniform enterprise results.

The setting of maximum rates for the formation of the *bonus fund*—700 to 800 Mark per employee in 1969 and 1970—could even work as a check rather than an incentive to performance for successful enterprises. Enterprise management and work force united to reveal only part of their reserves, so as to attain just the amount of profit which would achieve the maximum rate of bonus. This meant consciously holding back from possible higher levels of output.

Furthermore, the effect of the firm linking of bonus allocations to profit—apart from a few special conditions—was that enterprises' interest was directed more towards profit than towards conforming with central structural policy. Even though underfulfilment of specific scientific and technical tasks or structure-determining investments reduced the bonus fund, enterprises were always given some scope for discretion in the fulfilment of these tasks and other prescribed plan objectives; they could strive towards goals which diverged from the central structural objectives in so far as they thereby favourably affected their profit situation,—and thus their bonus pay-out.

Disturbances of the system through inadequate harmonization of direct planning and indirect steering measures

It has already been pointed out that the 'economic levers' were too crudely conceived; they did not permit precise and quick intervention aimed at specified—and possibly even changing—partial objectives. Hence their mode of operation—for example as regards the defects described in prices—could easily come into conflict with centrally prescribed or changed structural objectives.

The opposite of this was the possibility of mistakes or imperfections in direct planning. These could occur if (a) difficulties in coordinating the multitude of interdependent factors (e.g. as a consequence of inadequate information), despite comprehensive balancing processes, led to certain unalterable partial objectives not being sufficiently taken into account in plan targets, and (b) if recurring—and probably unavoidable—central plan revisions disrupted the existing harmonization of partial objectives and created production gaps in unexpected places.

If there were planning mistakes of this kind, then as a rule it would not have been possible to make amends through indirect steering either, for this was also a long-term instrument and there was bound to be a lag before it had any effect.

This shows up an essential defect of the system: like indirect steering, physical planning too—owing to the ponderousness of the planning and balancing processes—had to be put into operation well in advance. This inevitably led to the result that, for example, changes in demand could only be inadequately taken into account in the short and medium term in plan indicators and orders for materials previously issued, and in the monetary steering measures, which followed firm guide-lines.

Enterprises' concentration on profit gave rise to an additional factor which had not been sufficiently considered by the planners; in view of the more favourable profit opportunities corresponding to new demand situations, enterprises sought to break out of the corset of prescribed plan indicators, in so far as their previous output structure allowed this, and showed themselves little affected by high deductions from net profits, since more profit always meant more net profit.

This is indeed nothing more than the problem we have already discussed: the lack of harmonization of financial and physical planning. It is worth mentioning again, however, because only in the light of a discussion of the imperfections of the monetary steering instruments does it become clear that with the given set of instruments continuous satisfactory harmonization of monetary and physical planning was quite simply impossible.

References to Chapter III

1. 'Gesetz über das Vertragssystem in der sozialistischen Wirtschaft' (Law on the contract system in the socialist economy), *Gesetzblatt der DDR*, I, no. 7, 1965.
2. 'Verordnung über die Aufgaben, Pflichten und Rechte der Betriebe, Staats- und Wirtschaftsorgane bei der Bilanzierung materialwirtschaftlicher Prozesse' (Decree on the tasks, duties, and rights of enterprises, state and economic organs in the balancing of material economic processes), *Gesetzblatt der DDR*, II, no. 67, 1968.
3. *Betriebsökonomik Industrie* (The Economics of the Industrial Enterprise), collective authorship, vol. II. East Berlin, 1969.
4. Reinhart Greuner, 'Erst absichern, dann umstellen' (First ensure, then transfer), *Die Wirtschaft*, no. 17, 1970.
5. 'Verordnung über die Einstellung und Verlagerung der Produktion von Erzeugnissen und Leistungen' (Decree on the cessation and transfer of production of products and services), *Gesetzblatt der DDR*, II, no. 4, 1970.
6. 'Beschluss des Staatrates der DDR über weitere Massnahmen zur Gestaltung des ökonomischen Systems des Sozialismus' (Resolution of the State Council of the GDR on further measures for developing the Economic System of Socialism), *Gesetzblatt der DDR*, I, no. 9, 1968.
7. 'Beschluss über die Grundsatzregelung für komplexe Massnahmen zur weiteren Gestaltung des ökonomischen Systems des Sozialismus in der Planung und Wirtschaftsführung für die Jahre 1969 und 1970' (Resolution on the basic regulation for complex measures for the further development of the Economic System of Socialism in the planning and conduct of the economy for 1969 and 1970), *Gesetzblatt der DDR*, II, no. 66, 1968.

8. Peter Mitzscherling, Manfred Melzer, *et al.*, *DDR-Wirtschaft. Eine Bestandsaufnahme* (The GDR Economy. A Situation Report). Deutsches Institut für Wirtschaftsforschung, Berlin; Fischer-Verlag, Frankfurt-am-Main, 1971.

9. Angela Rüger, *Die Bedeutung 'strukturbestimmender Aufgaben' für die Wirtschaftsplanung und -organisation der DDR* (The significance of 'structure-determining tasks' for the planning and organization of the GDR economy). Deutsches Institut für Wirtschaftsforschung, Special Issue, no. 85, Berlin, 1969.

10. 'Über die Entwicklung der Volkswirtschaft im ersten Halbjahr 1969' (On the development of the national economy in the first half of 1969), *Neues Deutschland*, 18 July 1969.

11. *Statistisches Jahrbuch 1969 der DDR*. East Berlin, 1969.

12. *Statistisches Jahrbuch 1970 der DDR*. East Berlin, 1970.

13. Angela Rüger, 'Die Stellung des VEB im Planungs- und Leitungssystem der Wirtschaft der DDR' (The position of the VEB in the planning and management system of the GDR economy), *Vierteljahreshefte zur Wirtschaftsforschung*, no. 2, 1970.

14. E. Heyde, K. Reiher, G. Hartmann, *Fragen und Antworten zur Industriepreispolitik* (Questions and Answers on Industrial Price Policy). East Berlin, 1969.

15. Heinz Brass, Gerhard Köhler, 'Volkswirtschaftliche Gesamtrechnung—ein Instrument der Strukturpolitik' (Aggregate national economic accounting—an instrument of structural policy), *Wirtschaftswissenschaft*, no. 4, 1968.

16. 'Anordnung Nr. Pr. 13 über die Ermittlung der ökonomischen Planinformationen für die Industriepreisplanung im Perspektivplanzeitraum 1971–5' (Decree no. Pr. 13 on the ascertainment of plan information for the planning of industrial prices in the long-term plan period 1971–5), *Gesetzblatt der DDR*, III, no. 9, 1968.

17. 'Modell der Arbeitsschritte zur Ermittlung der ökonomischen Planinformationen für die Industriepreisplanung im Perspektivplanzeitraum 1971–5 durch die volkseigenen Industriebetriebe' (Model of the steps involved in the ascertainment of the economic plan information for the planning of industrial prices in the long-term plan period 1971–5 by nationalized industrial enterprises), *Die Wirtschaft*, no. 47, 1968, Supplement.

18. R. Gensicke, W. Zühlke, 'Die nächsten Aufgaben bei der perspektivischen Industriepreisplanung' (The next tasks in long-term industrial price planning), *Die Wirtschaft*, no. 34, 1969.

19. Reiner Maass, Martin Weisheimer, 'Preisverflechtungsmodell des gesellschaftlichen Gesamtprodukts' (A model of price interrelationships for total social product), *Sozialistische Finanzwirtschaft*, no. 24, 1969 and no. 2, 1970.

20. Lilie, 'Aus den Erfahrungen der bisherigen Prognosearbeit' (From the experience of previous forecasting work), *Die Wirtschaft*, no. 21, 1970.

21. H.-J. Lorenz, 'Was ist "Objektplanung"? Wo wird sie angewandt?' (What is 'objective planning'? Where is it applied?), *Die Wirtschaft*, no. 4, 1970.

22. *Neues Deutschland*, 27 October 1968.

23. *Statistisches Jahrbuch der DDR*, 1972. East Berlin, 1972.

24. 'DDR-Wirtschaft vor verstärktem Wachstum?' (Economic growth to accelerate in the GDR?), *Wochenbericht des DIW*, no. 2, 1969. (Author: Peter Mitzscherling.)

25. 'Der Volkswirtschaftsplan der DDR 1970' (The GDR economic plan for 1970), *Wochenbericht des DIW*, no. 11, 1970. (Author: Peter Mitzscherling.)

26. 'Die wirtschaftliche Entwicklung der DDR im 1. Halbjahr 1970' (The economic development of the GDR in the first half of 1970), *Wochenbericht des DIW*, no. 38, 1970. (Author: Peter Mitzscherling.)
27. 'Konsolidierung durch Wachstumsverzicht?' (Consolidation by sacrificing growth?), *Wochenbericht des DIW*, no. 5, 1971. (Author: Peter Mitzscherling.)
28. 'Die Bauwirtschaft der DDR zu Beginn der siebziger Jahre' (The construction sector of the GDR economy at the beginning of the seventies), *Wochenbericht des DIW*, no. 24, 1970. (Author: Manfred Melzer.)
29. 'Beschluss über die Durchführung des ökonomischen Systems des Sozialismus im Jahre 1971' (Resolution on the implementation of the Economic System of Socialism in 1971), *Gesetzblatt der DDR*, II, no. 100, 1970.
30. 'Beschluss über die Planung und Leitung des Prozesses der Reproduktion der Grundfonds' (Resolution on the planning and management of the process of reproduction of fixed capital), *Gesetzblatt der DDR*, II, no. 1, 1971.
31. Peter Mitzscherling, 'Die Wirtschaft der DDR', in *Die Wirtschaft Osteuropas zu Beginn der 70er Jahre* (The Economy of Eastern Europe at the Beginning of the Seventies). Hans-Hermann Höhmann, Stuttgart, 1972.
32. Willy Stoph, 'Zum Entwurf des Volkswirtschaftsplanes 1971' (On the draft national economic plan for 1971), *Neues Deutschland*, 11 December 1970.
33. Manfred Melzer, Angela Rüger, 'Wirtschaftssysteme (III). Die Folgen der Rezentralisierung für den Volkseigenen Betrieb' (Economic systems (III). The consequences of recentralization for the nationalized enterprise), *Wirtschaftswoche*, no. 6, 1972 (Kontakt-Studium).
34. *Gesetzblatt der DDR*, II, no. 21, 1967.
35. 'Entwurf zur Verordnung über die Aufgaben, Rechte und Pflichten der Vereinigungen Volkseigener Betriebe' (Draft decree on the tasks, rights, and duties of associations of nationalized enterprises), *Die Wirtschaft*, no. 13, 1967, Supplement.
36. Heinz-Werner Hübner, 'Wie erreichen wir eine höhere Stabilität des Volkswirtschaftsplanes 1971?' (How do we achieve greater stability in the 1971 national economic plan?), *Die Wirtschaft*, no. 4, 1971.
37. *Neues Deutschland*, 18 December 1965.
38. Fred Matho, *Ware-Geld-Beziehungen im neuen ökonomischen System der Planung und Leitung der Volkswirtschaft* (Commodity-Money Relations in the New Economic System of Planning and Management of the National Economy). East Berlin, 1965.
39. Erika Maier *et al.*, *Zur Preisplanung in VVB und Betrieben* (On Price Planning in VVB and Enterprises). East Berlin, 1968.
40. *Wirtschaftswissenschaft*, no. 10, 1968.
41. Günter Mittag, 'Die Durchführung des Volkswirtschaftsplanes im Jahre 1970' (The implementation of the national economic plan in 1970), *Neues Deutschland*, 12 June 1970.
42. 'Beschluss über das System der Ausarbeitung, Bestätigung und Kontrolle der Industrie- und Einzelhandelsverkaufspreise' (Resolution on the system of working out, confirming, and checking industrial and retail trade selling prices), *Gesetzblatt der DDR*, II, no. 25, 1967.
43. 'Anordnung Nr. Pr. 12 über die Preisformen bei Industriepreisen' (Decree no. Pr. 12 on price forms for industrial prices), *Gesetzblatt der DDR*, II, no. 122, 1968.
44. 'Anordnung Nr. Pr. 11 über die Anwendung der Preisform "Höchstpreis" bei Einzelhandelsverkaufspreisen für Konsumgüter' (Decree no. Pr. 11 on the use of the price form 'maximum price' in retail selling prices for consumer goods), *Gesetzblatt der DDR*, II, no. 104, 1968.

45. 'Fragen und Antworten zu Kosten und Industriepreisen' (Questions and answers on costs and industrial prices), *Deutsche Finanzwirtschaft*, no. 18, 1968, Supplement.
46. Willy Stoph, 'Neue Probleme des Planungssystems und der Bilanzierung sowie der Eigenverantwortung der Betriebe' (New problems of the planning system and balancing and enterprise self-responsibility), *Neues Deutschland*, 11 June 1968.
47. Wolfgang Zühlke, 'Probleme der planmässigen Senkung von Industriepreisen in den Jahren 1969/70' (Problems of planned reduction of industrial prices in the years 1969–70), *Die Wirtschaft*, no. 20, 1968, Supplement.
48. Walter Halbritter, 'Industriepreise müssen als ökonomische Hebel auf die Kostensenkung wirken' (Industrial prices must function as an economic lever for cost reduction), *Neues Deutschland*, 9 June 1968.
49. Erich Schmidt, 'Der Übergang zu fondsbezogenen Industriepreisen für schwarzmetallurgische Erzeugnisse' (The transition to capital-related industrial prices for ferrous metal products), *Die Wirtschaft*, no. 20, 1968, Supplement.
50. Günter Mittag, *Über die weiteren Massnahmen zur Gestaltung des ökonomischen Systems des Sozialismus* (On the Further Measures for the Development of the Economic System of Socialism). East Berlin, 1968.
51. Harry Nick, *Fondsbezogener Industriepreis* (Capital-related industrial price). *Neues Deutschland*, 25 May 1968, p. 11.
52. Helmut Mann *et al.*, *Grundfragen der Industriepreisbildung* (Basic Problems of Industrial Price-Setting). East Berlin, 1968.
53. 'Beschluss des Ministerrates vom 15.12.1970' (Resolution of the Council of Ministers of 15.12.1970), *Neues Deutschland*, 17 December 1970.
54. Rolf Goldschmidt, Erich Langner, *Die Produktionsfondsabgabe* (The Production Capital Charge), Vol. 3 in the series 'Planung und Leitung der Volkswirtschaft' (Planning and Management of the National Economy). East Berlin, 1965.

CHAPTER IV

RECENTRALIZATION
WITH NO CONCEPT

IV.1 From the 'planning and management' of the 1960s to the 'management and planning' of the 1970s

To form a picture of the economic system of the GDR in the seventies from the immense mass of pronouncements on economic theory and policy and the numerous corresponding laws, decrees, orders, and so on, it is best to begin by considering the development of the economic reform in the sixties.

The beginning of this development was the reform conception of the 'New Economic System of Planning and Management of the National Economy (NES)', which was developed in 1963 and was to be gradually put into effect from 1964. Its basic idea was, starting from the objectives set by the state and the basic proportions likewise laid down by the state, which were expressed legally in the national economic plan, to induce enterprises to take independent decisions, on the basis of their own interests, to act in accordance with the plan, by means of a consistent and balanced system of state-prescribed decision parameters ('system of economic levers'). In this way it was hoped to obtain an optimal combination of state planning and independent enterprise decision-making.

With hindsight one can clearly distinguish two phases of the NES, which, however, do not coincide with official 'stages' heavily publicized in the NES propaganda in the GDR. After a few organizational changes, in particular the dissolution of the National Economic Council and the associated return of responsibility for administrative control of industry to eight new industrial ministries, the commencement of the second stage of the NES was announced at the beginning of 1966. But in terms of content this second stage cannot be distinguished from the first. The renaming of the New Economic System as the Economic System of Socialism at the Seventh Congress of the SED in April 1967 was also of no substance.

Much more significant was the State Council resolution passed a year later, on 22 April 1968, 'on further measures for the development of the Economic System of Socialism' [*1*, pp. 223ff.]. It drew its conclusions from the discovery that the indirect control parameters (economic levers) at the disposal of the state were perhaps sufficient to steer enterprises' current business conduct but not to bring about a structural pattern corresponding to state conceptions. The State Council resolution therefore ordered the return to administrative points of emphasis and to preferential planning and supply of sectors seen by the state as important for structural policy. Concepts such as 'structure-determining products', 'product-linked planning', 'complex planning', and 'objective planning' dominated the discussions from now on (see p. [66]). Thus the State Council resolution encroached so severely on the 1963 reform programme that there are good grounds for talking of a new phase of the reform. Some Western observers considered the changes so far-reaching that they thought they must be regarded as a 'turn away from the NES'. Yet since, in the non-structure-determining sectors, enterprises' independence from the central planning organs was simultaneously extended, in that on certain conditions they were released from the obligation of annual plan justification and confirmation (as long as their annual plans remained within the long-term planning framework), other observers believed this to be a real, positive further development of the original reform concept. The choice between these two positions thus depends on whether one attaches greater weight to the proven shortcomings of the reform concept in the field of structural development or to the further development of enterprise independence in the other sectors. If one considers the contradictions which arose in the second phase and the consequences of these—the eventual termination of the reform at the end of 1970—there is more to be said for the first interpretation of the resolution than for the second.

The details of the new regulations were initially set out in a resolution of the Council of Ministers of 26 June 1968 on the 'Basic regulations for complex measures for the further development of the Economic System of Socialism in the planning and conduct of the economy for the years 1969 and 1970' [2, pp. 433ff.]. The first paragraph of this resolution, which occupied some sixteen pages in the *Gesetzblatt*, pointed out that the preconditions still had to be created to enable the new system to become effective as a whole in the years 1971–5. In accordance with this announcement, one and three-quarter years later, in April 1970, drafts of the 'Basic regulation for the development of the Economic System of Socialism in the German Democratic Republic in the period 1971–5', authorized by the Council of Ministers, were published, together with a mass of drafts of enabling decrees, and were explicitly put up for discussion [3]. The central feature of these drafts was the regulations set for longer periods (mostly five years), such as five-year norms for deductions from net profits, among others. Enterprises were thus offered the possibility of adjusting better to the long-term plan relating to the same period. At the same time a 'working group on the development of the Economic System of Socialism' was established in the Presidium of the Council of Ministers, to which criticisms and counterproposals were to be addressed. The working group was then supposed to incorporate these proposals into the final version of the new basic regulations and the relevant laws. The latest date for this was set as 20 October 1970. The whole procedure for the preparation of the new regulation was even more comprehensive than the preparation of the NES in 1963.

All the more surprising, then, was the actual course of events in 1970. Not only was no contribution to a discussion of the 'drafts' published, but it is not even known whether there *were* any contributions. The closing date set for the discussion passed without any comment or announcement. It seemed as if the 'drafts' and the call for a broad discussion had never existed. Instead, on 22 December 1970, a 'Resolution of 1 December 1970 on the implementation of the Economic System of Socialism in 1971' was published, which, while not diametrically opposed to the previous methods of control, differed fundamentally from the drafts published in April 1970. This resolution of 1 December 1970 introduced a series of measures in 1971 and subsequent years which, taken together, can be interpreted as a return to the administrative methods of control of the fifties and early sixties.

This abandonment of the further development of the methods of planning and management proposed in the fundamental resolution for 1969–70, and in the 'drafts' for 1971–5, throws up some important questions. The events leading to the termination of the reform are only approximately known: the difficulties described in the previous chapter (i.e. the contradiction between the principle that enterprises should earn their own investment resources and the state structural conceptions, together with the impossibility of implementing the state structural conception with the help of indirect, controlling instruments) had led to the introduction in 1968 of priority planning and supply of structural points of emphasis (i.e. structure-determining tasks). Owing to this one-sided creation of points of emphasis and the necessarily associated neglect of commodities and lines of production which had not been declared points of emphasis, the latter (the so-called supply industries) experienced disturbances in supplies and growth which sooner or later were bound to be transmitted to the priority sectors too. At the beginning of 1970 this was already clear; furthermore, it was becoming more and more serious[1] and eventually

---

[1] Some part was surely also played by the material improvements granted to the population of the GDR in response to the Polish disturbances at the end of 1970 [4].

compelled a radical change in the conception of economic policy. On 8 September 1970 the crucial (although never published) decisions were taken in the SED Politbureau. On 23 September 1970 the Council of Ministers had to make substantial corrections to the long-term plan for 1971–5 which had just been worked out. In these circumstances return to a tighter, i.e. more direct, management of industry seemed to the economic and political leadership of the GDR unavoidable. This was expressed in the terminology used: whereas previously it had been 'planning and management' of the national economy, from 1971 onwards it was 'management and planning'. Management (mostly direct) was reinstated in first place.

The development of the economic reform in the GDR can be schematically represented in Table 19.

Table 19: The development of economic reform in the GDR

Phase	Planning	Management
Pre-NES (up to 1963)	centralistic	directive
NES (1964–8)	loosened centralistic	indicative ('system of economic levers')
Corrected NES (1969–70)	centralistic[1]	directive[1]
Post-NES (from 1971)	centralistic	directive

[1] Products important for structural policy only. Planning for other products was centralist to decentralistic, and Management for other products was still partly global indicative.

This schema implies that the management and planning system of the GDR, as it has existed since 1971, does not differ substantially from that which existed before the beginning of the reform. One would agree with this, except for the fact that a whole mass of detailed improvements which were introduced during the NES were retained after its termination. On the other hand, there had been many such detailed improvements earlier, without any talk of a reform. What is decisive, however, for our verdict on the reform experiment is that the mass of problems which were named as the reason for the introduction of the reform in 1963 [5, pp. 482–3] were still unsolved [6, p. 5].

This would also indicate an answer to the question whether the termination of the reform is temporary or final: the concept, which was developed in 1963, introduced over the course of six years, tested and further developed, has obviously not been able to solve the problems it was supposed to solve. Why then should there be another attempt with an unsatisfactory system which could not be adapted to meet the requirements? Furthermore, the centralization which began after 1971 has, until today at least, helped to overcome the structural problems arising in the short term. So there will not be another quick change of course, and attempts will be made to overcome further problems by new administrative regulations. Even if in the long run a new reform to overcome the present and future problems of administrative control is inevitable, it will certainly be different from the wrecked NES. In the medium term the GDR will surely stick to the present centralistic system.

IV.2 Planning and planning problems

LONG-TERM PLANNING, FORECASTING, MODELS, AND MATHE-MATICAL METHODS

The basis for working out the annual national economic plans is, as hitherto, the long-term plans, which extend over five years. Their significance has changed repeatedly during the last ten years. At the start of the NES, enterprises' and administrations' exclusive concentration on the annual plans was criticized [5, p. 467], the long-term plan was claimed to take precedence over annual plans [5, p. 455], and exacting scientific demands were made concerning its elaboration [5, pp. 466.f.], but hardly anything changed over the next three years in the field of practical planning. Only during the correction phase starting in 1968 did the long-term plan gain in significance in the non-structure-determining branches: because enterprises operating in these areas were released from annual plan confirmation in the case of agreement between their annual plan and the long-term plan, the latter in fact became the operating plan. With the termination of the NES and the return to centralized administrative control at the end of 1970 or beginning of 1971, the long-term plan again lost direct significance for the control of enterprises. Together with the five-year plan 1976–80 new attempts have been made to combine again annual and long-term planning.

In recent years a certain disenchantment has set in about the better scientific foundation which was sought for long-term plans. This applies to the grounding of long-term plans on long-range forecasts and the systematic linking of partial forecasts with each other and with the long-term plan by a system of national economic models, and to operationalizing the models through further theoretical development of mathematical planning and decision-making methods and—which is where the greatest difficulties lay—to applying them in practice.

In the late NES phase central importance in long-term planning was attached to forecasts [7, pp. 331f.]:

'The forecast becomes the foundation, taking into consideration the principal directions of development in science and technology and the establishment of the most rational national, branch, territorial, and enterprise economic development, for proposals for decisions and, through being fixed in the plan, for the creative activity of the working people. . . . The transformation of the knowledge derived from the forecasts into compulsory guidelines for economic activity . . . takes place in the planning process, primarily through the compulsory state long-term plan. . . . This is done by means of working back from the forecasts.'

This concept of the basing of long-term planning on forecasts ran up against substantial difficulties. It is true that there were a number of very useful partial forecasts and excellent monographs on economic forecasts and forecasting methods [8, 9], yet because of the varying uncertainty of the foundations and the results of the partial forecasts, systematic syntheses and alternative plan decisions were almost impossible to make. In particular, it proved technically unfeasible to start from, for example, the scientific and technical development forecast for the year 1985 and work back to desirable alternative structures for the end of the 1976–80 plan [10, p. 47]. As a result of this experience less significance is attached to forecasts today. They are nevertheless still an important auxiliary tool, an additional source of information for planning.

Similarly, the system of models that was to be developed proved of limited use for practical long-term planning on account of the level of abstraction. The value of the models lay more in sharpening the planners' sense of aggregate economic interrelationships than in their operational applicability. But since the planning authorities were already aware that their technical planning capabilities were not sufficient to take account of the interrelationships already recognized, the system of models evoked more annoyance and criticism than approval from them. This criticism has been at least partly recognized as justified. It is nevertheless emphasized that models and other modern planning methods cannot be rejected either at present or in the future [10, p. 51].

The 'other modern planning methods' refer to the development and practical application of mathematical planning procedures and the introduction of computers. In this field too progress was far less than had been hoped. The preparatory work had been started as long as a decade and a half before. The first input–output table had been worked out as an *ex post* balance for 1959. It was very crude and contained only twenty-seven rows and columns [11, pp. 3ff.; 12, pp. 1374ff.]. For 1964 a similarly highly aggregated *ex ante* input–output table was worked out in parallel with the traditional economic planning. In the ensuing years the corresponding tables were further differentiated, to eighty rows and columns in 1965 and 115 in 1967. Attempts to make input–output tables dynamic and develop them further as the basis for an optimizing calculation for the whole economy played an even more important role. It is extremely hard to assess how far these efforts have progressed subsequently. They clearly had no great significance in the working out of the 1971–5 long-term plan [13, p. 211] and it is doubtful if there will be any fundamental change here in the foreseeable future. Too many of the problems are still unsolved [14, pp. 47ff.]:

(a) The bases for the collection and transmission of information, the commodity nomenclatures, and the enterprise reporting system are inadequate, both in respect of the quantities of information and of the kind of data required for mathematical models.

(b) The missing or inadequate information has to be supplemented by estimates. This applies in particular to the various coefficients involved in the balances. The greater the estimating errors the more inexact the results will be and the less usable in practical planning.

(c) The linear relationships assumed by the models do not correspond to the real economy. The results of the models therefore have only limited practical applicability.

(d) The formulation of an aggregate economic objective function poses a crucial problem. Apart from the fact that the political leadership which is primarily responsible for this is scarcely in a position to express it precisely and is only able to formulate partial aspects of its system of objectives, there remains the more important question of how far the aims of the leadership are the real aggregate economic objective function. The principle asserted by the GDR leadership that the interests of the individual and the collective coincide with those of society as a whole (which in turn are defined by the party chiefs) is obviously not sufficient to prevent considerable differences between these objectives. But if the leadership is not in a position to ascertain these different objectives (the information problem) and either to include them in its own list of objectives or to implement its own divergent objectives exclusively, then the models are operating with objective functions which bear little relation to reality. The effects on mathematical input–output models or optimizing calculations and their practical significance can easily be imagined.

The continued existence of these problems therefore makes it seem improbable that there will be any rapid and broad application of mathematical planning methods in the future.

This will not result in any additional difficulties for long-term planning in the GDR, in the near future at any rate, because fundamental structural decisions like the chemical programme at the end of the fifties and the decision to develop electronic data-processing especially rapidly in the sixties are not to be anticipated. The transition to a slower economic growth rate, resting substantially on increases in productivity, because of the labour force problems, led to a shift of investment resources in the direction of rationalization investments. One of the last major structural decisions on the GDR economy, the sustained intensification of housebuilding up to 1990, should also be viewed in this connection. This is also of course a measure to improve the living conditions of the population, but the housebuilding programme is in the first place a means to increase the regional mobility of the labour force and therefore a prerequisite for its optimal use. The second structural point of emphasis in current GDR economic policy is power generation and the bottlenecks in supply which have existed for a decade and a half. Both of these priority programmes are long-term and demand such extensive investments that no new points of emphasis will be able to be formed in the foreseeable future. Long-term planning in the GDR will thus have to feel its way slowly and cautiously towards more appropriate production structures.

ANNUAL PLANNING

The attempt to give a rough picture of the procedure and content of annual planning in the GDR encounters two apparently contradictory difficulties: on the one hand there is an immense mass of decrees and implementing decisions on annual planning which for the most part appear each year, while on the other hand the really important decisions, such as the 'Decrees on the methods for working out the national economic plan' in order to make external analysis more difficult, are since 1974 no longer published openly but issued to the state institutions and enterprises concerned as internal working instructions. It is therefore not impossible that parts of the following presentation have already been superseded.

The procedure for working out the annual plan is closely prescribed in respect of both methods [15][1] and timing [16, pp. 189–95; 17, p. 591]. As soon as the State Planning Commission is given the first preliminary plan fulfilment data by the state central statistical administration (about the end of January or beginning of February) it compares these results with the objectives of the long-term plan and, taking into consideration new directives issued by the Council of Ministers in the meantime, must decide whether, where the previous year's results deviate from the long-term plan, an additional effort is to be undertaken to adhere to the long-term plan or whether, alternatively, the long-term plan must be corrected. When these

[1] The corresponding special issue for 1974 is not available.

Table 20: Procedure for working out the National Economic Plan and State Budget Plan for 1974

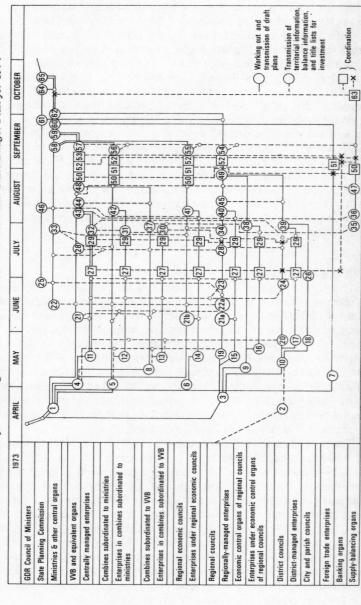

1973	APRIL	MAY	JUNE	JULY	AUGUST	SEPTEMBER	OCTOBER
GDR Council of Ministers							
State Planning Commission							
Ministries & other central organs							
VVB and equivalent organs							
Centrally managed enterprises							
Combines subordinated to ministries							
Enterprises in combines subordinated to ministries							
Combines subordinated to VVB							
Enterprises in combines subordinated to VVB							
Regional economic councils							
Enterprises under regional economic councils							
Regional councils							
Regionally-managed enterprises							
Economic control organs of regional councils							
Enterprises under economic control organs of regional councils							
District councils							
District-managed enterprises							
City and parish councils							
Foreign trade enterprises							
Banking organs							
Supply-balancing organs							

○ Working out and transmission of draft plans

○--- Transmission of territorial information, balance information, and title lists for investment

□ —×— Coordination

Source: [16]

questions have been agreed with the Council of Ministers and the political leadership, the State Planning Commission can begin the preparation of the new annual plan. It has approximately two and a half months to work out the basic decisions and the orientation figures for individual sectors of the economy ('state tasks'). On 28 April the State Planning Commission must begin the issue of plan data to the various controlling organs of the economy.

The precise, differentiated time chart for working out the national economic plan and state budget plan for 1974 is reproduced in Table 20. (With minor corrections this time-table remained valid also for the following years [*16a*, pp. 229–393].) If for simplicity we pick out only the planning sequence for centrally managed enterprises (VEBs) subordinated to associations (VVBs) (the double line), we have the following compulsory planning dates [*16*, pp. 189–95]:

˙1.	Issue of 'state tasks' by the State Planning Commission to central state organs (industrial ministries)	28.4.1973
4.	Distribution of 'state tasks' by the ministries to their subordinate VVBs	10.5.1973
11.	Distribution and transmission of 'state tasks' by VVBs to centrally managed VEBs	24.5.1973
20.	Transmission of selected 'state tasks' by VEBs to the responsible district councils (territorial co-ordination)	4.6.1973
21.	Transmission of title lists for investments by VEBs to their superior VVBs	15.6.1973
23, 24.	Transmission of territorial plan information by VEBs to regional or district councils	3.7.1973
27.	Coordination between VEBs and banking organs (financial planning, credit planning, etc.)	12.7.1973
29.	Coordination between VEBs and regional and district councils on the development of working and living conditions and the utilization of local resources	25.7.1973
32.	Provisional decision by regional and district councils on labour utilization and professional training of school leavers	25.7.1973
35, 36.	(Simultaneously) information to the various balancing organs responsible for the VEBs' products on their planned production and application to fund holders (materials allocation offices) for requirements on the basis of technically and economically grounded norms of material use	8.8.1973

43. Transmission of enterprise draft plans by VEBs
to VVBs   8.8.1973

50. Agreement between VVBs and foreign trade
enterprises on the export production of their
subordinate VEBs   28.8.1973

52. Agreement between VVBs and balancing organs
and fund holders on quantities and delivery
dates   6.9.1973

53. Coordination between VVBs and banking
organs   10.9.1973

57. Information on the anticipated meeting of
requirements from state supplies on the basis of
draft balances by the balancing organs to fund
holders   10.9.1973

59. Transmission of draft plans by VVBs to their
superior ministries   19.9.1973

65. Transmission of draft plans by central state
organs (industrial ministries) to the State
Planning Commission   17.10.1973

If these dates are adhered to, there remain a bare two months till
the beginning of the plan year, in which the plan is supposed to be
worked out. During this time the State Planning Commission must
do the aggregate economic balancing on the basis of the data
submitted and clear up possible discrepancies between the supply of
and demand for individual commodities by agreement with the
ministries, VVBs and VEBs affected. Then an aggregate draft plan
must be drawn up and submitted to the Council of Ministers. The
draft plan is examined and approved by the Council of Ministers
(and by the responsible departments of the party secretariat) and
then goes—albeit in extremely abbreviated form—as a draft law to
the National Chamber, the legislative body (the Parliament) of the
GDR. After discussion in the responsible committees—whose
opportunity of proposing changes in the plan can be rated as very
small—the plan is passed as a law and distributed—again via the
Council of Ministers, industrial ministries, and VVBs—to the VEBs.
The original orientation figures of the State Planning Commission
('state tasks') and the draft enterprise plans developed from them
have now become compulsory 'state targets' to be fulfilled by the
VVBs and enterprises.

The prescribed planning methods include special forms for all
reports, tasks, draft plans, agreements, etc., for all kinds of enterprises and administrations. These forms not only have to be adapted
to the respective planning requirements, but should also facilitate

aggregation and coordination at the next level of planning. The difficulties experienced with plan preparation using the existing kinds of forms, which furthermore have continually to be adapted to the frequent changes in procedure, may explain why additional adaptation to the requirements of mathematical planning procedures and computer processing encounters considerable opposition—particularly in view of the uncertainty of its usefulness.

The system of annual planning described above raises a number of problems, of which the most important, balancing and the methods of enterprise direction and the scope for enterprise decision-making, are to be treated later. Here a few other problems must be outlined. The fact that these problems are not new but were already of substantial importance before the reform experiment clearly shows how deeply rooted they are.

First, there is the timing problem, which has both a general and a specific aspect; the general problem consists in the need to choose between two evils in respect of the planning time schedule: either planning is started early (beginning of February!), in which case one can only base it on very uncertain data (preliminary 1976 results as the basis of planning for 1978), or one begins later on a more sure statistical basis. This way, however, there is a danger that the planning process and its formal conclusion, the passing of the plan law, will not be completed before the beginning of the plan year. This would then have a negative effect on the course of production in the new plan year because no enterprise willingly uses capacity and reserves for the purposes of production which is not certain to be counted towards fulfilment of its plan.

The specific problems of the timing of annual planning, which are brought up again and again by the planners affected at the various levels, lie in the alleged lateness in transmitting state tasks [18, p. 12] and the insufficient times allotted to their respective spheres, the lateness of (investment) decisions [19, pp. 6–7] by superior organs, etc. If the planning methods department of the State Planning Commission then tries to meet these desires and changes the dates or procedures, understandable demands are certain to arise from the other side for clarity [20, p. 9] and long-term stability [21, pp. 616–20] in planning methods.

Another problem concerns the planning of enterprise production structure, which during the NES period was largely left to enterprises. After the termination of the NES in 1970–71 enterprise assortments were again compulsorily prescribed. This was inevitable because from the price freeze ordered in November 1971 till the end of the 1971–5 plan, meanwhile prolonged until 1980 [22, pp. 669–73], enterprises' efforts to raise their profits by shifting their assortment to the most profitable products or by product changes had to be counteracted. This policy was accompanied by the negative phenomenon that enterprises could no longer undertake any adaptation to changes in demand by themselves, and gaps in supply came about. Thus some severe criticism of state assortment planning came from enterprises [23, p. 12]:

'Gaps in supply ... are in the main due to gaps in assortment and cannot be ascribed to an insufficient overall volume of production in particular branches of industry. However, the detailed assortment cannot be planned centrally. All the problems connected with this belong within the competence of enterprises and combines. Likewise only the production enterprises can exercise responsibility for changes in assortment which become necessary owing to new or altered demands in the course of the plan year as only they, in cooperation with their contractual partners, have the concrete information.'

The connection between aggregate economic and enterprise planning, which was a central point in the Liberman proposals in 1962 and a principal feature of the NES in 1963, still plays an equally crucial role: today, as then, the problem is enterprise motivation. What is to be promoted by enterprise bonuses: absolute, quantitative output growth, output growth and cost reduction (i.e. profit growth), or plan fulfilment and overfulfilment? Quantitative output growth is eliminated because it is determined more by state structural policy and the long-term plan than by enterprise performance. Concentration on profit was tried during the NES and for the reasons described (principally because of price problems) did not lead to the results hoped. There remain bonuses for plan fulfilment and over-fulfilment [24, p. 5]: 'However, concentration on overfulfilment includes the possibility of aiming for low plan targets, and he who wants to overfulfil needs either more supplies or correspondingly high stocks.' This policy induces enterprises to strive for 'soft plans' and to build up the highest possible reserves of materials.

A way out of this dilemma is no more in sight today than it was fifteen years ago. The most recent attempt in the GDR, as in the Soviet Union, to induce enterprises to take on additional competitive obligations in the form of 'counterplans' [25], i.e. offers of performance exceeding enterprise draft plans, have no great chance of success. Although from 1974 enterprises were obliged to put up counterplans [26, pp. 1–3, p. 4ff.], their effect is likely to have been little since one can assume that in expectation of this development enterprises will have submitted draft plans which left a certain amount of scope for the subsequent incorporation of counterplans.

BALANCING

The most important instrument with which annual planning operates and establishes the relationships between the various different sectors of the whole economy is balances.[1] Balances are comparisons, disaggregated by function and time, of the anticipated supply of, and the consumption resulting from planned demands for, goods and services for the respective plan year. The task of annual planning can also be described as the establishment of a consistent system of balances, with no gaps in their interconnections, showing neither deficits nor surpluses.

The procedure of balancing is accordingly closely linked with the planning process. It consists in essence of the following principal sections [28, p. 384]:

(a) Elaboration and issue of provisional or target balances by the State Planning Commission and other central state organs in accordance with decisions on planning methods. The basis of the provisional balances is the orientation figures of the draft national economic plan.

(b) The supply and consumption resulting from the provisional balances are 'state tasks' and are to form the basis for working out plans.

(c) The balancing organs work out draft balances and coordinate them with those involved in the balancing process.

(d) The suppliers and consumers of the goods contained in the balance list must make the necessary plan information available to the balancing organs.

(e) The draft balances must be coordinated with other parts of the plan and discrepancies cleared up by decisions of the responsible planning organs.

(f) The draft balances, together with the draft plans, have to be defended before the superior organs and are checked by the latter through counter-calculations.

(g) The draft balances are confirmed, depending on their importance, by the Council of Ministers ('state plan positions'), the State Planning Commission, and the industrial ministries, and thus become an obligatory part of state plans.

Since the beginning of the sixties GDR balances have been drawn up for about 4,500 commodities [29, p. 11]. They were supposed to form a pyramid of balances, depending on their importance and the administrative responsibility for working them out: at the peak of the pyramid a few important balances ('state plan positions') were supposed to be worked out by the State Planning Commission; below

[1] The Chairman of the State Planning Commission described balances as the principal instrument of planning [27, p. 5].

them an intermediate group of balances by central state organs (ministries) and finally at the base the great mass of assortment balances elaborated by VVBs or individual enterprises. However, this intention did not last long. According to the current balance list [30], the number of state plan positions has again climbed to around 300. With about 500 balances worked out by the ministries, this gives 800 central balances. This compares with 3,700 assortment balances.

Yet these 4,500 balanced commodities represent only a small part of the total number of products produced in the GDR. Even if one regards the figure of 80 million different commodities calculated in connection with the new central catalogue of items prepared for 1977 as exaggerated [31, p. 11], it is nevertheless clear that for a great number of commodities which are not balanced in physical terms broader, i.e. aggregated, balance units have to be established. Here, however, the price problem acquires central importance at the planning level too, for commodity aggregation is not possible without valuation by means of prices. Planned prices therefore not only have a (not precisely definable) guiding function at the level of associations and enterprises but also to a certain extent determine the (supposedly purely physical) plan decisions of the central planning organs.[1]

When it comes to balancing in detail a mass of problems arises. They stem partly from value balancing and start with the determination of demand [32, pp. 8f.]: 'If someone orders two 6·3 ton motor cranes and one 40 ton mobile crane this appears in the statement of demand as the number of items, three, and the total value. It is easy to imagine what balancing means in these circumstances.' If, however, one tries to plan not in value but in use-value terms, i.e. starting from technical performance parameters, other insoluble difficulties emerge [33, p. 6]: 'Experiments show that for a single crane, which has hitherto been planned and balanced with a single form, eighteen forms are necessary with use-value planning.' In these circumstances it is not surprising that, despite the participation of 350 balancing organs and 250 fund holders in twenty sectors of supply, the quality of demand determination and demand planning was described as inadequate [34, pp. 7–8].

One major balancing problem which was said to be completely unsolved in the middle of 1971 [35, p. 549] is the interconnection of the individual balances. This was supposed to be done by material use

---

[1] Presumably the effect of prices is in any case greater at the central level than at that of enterprises. In addition, this problem shows that within the foreseeable future abandonment of commodity-money relations and in particular of the use of prices is completely excluded.

norms (MVNs) which established the amounts of various inputs necessary for production of one unit of output. But as a rule they were not technically and economically grounded, but merely based on statistical experience [36, p. 12]. At the beginning of 1972 it was announced that about 450 norms (MVNs) for eighty balance positions (input commodities) were to be worked out, relating to 150 product groups [37, p. 7]. In the main this was successfully completed—for the first time for the 1973 plan [38, p. 6; 39, p. 8]. Yet this small number of technically and economically grounded material use norms—in relation to the total number of balances or even more the number of important commodities—speaks volumes about the quality of balance interconnection.

Another problem concerns the methods of balancing the balances. In view of the immense secondary effects which accompany any attempt to balance balances on the supply side by production increases, the balancing organs concentrate mostly on the consumption side. This means that they cut out completely what they regard as less important uses or reduce the supply of inputs to different users by varying amounts. The undesired secondary effects on the consumption side—smaller output at subsequent production stages—are then mostly avoided by statistically tightening the material use norms: the consuming enterprises have to produce their planned output with less inputs. This procedure evokes a great deal of irritation on the part of the producing enterprises and explains why the repeated attacks on these methods of balancing balances come only from the users' side [35, p. 548].

The discussion of the technical problems of balancing, as conducted in the GDR and other East European countries, makes it clear that the mathematical planning procedures, which are so much the centre of interest in the academic field, and the hopes of concentrated introduction of computers can hardly help here. A prerequisite for both would be a transition from physical, use-value balancing to pure value calculation. But it is precisely value calculation which causes problems with the results of balancing.

IV.3 Management

ORGANIZATION

The terminological shift of emphasis in the official interpretations of the GDR economic system from the so-called 'system of planning and management' to the 'management and planning of the national economy'[1] and the repeated description of planning as 'the kernel of management' [40, p. 1350; 41, p. 1425] put the management function

[1] See IV. 1.

of the state clearly at the head of its list of tasks. Particular importance is thereby attached to the organization of the state and economic administration by which this management function is discharged.

A general view of the present—simplified—administrative organization of the industrial sector is given in Table 21. It shows first the level of political decision, above the pure administration, which in turn is controlled by the Council of Ministers. Of the four institutions listed here—the Politbureau, the Central Committee, the State Council, and the National Chamber—the Politbureau is undoubtedly the most important, in the field of economic as well as political control. It is small enough (nineteen members, nine candidates) to conduct real, problem-oriented discussions. Moreover, it has at its disposal in its secretariat an apparatus which makes it to some extent independent of the state administration for specialist knowledge. As long, therefore, as the Politbureau is in agreement, the relatively large Central Committee (189 members and candidates) has been limited to giving formal approval. The comparatively small State Council (twenty-four members), which during the Ulbricht era became the most influential state organ because of his personal position, has declined considerably in importance under his successor Stoph. Also when SED General-Secretary Honecker became chairman in 1976, the State Council did not regain its former importance. One of the main reasons for this, besides the slight political weight of its members, may be the lack of an administrative apparatus of its own like the one its secretariat provides for the Politbureau. The National Chamber, the GDR Parliament (500 deputies), which formally has to pass the law on the national economic plan, is essentially a confirmatory organ. Neither is there the necessary time available for extensive discussion in its committees, nor are they in a position to examine independently the possibilities and consequences of a change in a plan.

The real administrative apparatus of industry (and of the economy in general) begins at the level of the Council of Ministers, which—despite the recent reassessment of its significance—is more the top administrative organ than a centre of political decision. In the sphere of economic administration three levels can be distinguished. The first consists of the central planning and controlling authorities of the Council of Ministers which comprise, besides the State Planning Commission, the industrial ministries and the other ministries and offices which are important for economic control. At the second level the intermediate economic administrations include the regional economic councils, the VVBs and also nationalized combines (VEKs) in so far as there are other independent enterprises subordinated to them. The lowest level consists of the economically and legally

Table 21: Industrial administration in the GDR

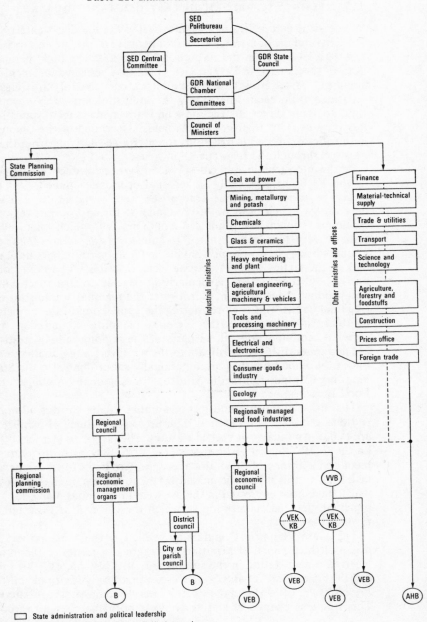

State administration and political leadership
Legally independent economic units (juridical persons)

VEB—Nationalised enterprise
VVB—Association of nationalised enterprises
VEK—Nationalised combine

KB—Combined enterprise
B—Non-state enterprise
AHB—Nationalised foreign trade enterprise

Source: Leptin and Melzer.

independent enterprises of the state sector (nationalized enterprises —VEBs) and the non-state sector (cooperative or private enterprises).

At the level of the central authorities' overall economic planning duties, specialized tasks (finance, planning and management of supplies, price-setting) and administrative control are clearly separated from each other. Only the industrial ministries have the right to issue direct instructions, and direct personal responsibilities only exist in their respective fields. Decisions of the planning authorities or special instructions to enterprises deriving from them[1] must go through the respective ministries.

At the intermediate level enterprises are grouped either by branches in the VVBs or regionally in regional economic councils: all the larger or more important enterprises were assigned to a VVB, depending on their branch, the remainder to the appropriate regional economic council. Nationalized combines, of which there were initially very few, subordinated to ministries (e.g. Carl Zeiss, the Leuna works, etc.), were not established in larger numbers until the end of the sixties when it became clear that the VVBs could only partly fulfil their duties, particularly in relation to structural policy and product specialization. Apropos of the regional administrations (regional councils) it is worth noting the application of the 'principle of dual subordination': the regional planning commission and regional economic council, as parts of the regional administration, are administratively subordinate to their respective regional council, but at the same time they are functionally subordinated to the State Planning Commission or the Ministry for Regionally Managed and Food Industries.

The tasks, authority, and responsibilities of the various administrations, offices, and ministries, right up to the Council of Ministers, are laid down in laws or special statutes. The law of 16 October 1972 on the GDR Council of Ministers [42, p. 253] declares the management and planning of the national economy to be its most important task (§1). In this it is to be guided by the directives of the SED (§3) which have been expressed in the five-year and annual plans, for the punctual, detailed elaboration of which the Council of Ministers is responsible (§4).

The State Planning Commission, which is the most important organ of the Council of Ministers for aggregate economic planning, received a new statute in the summer of 1973 [43, pp. 417–20]—the eighth since 1958, counting the corresponding provisions in the *Principles* . . . of 1963 and the various later 'fundamental regulations'. This frequent change of statutes reflects both the changes in con-

---

[1] General decisions and instructions directed to all enterprises and administrations within the framework of specialized competence can be issued directly.

ceptions of economic policy and the various problems in implementing them. While the last statute, issued in 1968, still upheld the emphatic concentration of the work of the State Planning Commission on long-term planning, 'structure-determining tasks' and the relatively great independence of 'economic units' (VEBs and VVBs), the new statute clearly shows the centralization of all important decision-making which has set in since 1971. Not only may the Chairman of the State Planning Commission give instructions to the regional planning commissions directly subordinated to him, but he may also issue direct orders, within the framework of his tasks, to the ministers and heads of other central state organs with whom he previously had to cooperate on a basis of equal rights (§2, 7). Fundamental economic problems on which differences of opinion exist between ministries are decided in the Council of Ministers on the basis of reports by the State Planning Commission (§3, 1). The element of prior decision which this involves makes it particularly clear how the position of the State Planning Commission has been strengthened.

There are similar statutes for each ministry[1] and for the different central offices and state secretariats.

The rights and duties of regional economic councils and the corresponding administrations at district and parish level were laid down by a new law in July 1973 [45, pp. 313–35]. The essence of this law is that while the regional, district, and parish organs are allotted a whole series of tasks and responsibilities together with the necessary authority, the Council of Ministers has a right to guide and check all important questions (§9), and the local councils are closely bound to the centrally determined national economic plans where problems of economic planning and control are concerned. In this respect they do not have significantly greater decision-making scope than the VVBs and VEKs.

For years the greatest difficulties of a legally fixed delimitation of authority have concerned the relationship of VEB, VEK, and VVB. After the failure to supplement the decree on the legal position of the VEB, passed in 1967 [46, pp. 121ff.], by a corresponding regulation for the VVB, and after the formation of combines (VEK) which occurred in 1968–9 was enabled by a number of special decrees, a new attempt at legal regulation of this difficult area could follow the centralization of decision-making powers introduced in 1971. The 'decree of 28 March 1973 on the tasks, rights, and duties of nationalized enterprises, combines, and VVBs' [47, pp. 129–41] clearly reflects this centralization. Thus, in particular, the new law omits a number of rights which had been given to enterprises in

[1] For an example see [44, pp. 385–9].

connection with planning: the right to receive consistent plan indicators and a right of protest against state plan tasks which diverged substantially from enterprise plan proposals. The right to claim compensation for losses caused by imposed plan changes, which enterprises enjoyed *vis-à-vis* their superior organ (§15 of the 1967 decree) was placed at the discretion of the superior organ in the new 1973 decree (§12, 4).

Many other provisions of the new decree also reflect the concentration of decision-making powers.

Although considerable importance has been attached here to the organizational structure of the state economic administration and the legal regulations on its tasks and powers, it must nevertheless be admitted that informal relationships, personal acquaintance, and mutual help outside plans and organizations play a large part. One cannot go so far as to assert that *only* such informal relations make the planning organization function, but their influence must not be underestimated.

THE INDICATOR SYSTEM

In our discussion of the NES—despite our cautious assessment—the reduction of the number of plan indicators compulsorily prescribed for enterprises was depicted as an essential element of the reform.[1] It was therefore inevitable that the recentralization of economic decision-making powers and the restriction of enterprise rights would lead to a substantial increase in those enterprise plan indicators. Most of the indicators involved did not need to be newly introduced because even during the NES they had been determined by enterprises and had had to be communicated to their superior planning authorities. They were nevertheless not compulsory planning magnitudes or measures of enterprise results, but only parts of the system of 'economic plan information' and thus the basis for plan elaboration by the central planning organs. For the 1969–70 plan enterprises had to send in 167 indicators which, with their subdivisions, required 391 separate items of data [48, p. 20].

The return to administrative management of enterprises made most of these indicators compulsory planning magnitudes again, i.e. they had to be incorporated by enterprises in their independently drawn up plans and at the same time were used—at least partly—as measures of enterprise plan fulfilment. This was to 'increase the role and authority of the plan and accomplish its implementation through qualified and highly disciplined state management at all levels' [49, p. 732].

[1] See II. 1, 'Enterprise planning', pp. 19ff.

For the first plan year after the recentralization, the resolution of 1 December 1970 laid down twenty-two state plan indicators, ten state norms, and fifteen national economic calculation indicators for the majority of VEBs.

The most important state plan indicators are:

1. Industrial commodity production (by value)
2. Trend in labour productivity (in per cent)
3. Relation of productivity growth to growth in average wage
4. Wage fund
5. Net profit
6. Deduction from net profit payable to the state
7. Production target for major products by quantity or quantity and value
8. Delivery targets for major products by quantity
9. Production of finished consumer goods sold (by value)
10. Exports, subdivided by economic and current areas and for the USSR

Economic areas   Socialist countries—
                  of which: USSR
                  Capitalist countries—
                  of which: Federal Republic of
                            Germany
                            West Berlin
                  Developing countries
Currency areas: Socialist currency area—
                  of which: USSR
                  Non-socialist currency area—
                  of which: convertible hard
                            currencies
                            accounting currencies
                            Federal Republic of
                            Germany
                            West Berlin

11. Export profitability, subdivided by currency areas
12. Export of major products and services (by quantity), correspondingly subdivided
13–14. As 10 and 12 for imports
15. Balance shares (i.e. material quotas)
18. Investments
20. Number of blue- and white-collar workers

With few exceptions these indicators, which are already partially disaggregated from functional viewpoints, have in addition to be subdivided monthly.

State norms, i.e. planning magnitudes set uniformly for several or all enterprises, include among others:

1. Norm for the production and trade capital charge (in per cent)
2. Norm for the deduction from net profits (for overfulfilment of net profit indicator—see 5 above) (in per cent)
5. Norm for the bonus fund
6. Norm for the cultural and social fund
8. Norm for export support
10. Norm for amortization deductions (in per cent)

National economic calculation indicators serve less to determine enterprise activity—although they are supposed to have some effect on this too—than to provide information for the superior planning organs. They include, for example:

1. The trend of the capital/output ratio (the ratio of volume of output to value of production capital)
2. Expenditures on science and technology
3. Degree of automation and mechanization
4. Material cost intensity (in per cent)
5. Inputs of rolled steel, copper, and aluminium
6. Shift coefficient, to determine capital utilization in the multi-shift enterprise
7. Growth of capacity through investment
8–11. Various export and import data
12. Change in the volume of credit
15. Employment of school-leavers

The indicators of which a selection is listed here represented only the beginning. In the course of the next few years they were greatly altered, mostly expanded, although occasionally restricted again. A substantial extension of the indicator system was brought about, for example, by a decree of 15 September 1971 on the planning of use of materials [50, pp. 589–95]. In addition to the existing indicators whole groups of new ones had to be planned, defended, and confirmed: material use norms, aggregated material use norms, indicators of material extraction, material cost reduction indicators, stock norms, indicators of the trend in the level of unfinished products, etc.

A further tightening up of the indicator system came with the planning methods for 1973 [15, pp. 10–11]. Not only were most of the state norms transformed into plan indicators; the character of some was changed too. Thus the bonus fund and the social and cultural fund no longer had norms planned; these had been used to calculate the size of the funds and had therefore opened up the possibility of enterprise influence, but they were now set in absolute quantities as plan indicators. This tendency continued in the years thereafter and found its clearest expression at the beginning of the five-year plan for 1976–80 in the voluminous 'Decree of 20 November 1974 Concerning Organization and Planning of the National Economy of the GDR from 1976 to 1980' (in *Gesetzblatt der DDR*, Special Issue, no. 775a, 15 December 1974). In particular, indicators which have become important are of the type that make it possible to demonstrate efficiency *vis-à-vis* superior organs (e.g. productivity of labour on the basis of value added, or total costs for each 100 Mark of commodity production realized).

On the other hand, there were also relaxations in the system of indicators which in a way can be seen as directly symptomatic of the development of the GDR planning system: a footnote to the plan methods for 1973 pointed out that from 1973 the state plan indicator 'deduction from net profit' was to be treated only as a national economic calculation indicator. It could be deduced from another, later source that the same applied to the indicator 'net profit' [*23*, p. 12]. Thus, exactly ten years after the beginning of the NES—the outward characteristic of which was widely seen as the orientation of enterprises towards profit and in which profit did at least take on the function of chief indicator—this indicator was completely eliminated as a compulsory element in enterprise planning. As far as indicators are concerned, the enterprise planning system is therefore constructed in exactly the same way in the middle of the seventies as it was at the beginning of the sixties. The only important difference lies in a considerable higher number of plan indicators.

All the problems which dominated the discussions at that time, in particular those following the Liberman proposals, have thus naturally regained importance. On the indicator problem Liberman had stated [*51*]: 'No doubt many indicators need improvement, yet even "ideally" constructed indicators yield nothing by themselves. The problem is not the indicators but the system of linking enterprises to the national economy, the planning methods, the evaluation and award of bonuses for the work of the production collective.'

THE SYSTEM OF 'ECONOMIC LEVERS' TODAY

The present system of indirect steering instruments can be briefly summed up and compared with that of the NES as follows: of the 'economic levers' originally developed only the production capital charge [*52*, pp. 33ff.] and a small portion of the VEB and VVB fund formation still operate unchanged after the recentralization at the end of 1970. The preponderant part of the funds—like the deduction from net profit and the unified enterprise result—have been modified. The measures to make prices dynamic have lapsed completely, the further introduction of 'capital-related' prices was suspended for the time being, and a new fund, the so-called performance fund, appeared.

The diminished role of profit

In order to attain better harmonization of physical and financial planning and broad implementation of state objectives, the economic leadership of the GDR embarked on a drastic restriction of the role of profit. In 1971–2 the profit to be earned by the enterprise was made a compulsory plan indicator and firmly incorporated into financial planning; even after its transformation into a calculation indicator from 1973 onwards nothing changed here. Its level is now no longer directly planned but is derived indirectly from the other compulsory plan indicators. This means that changes in compulsory plan indicators are accompanied by a change in net profit.

If the enterprise exceeds the planned net profit it has few worthwhile possibilities—in respect of its own development aims—for spending the surplus profit which remains after deduction of a 50 per cent levy. The possibilities are: improvements in work organization (in particular in care for shift workers), raising the proportion of self-financing of planned investments, early repayment of credits, financing of rationalization measures carried out by the enterprise itself—which are therefore not always very efficient—purchase of second-hand capital goods, adoption of certain scientific innovations to apparatus and instruments in the production process, implementation of proposals for innovation up to a level of 10,000 Mark each, and additional payments into the bonus fund[1] [53, p. 686]. As a rule, these possibilities for spending surplus profits are unlikely to have stimulated any significant enterprise drive to overfulfil the physical plan tasks and thus the planned profit indicator.[2]

Close coordination of financial and physical planning has particularly unpleasant consequences for the enterprise in the case of nonfulfilment or underfulfilment of predetermined production tasks: in such a situation—just as with cost overruns—it obtains only part of the planned profit and thus cannot form funds of the size planned; in particular, it faces substantial financing problems in continuing to carry out planned investment projects if the profit earned is not, or is only just, sufficient to meet the prescribed fixed

[1] Recently, financing of joint measures of enterprises and local councils has been added to the permitted spending possibilities [54, p. 471]. These measures must be carried out on top of the state 'volume of investment' indicator.

[2] On the contrary, some criticism has pointed out that this regulation directs 'material interest' more towards obtaining higher bonuses than towards enterprise investment [55, pp. 1420–21].

sum deduction from net profit. Since future profits depend in turn on investment, the enterprise can meet this calamity only by short-term—and therefore more expensive—bridging credits. These credits, however, are restricted both by the level of enterprise financing demanded by the bank—which corresponds to the level of efficiency reached—and by adherence to predetermined indicators of use of credit and a maximum credit duration. Furthermore, resort to additional credit is limited in so far as the enterprise is allowed only a certain amount of scope by its 'change in the volume of credit for fixed capital' indicator.

In view of these problems the pressure on the enterprise to fulfil its profit plan, which stemmed from the fixed sum deduction from net profit, has been relaxed again since 1972: while in 1971 the enterprise which did not reach its planned net profit still had to pay the full deduction, it was allowed to reduce this by 30 per cent in 1972 [53, p. 686], and by as much as 50 per cent since 1973 [54, p. 472], of the shortfall in planned profit. Thus the cuts in the planned allocations to the enterprise's funds were reduced in cases of underfulfilment of the profit plan from 70 per cent in 1972 to half of the profit shortfall since then. Furthermore, to combat a long-criticized practice of enterprises, they were now required to pay over completely to the state budget 'illegal' profits not derived from planned enterprise performance (e.g. from price violations, illegal changes of assortment, or failure to adhere to export targets—which were differentiated by groups of countries [56, p. 11]).

Finally, it was laid down that in a case where the enterprise achieved such a small net profit that it did not even cover the due deduction from net profit, the whole net profit was paid over and the resultant financial debt to the state, equal to the size of the difference, was liable to 5 per cent per annum interest and had to be extinguished during the following year—basically by earning overplan profits.

The reduction in the significance of profit for the enterprise is also clearly shown by the fact that—after the cancellation of the regulations on foreign currency entitlements for successful export enterprises—with effect from January 1971, fulfilment of the foreign currency revenue plan, subdivided into currencies of socialist and non-socialist countries, became the primary measure of the performance of export enterprises instead of actual export profit in Marks [49, p. 742]. In 1971 underfulfilment was followed by drastic cuts and overfulfilment earned special payments to the bonus fund. At that time it was expressly stated in the bonus decree that for enterprises whose exports exceeded 10 per cent of their commodity production the allocations to the bonus fund depended particularly on fulfilment of their export targets [57, p. 106]. In more recent regulations this point is missing, yet it is explicitly pointed out that, instead of linking the bonus fund to the commodity production and net profit plan indicators, other indicators can also be set by central organs 'if they express enterprises' performance better' [*58*, p. 50]. Thus among the plan indicators for foreign trade enterprises 'foreign currency revenue and foreign currency requirement in Mark or foreign currency Mark' are mentioned first, now as before, besides indicators of credit granted and received in Mark or foreign currency Mark, volume of exports and imports by groups of countries, import profitability, export profitability, industrial commodity production, etc. [*15*, pp. 10, 14].

Furthermore, foreign trade enterprises and enterprises which are charged by the Ministry of Foreign Trade with carrying out particular foreign trade tasks and which instead of a unified enterprise result (see p. 44) have to draw up a specific foreign trade result are allowed to use only 40 per cent of any surplus over their profit target for their own funds [*59*, pp. 174ff.]. Here too the principle of full payment of the deduction from net profits in the case of underfulfilment of export obligations applies; if the profit earned is not sufficient, an interest-bearing debt to the state budget is created.

In these measures a complete change in the role of profit can be recognized. From an internal driving force for enterprises to exercise their own initiative it was reduced to a state target to ensure enterprises' financial contributions. This was clearly expressed in changes in the system of indirect steering: with a multitude of physical targets set in advance, the modified 'system of economic levers' today attempts to exert indirect pressure on the enterprise for improvements in performance and better execution of its tasks through a kind of financial planning which gives it relatively little freedom (in particular planning of profit and the use of profit and also credit planning).

This dual pressure through physical targets on the one hand and financial restrictions on the other can be countered by the enterprise in practice only by cost reductions—and its investment is also limited and predetermined. This intensified concentration of monetary steering instruments on cost savings represents a significant step towards an attempt to measure enterprise efficiency mainly by the extent of cost reductions.

Precisely for this reason, from the period when enterprise plans for 1974 were worked out, it was made a duty of enterprises not only to undertake detailed cost planning but also to devote the fullest attention to *prime cost reduction* [*60*, pp. 70ff.]. This was intended to make 'economic accounting' more effective and induce general economies: the relevant new order instructs enterprises to make a compulsory breakdown of costs by kinds in the process of planning costs in advance, to draw up a register of costs and to make an estimated allocation of costs to products or product groups. The advance payments to be made and the planned profit rates on each product are also to be determined—the latter by comparing planned costs with anticipated revenues. Since with the passage of time planned reductions in prime cost are sought, the enterprise must set the planned prime cost for the plan year lower than the 'basis costs',[1] in accordance with the rationalization measures that have been introduced (e.g. improvement of production and labour organization, increase in product quality, saving on raw materials or on administrative costs). The planned cost reductions must also be disaggregated by kinds of costs and by rationalization measures [60, p. 73].

Minimum requirements are placed on enterprises with this cost planning; in particular, besides their plan tasks, the norms for use of materials and components (e.g. the technically and economically grounded norms of material use [61], the materials use indicators set by the general directors of VVBs or other organs of economic management, or confirmed by VEB directors [50, pp. 589ff.; 62, p. 444]), the planning of wage costs according to the technically based work and manning norms, and the overhead cost norms confirmed by superior organs [63, pp. 661ff.] must be observed. While the additional costs arising in connection with the introduction of new or improved products or processes[2] are taken into account in cost planning, the so-called unplannable costs[3] which enterprises have to bear may not be included. This could certainly lead enterprises to see the possibility of reckoning additional costs on product improvements as an incentive to general product changes in order to conceal the costs which cannot otherwise be hidden behind illusory or minor changes.

This very detailed cost planning is intended to promote more efficient use of the given resources and also to uncover intra-enterprise reserves. Furthermore, not only does the advance information on future enterprise costs give the management organs outstanding data for comparisons between enterprises of the same branch, enabling them to attack possible sources of trouble revealed in this

---

[1] These are the planned prime costs of the previous year per product, related to the quantity of output laid down for the plan year.

[2] For example, starting costs, increased depreciation allowances for plant to be replaced, extra costs of—authorized—higher stocks of raw and other materials or quality improvements.

[3] For example, extra costs resulting from unsatisfactory investment or inadequate design, contract penalties, economic sanctions and compensation, devaluations, interest on unplanned credit, or debts and costs of services or repairs on warranty claims.

way, but, more importantly, they also get information on intended or possible enterprise initiatives inconsistent with central objectives, long before they are actually begun.

Table 22: Use of profit and fund formation in the nationalized enterprise

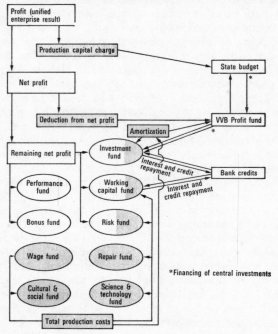

The reform of fund formation

Fund formation commits financial resources of VEBs, combines, and VVBs for specific purposes and uses them according to detailed legal regulations. Because the large number of funds and the differences that exist between individual enterprises, combines, and economic management organs require extensive discussion, what can be provided here is only a general survey of the more important funds which characterized the system of financing in the state-owned enterprises in the mid-1970s. The changes which have occurred since then in the individual regulations governing the formation and utilization of the various funds are of a narrow scope and do not touch the fundamental elements of the system. The following discussion is based on the state of affairs as it existed in 1973–4.

(a) **The investment fund** [54, pp. 472–3]: This fund consists of amortization allowances, the profit the enterprise has left after forming the other funds, investment credits permitted and granted, and, for particular tasks, allocations from budgetary funds or from the VVB investment fund.[1] The investment fund finances the preparation and execution of planned investments, instalment payments for completed parts of projects, repayment of investment credits and bridging credits, purchase of second-hand capital goods, and projects carried out jointly with local councils [60, p. 74].

(b) **The risk fund** [64, pp. 265ff.; 65, p. 445]: Producers of industrial plant, technological components of plants, buildings, and other capital structures form this fund out of the margins laid down for risks in price calculations, as well as from extra profits they earn. It is immaterial whether they are operating as general or principal contractor or as sub-contractors responsible only for parts of projects.

The fund serves to insure against scientific, technical, and also economic losses (e.g. losses resulting from insufficient testing for exceptional conditions, or from the use of new processes or raw materials). It is also to cover, in particular, losses which arise from giving a binding price quotation[2] for investment projects. Since not all the details of an investment project, for example, can be known to the enterprise in advance, it runs the risk that when it carries out the project additional costs may arise which it cannot pass on.

(c) **The science and technology fund** [67, pp. 839ff.]: Enterprises which put new scientific and technical developments directly into practice or introduce new processes are allowed, in accordance with the scales laid down in the *science and technology* plan for financing these innovations, to form this fund to the prescribed extent out of costs. It also includes revenue from research and development work performed and from state budget resources designated for special projects—after approval by the Minister for Science and Technology—and funds reallocated by the VVB.

This fund is formed to the full extent even when the enterprise's physical targets are underfulfilled, in which case the enterprise is allowed bank credits—particularly if it is extending its tasks.

(d) **The culture and social fund** [58, pp. 52ff.]: This fund is laid down as an absolute amount, coming out of costs, by the superior

[1] If prescribed efficiency criteria are observed, investment projects which are important for a whole branch and exceed the financial capacity of the individual enterprise can be financed from this fund.

[2] The following passage shows how unsatisfactory the quoting of binding prices was still in 1971 [66, p. 10]: 'After investigations in the first half of 1971 the Industry and Trade Bank had to report that for only 20 per cent of the investment projects started or scheduled for 1971 were there binding price quotations. In the Halle district, out of eighteen investments started in the second half of 1970 there was a confirmed binding price quotation in February 1971 for only one. That means that the customer has started building without clear knowledge of the cost, and even encourages the contractor to begin work without documentation.'

organs—taking into consideration the level of cultural and social care reached by the enterprise. Increases are supposed to be made primarily where the proportion of women and shift-workers employed is high.

This fund serves principally to finance measures to improve working and living conditions of people doing shift-work in the enterprise, for cultural and social assistance to working women and mothers and also young people, and for the promotion of sport and health care. Allocations are also granted from the cultural and social fund for workers' days and for enterprise housing construction.

(e) **The bonus fund**[1] [*58*, pp. 49ff.; *68*, pp. 379ff.; *69*, pp. 549–50; *70*, pp. 485–6; *71*, p. 810; *72*, p. 293]: The present bonus fund, formed from enterprise net profit—and basically set as a state plan indicator—is intended to stimulate the workers' interest through bonuses for particular actions (such as proposals for rationalization, organizational improvements, cost savings, etc.) and also through annual bonuses.[2]

Today this fund is no longer as tightly linked to the trend of enterprise net profits as it was before 1970. In 1971 the bonus fund was already tied to the fulfilment of two other targets, to be chosen in advance by the enterprise (e.g. planned exports, capital productivity), as well as to the achievement of the planned net profit;[3] since 1972 it has, in addition, been coupled to the achievement of planned commodity production; now only increases in the bonus fund depend on fulfilment of two supplementary targets.

There are detailed provisions for reductions in the bonus fund if the planned commodity production and net profit indicators are not reached, and for increases if they are overfulfilled. For every one per cent over- or underfulfilment of commodity production it is changed by 1·5 per cent and for net profit by 0·5 per cent.[4]

---

[1] The bonus fund decree for 1972 also applied for 1973 and 1974.

[2] Here a minimum bonus per employee of the level planned in the previous year is to be guaranteed.

[3] For over- or underfulfilment of the profit plan the bonus fund could be changed by up to 25 per cent and, for failure to achieve particular physical targets, reduced by up to 30 per cent. Overspending of the planned wage fund was also—as it had been earlier—deducted from the bonus fund [*57*, pp. 105–6].

[4] But reductions may amount to a maximum of 20 per cent of the bonus fund. Increases depend basically on fulfilment of two targets selected from the following list: exports by economic areas, commodity production for sale to the public, labour productivity, plan fulfilment for specific products (e.g. spare parts, important consumer goods). It is interesting that the regulation still in force in 1971, reducing the bonus fund when planned wage costs were exceeded by the amount overspent, was replaced by the following: in such a case reduction of the enterprise director's and the responsible managers' bonuses only, by a maximum of 50 per cent, is provided.

The regulations on work with counterplans for 1974 even provide [26, pp. 1ff.] that in the case of overfulfilments of state-prescribed tasks which were already embodied in counterplans (up to February–March 1974) the bonus fund plan indicator is to be raised subsequently by 2·5 per cent for one per cent overfulfilment of commodity production and 0·8 per cent for one per cent overfulfilment of planned net profit, but only by the amount of the overfulfilment actually achieved. If the overfulfilment achieved is higher than that anticipated in the counterplan (or there is no counterplan), then the arrangements mentioned in the previous paragraph apply also to the difference.[1]

The maximum allocation to the bonus fund for full-time blue- and white-collar workers (three apprentices are reckoned as one worker) is set at 900 Mark. Of course, this sum might be exceeded by the bonus allocations resulting from overfulfilling state targets.[2] The basic principle then is that annual bonuses per employee may amount to at least one-third of monthly average earnings, and bonuses for particular activities may amount, at most, to two months' salary.

Some 3·7 million blue- and white-collar workers received an annual bonus of 650 Mark for 1972 [73], about 60 Mark more than in 1971 and around 210 Mark more than in 1969. For 1973 the average annual bonus for an unchanged 3·7 million workers is said to have come to 725 Mark. It reached 755 Mark in 1974 and 764 Mark in 1975.[3]

(f) The performance fund [74, pp. 467ff.]: In order to spur groups of workers or whole enterprises to additional performance beyond state plan targets the so-called performance fund was created in mid-1972. Initially it was only to be for nationalized enterprises in industry and construction, but since 1974 it has also been applied to selected agricultural and transport enterprises and to regionally managed enterprises—working on an economic accounting basis. This fund is intended to 'make economic accounting effective right down to the workbench' [75, pp. 2–3], by prompting initiatives, above and beyond the stimulation of the bonus fund, towards cost reductions through increases in labour productivity or savings of materials or quality improvements.[4]

[1] The position on financing is that increases in bonus fund allocations, which result when state plan targets exceed the state tasks set in draft plans, are to be covered in full from the deduction from net profits set for 1974. On the other hand, additional bonus fund allocations which arise subsequently through counterplans must be financed by earning additional profits (after meeting the full deduction obligation).

[2] Since the principle is that the planned bonus fund should be at least as high as the prescribed amount of bonus the previous year, the actual over- or underfulfilments cannot be the basis of planning the following year.

[3] According to statements by Karl Heinz Gerstner on GDR Radio.

[4] On this see Siegfried Böhm's fundamental article on the performance fund [76, pp. 2ff.].

Allocations to the performance fund, to be financed out of net profit, are possible in the following three cases:

(i) For each one per cent rise in labour productivity above the state plan targets allocations to the performance fund may be made amounting to 0·8 per cent of the planned wage fund for production workers.[1] The allocations amount to as much as 1·2 per cent if the plan overfulfilment is set at the time the plan is under discussion and is fixed in the enterprise annual plan or in the counterplan; in case of failure to achieve the anticipated excess this rate of allocation then applies to the improvement actually achieved.

(ii) In the case of cost savings as a consequence of reducing specific material use below the planned use of the previous year,[2] while complying with the compulsory norms for use of materials and power, the enterprise may make allocations to the performance fund; the rates provided are 50 per cent of the cost savings for power and 20 per cent for certain other materials.[3] Since 1974 the basis of performance fund allocations has been the difference between the actual cost savings on some materials and any cost excesses that have arisen on other materials [77, p. 66]. It is a precondition for every allocation that the enterprises pledged themselves to the materials savings in advance in the plan.

(iii) If the enterprise achieves additional profits from an improvement in the standard of quality above the planned level of the previous year, while adhering to the planned output of important products in quantity, value, and price groups, up to 50 per cent of these profits can be allocated to the performance fund.[4]

In a sense this fund was accorded a priority in the years 1972 and 1973: if overplan allocations were due to it but could not be covered out of overplan profits—after making any additional payments required for the bonus fund—they were to be financed at the expense of the deduction from net profits, when the labour productivity indicator was overfulfilled, and in the case of quality improvements out of the profit fund or the reserve fund of the VVB or combine

---

[1] This basis of measurement was chosen in order to favour enterprises with relatively low administrative expenses—and therefore a high proportion of productive labour. This is supposed to 'reward' enterprise efforts to reduce administrative expenses.

[2] For 1972 materials savings were to be determined by comparison with the respective actual use in 1971.

[3] The responsible Minister lays down three to five specific materials for individual branches (after coordination with the Minister for Planning and Management of Supplies and the Chairman of the State Planning Commission).

[4] The precise percentage is set by the enterprise's superiors, depending on the demands on the enterprise work force which the quality improvement required.

[54, pp. 471–2]. These priorities were subsequently cancelled again [77, p. 66], so that from 1974 all payments to the performance fund have to be made exclusively out of net profits earned—after making the deduction from net profits.

The performance fund is intended to be used for the following purposes:

(a) Improvement of 'the working and living conditions of the workforce'. This includes improvement of provision for shift workers, general social and cultural provision for employees, subsidies for workers to build their own homes, financing of investments to improve working conditions (from reserves), and allocation of funds for joint measures with local councils.

(b) Implementation of enterprise rationalization measures.[1] Improvements in organization, production of means of rationalization by the enterprise itself, and purchase of second-hand equipment are important, but the main goal here is technical innovation.[2]

(c) Central trade union measures, such as the construction of holiday villages and rest homes.

Every expenditure from the performance fund must be made with the agreement of the enterprise trade union leadership.

The revised system of indirect steering

The reduction of the significance of profit brought about not only a substantial curbing of its stimulation function and thus a restriction of enterprise initiatives, but also, and more important, through being tightly fitted into planning, profit was 'degraded' to a mere instrument for securing financial requirements. This is, as it were, the 'price' for the attempt to obtain better harmonization of physical and financial planning.

Persistent pressure is now exerted on enterprises, through financial planning and the enlarged number of indicators used in physical planning, together with further 'economic levers', to fulfil their plan and cost targets. The new cost planning and prime cost reduction measures reinforce the pressure to extract all available enterprise reserves and thus achieve cost savings. They are also supposed to provide advance information to state bodies about intended initiatives which do not accord with the structure of central objectives.

---

[1] But no construction capacity included in planned balances may be used for this purpose.

[2] The annual benefit from the introduction of such innovations is said to have amounted to 2·9 mlrd Mark in 1971 and in 1972—after the introduction of the performance fund—to 3·2 mlrd Mark [78, p. 3]. In 1973 it is said to have been around 3·6 mlrd Mark [79, pp. 65ff.].

Thus indirect stimulation of enterprises' own initiatives has been replaced by strong pressure for precise fulfilment of centrally set targets. Deviations are closely checked. In order to stimulate extra performance the relative value attached to *overfulfilment of state plan targets* was raised—although there has been very limited success in developing effective incentives for this. For the diminution in the 'profit' motive, and in particular the loss of the scope for free enterprise investment decision-making, removed enterprise managers' interest in taking increased risks and sounding out the possibilities of 'new factor combinations'.

Furthermore, the desire for overfulfilment in a planning system which was again strongly centralized brought new requirements for ensuring plan implementation, namely the necessity of balancing the inputs for these additional output increases and coordinating them with other plan goals. In order to meet these new prerequisites of efficient plan coordination *advance declaration* of additional performance had to be particularly encouraged. A substantial part of the modifications to the incentive system made between 1972 and 1976 concentrate on this: when additional tasks are taken on in advance, higher fund allocations are granted.

Since, as already explained above, the only real incentive to enterprise managements for extra performance would be increased enterprise decision-making rights—which is precisely what the economic leadership is not prepared to grant—it is thought that a substitute solution can be found by *shifting incentives* to labour. In a situation of limited and centrally laid down investment the creation of the performance fund, the further development of the bonus fund, and the increasing significance of counterplans and personal plans (pledges of higher performance by individual workers) are intended chiefly to mobilize the performance reserves of the enterprise work force and induce individual employees to greater efforts.

Yet the function of the performance fund as a stimulus is limited. Large labour productivity increases, continuous materials savings, and cost-neutral quality improvements are scarcely conceivable over the long run as they are to be achieved with little additional capital and principally through improved labour organization and increased efforts by the workers. Their 'performance reserves', particularly in respect of quality of work, organization of the work process, reduction of sub-standard output, avoidance of lost time, saving of materials—even with the best will of those concerned—are surely bound to be exhausted after a certain time. At any rate, much greater performance increases could be obtained through technical progress (use of improved processes), additional investment, development of new products, etc.

There is a danger that the result of exceptional efforts by enterprise work forces will be to set standards which they cannot keep up permanently. Besides, the incentive to higher efforts created by the performance fund is small, because of the one-sided possibilities for using the fund's resources—with the sole exception of the subsidy for workers to build their own homes. Therefore, as a rule, instead of persistent efforts enterprises will attempt rather to switch over to the lowest possible plan tenders when plans are being worked out. For, by holding back reserves, the enterprise management succeeds to a certain extent in defending itself against the pressure of physical and financial planning and it becomes relatively easy for the enterprise work force to plead for extra performance. Overfulfilments incorporated in 'counterplans' can then be achieved without excessive effort and the work force still succeeds in enjoying resources from the performance fund.

The bonus fund's stimulation effect is also limited. Individual initiatives or special efforts by individual employees are definitely encouraged, but the annual bonus for all employees presents as many problems as before: thus the linking of allocations to the bonus fund to the degree of fulfilment of the net profit and industrial commodity production plans leads to an assortment in which fulfilment of these two indicators takes priority over consumer demand. Furthermore, the present maximum rate of 900 Mark per employee is likely to have a certain restrictive effect in successful enterprises. As a rule their work forces are likely to use their reserves only to the extent required to obtain the maximum rate.

To be sure, the new regulation that additional bonus allocations above 900 Mark are possible for fulfilment of additional tasks incorporated into counterplans could give rise to incentives for higher performance. But this is unlikely to occur on a wide scale because enterprises are bound to be afraid that overplan increases in performance achieved in counterplans today will be set as their targets tomorrow, or used as target figures which should be easily attainable by other enterprises ('planning from reported levels').

Besides, there is another point to be considered: a sharply growing gap between the maximum bonuses achieved by successful enterprises and the very much lower average bonus in weaker enterprises could spark off a feeling of injustice among a number of groups of workers in a system 'directed primarily toward the interests of the workers'. Precisely because the defects in the measures of efficiency and in the plan indicators used make an economically sound measurement of performance virtually impossible, too sharp differences in bonuses between workers are likely to be met with the demand for equal 'thirteenth month's' salary for similar groups of employees in different enterprises.

The present system of 'economic levers' still fails to stimulate work force performance (quite apart from the limited possibilities for this) adequately and in the case of capital—where there really would be numerous possibilities for incentives—is completely unsatisfactory. Thus the production capital charge was unable to fulfil its function since it is based on a valuation of capital which is not uniform because of the prevailing price distortions—especially after the failure to complete the introduction of capital-related prices. What is worse, this unsatisfactory measure of value for capital goods hinders the economically meaningful calculation of capital productivity and profitability. It is therefore doubtful whether the economic leadership will succeed in developing more or less 'optimal' macroeconomic investment structures and whether the intermediate decision-making bodies and the banks will create justifiable microeconomic investment structures—while also taking into consideration enterprise proposals and expert appraisals.

A further substantial defect is that in view of the intensive checks and inter-enterprise cost comparisons there is a tendency for weaker enterprises to catch up with the performance of better enterprises, but there is insufficient incentive for successful enterprises to make further efforts. Moreover, allowing an increased profit margin in the price for new or considerably developed products is insufficient to induce innovations, because the possibilities of spending such additional profits are scarcely of interest to dynamic enterprises.

PRESENT-DAY PRICE-SETTING AND ITS PROBLEMS
Price-setting problems up to 1975

Recentralization affected the price system particularly adversely; just when the reform trends were on the point of making prices into an active element in the system [80, pp. 332–48], the NES was terminated. The industrial price regulation system and the 'declining' ('stepped') prices for new and improved products were abolished [81, p. 761], the further introduction of capital-related prices was stopped, and it was laid down that the prices of all commodities produced in 1971 were to remain constant until 1975 [82, pp. 669ff.]. Thus prices relapsed again into the role of a passive element in planning, which by itself could scarcely spark off any impulse to greater national economic efficiency.

An important consequent defect is that the price freeze, which has now been prolonged until 1980, maintains the previous price distortions. At the same time financing problems have arisen in capital-intensive enterprises, since, owing to the interruption of the transition to capital-related prices, the prices for a number of product-groups still do not take account of the capital employed— and this is increasing with the passage of time. Enterprises in the branches affected can only pay the capital charge, levied at a uniform rate of 6 per cent since 1971, by restricting their fund formation. For this reason the introduction of differentiated 'production capital charge coefficients'—lower for capital-intensive enterprises—was discussed in 1972 [*83*, p. 6]. This proposal has not been accepted, however, and reduced deductions from net profits, or subsidies for specific enterprises, are used instead.

Since, in a price freeze, setting prices for new and improved products becomes a problem, a complicated and extremely bureaucratic price proposal and confirmation procedure has been developed.

For *consumer goods* it was decided [*84*, pp. 674ff.] that prices for new or improved products were to be confirmed by central bodies, on the basis of enterprise price proposals, after prior checking of the cost and price calculations. A Central Price Advisory Board was created, attached to the Prices Office, for specialist preparation of price decisions.[1] In the case of changes in consumer goods which are purely within the normal alteration of assortment, and only involve negligible increases in use value, they are classified according to predetermined sets of prices, other statistical norms, or price lists. Either central organs,[2] or even enterprises themselves,[3] are responsible for doing this. As a rule the complicated procedure of price confirmation or classification begins with a price proposal[4] to be made by the

[1] Its members are: one representative each of the Minister of Trade and Supply, the Minister of Finance, the responsible Industrial Minister, the Minister for Construction, the Minister for Agriculture, Forestry, and Foodstuffs, or the Minister for Foreign Trade and the President of the Office for Measures and Goods Testing.

[2] For specified product ranges (e.g. furniture, domestic china, shoes, household electrical appliances) economic management organs in trade or industry are responsible. For others it is specialized ministers (e.g. for printed products, records, etc., the Minister for Culture; for medicines, bandaging materials, and medical instruments, the Minister for Health; and for seasonal prices of fresh fruit and vegetables the Minister for Trade and Supply). Perishable goods or goods peculiar to particular regions are classified by the chairman of the regional board in the price hierarchy.

[3] Enterprises may carry out price classification themselves for a number of commodity groups (e.g. products of the food and luxuries industry, men's outer clothing, hosiery, domestic chemical goods) on the basis of state price catalogues or, for other groups (e.g. knitted outer wear and underwear, soft furnishings, materials), on the basis of price calculation regulations with sets of price norms.

[4] This comprises, besides a detailed product description, data on the anticipated volume of production, the demand to be expected, the level of costs, and in particular a price proposal agreed with the principal customers.

enterprise [85 pp. 257ff]. This proposal goes first to the management organs of the industry, then to those of the trade network, which are assisted by Price Advisory Boards, then to the Ministry for Trade and Supply, and finally to the Prices Office or the Council of Ministers. At every stage a thorough check is to be made—particularly to ensure that prescribed cost norms and other regulations of the current calculation principles [86, pp. 741ff.] have been observed—and proposals are to be worked out and passed on to the immediately superior organs. For price classification only, the process ends with the trade management organs (e.g. Central Commodity Office, wholesale directorates for particular commodity groups), in so far as for some product groups the enterprise may not itself perform price classification on the basis of price calculation regulations.

For *industrial prices* the procedure for confirmation or classification is in principle exactly the same as for consumer goods prices. The only difference is that, instead of the trade organs and the Ministry for Trade and Supply, the series of bodies which check the enterprise price proposal, after the management organ of the industry, includes the responsible Industrial Ministry, which is assisted by working groups or temporary expert commissions.[1] While classification of prices in the existing price structure is as a rule done by the price coordination organ of the industry—for some products by enterprises themselves even—price confirmation for new or improved products is performed either by the corresponding Industrial Ministry or, for particular product groups, by the Prices Office, the head of the Prices Office, or the Council of Ministers.[2]

For those products the principle is that the price rise on the new product must be smaller than the quality improvement, so that the user obtains an increase in utility—in relation to his costs—in comparison with the previous product.[3] Furthermore, an additional profit margin may be approved in the price of new or improved products—usually for three years—on the basis of close adherence to differential norms for processing and overhead costs [82, p. 673]. For products with the official quality mark 'C' or '1' price surcharges may be applied—after confirmation by the Prices Office [87, pp. 752–3].

[1] Besides representatives of the price coordinating organ for industry, representatives of the principal customers and of the Prices Office are called in for these commissions.

[2] The responsibility of the respective central organs for price confirmation and that of the industrial price coordination organs and enterprises themselves for price classification is set out in special unpublished product-groups catalogues.

[3] Despite this, additional costs of improving the protection of labour or of the environment may nevertheless be confirmed in the price in full.

New and comprehensive *calculation regulations* occupy a crucial place in this complicated price-setting procedure: on the one hand, they are an attempt to establish uniform yardsticks for price-setting, and, on the other, they are intended to exert a strong pressure on costs—as with cost planning. Thus enterprises, VVBs, and combines are obliged at least once a year to make an *ex post* analysis of the trends in their costs, profits, and prices and a comparison of actual and planned costs. Cost comparisons between enterprises, and investigation of the extent and causes of deviations, are to play a prominent part here.

For new products *price limits* are to be established at the development stage, with the participation of the principal customers and important suppliers. For whole investment projects, where exact advance calculation would involve considerable difficulties, part of the responsibility for price is transferred to the customer and the general or principal contractor jointly: they are allowed to set an *agreed price* [*88*, pp. 259ff.], in accordance with the regulations in the calculation principles, the current cost norms, and the prices set for parts of projects, after submission of a binding and detailed price quotation by the contractor. The customer has the right to inspect the relevant data underlying the calculation.

The growing significance of state price control organs has also increased the importance of the Prices Office. In conjunction with the State Planning Commission and the Ministry of Finance it determines the profit norms laid down for price-setting and has an appreciable influence on the principles of cost calculation. In addition, this office carries out continual price checks in enterprises and combines, sets penalties for price manipulation, and submits an annual analysis of the trends of costs, profits, and prices to the Council of Ministers.

Both the abandonment of important conceptions of price-setting from the NES period and the 1971 price freeze have aggravated the prevailing price distortions (cf. pp. 83ff.) and perpetuated them into the future. Thus the defects of price, which the industrial price reform, despite its imperfections, did reduce, have clearly increased again. They are affecting the measures of performance and efficiency more and more. Owing to the continual changing of costs and use of materials the relative values of commodities alter, but not noticeably, as prices remain basically unchanged. This is all the more serious in that inflationary phenomena are also concealed behind the reliance on formally constant prices. Economically sound evaluation of performance—i.e. at least according to costs—is scarcely possible.

Since financial and physical planning are interconnected by prices, price defects cause trouble with planning in general. 'Wrong' prices lead to economically wasteful production, obstruct necessary processes of innovation, or guide them in wrong directions [*89*, p. 667]: 'One form in which this shows up is the retention of old techniques and technologies, insufficient scrapping of obsolete capital, and inadequate efforts to release labour.' The following specific price defects can be distinguished:

(a) At present there are in principle three groups of prices in force side by side: for a large proportion of products prices set in the industrial price reform are still used; there is a group of products with 'capital-related' prices; and another group of new or improved products with new—although not as a rule 'capital-related'—prices. Present-day costs are thus inadequately reflected and are also distorted.

(b) The valuation of the gross capital stock in 1962 prices is no longer up to date, as the prices used in the revaluation no longer correspond to the replacement cost, nor indeed to the actual cost of capital goods. Thus not only are depreciation allowances wrong but, more important, even for those goods which do have capital-related prices, neither this price type nor the production capital charge can be fully effective as economic levers. For products which still do not have capital-related prices the economically necessary capital input is not taken into account in price.

(c) The prevailing prices do not express sufficiently the relative scarcities of factors of production, because the prices of the latter are influenced only by their approximate costs, and even that inadequately, but not by the pressure of demand for them. This applies above all to the factor which is especially scarce in the GDR, labour, which, because wages are low, is often employed where greater use of capital goods would be economically more efficient.

(d) The level and branch structure of wages do not correspond to those of labour productivity. Proposals for a so-called labour-power charge, which would be related to the wage fund,[1] and for extension of the concept of capital-related price to labour too (inclusion of a specified proportion of profit in relation to the respective economically necessary wage fund) [*93*, pp. 68–9] have not been officially followed up.[2]

(e) The scarcities created on the demand side with the given supply structure, i.e. the urgency of demand, continue to be left out of account in price-setting now as before.

---

[1] This charge, based on the actual amount of wages, which in principle is very similar to the production capital charge related to capital, was proposed, for example, by [*90*, p. 1775; *91*, pp. 46–7; *92*, pp. 1559ff.].

[2] The necessity for further development of this so-called *resource price* is nevertheless emphasized more and more from the theoretical side.

(f) The present price system is unable—either by allowing a higher initial profit for new or improved products or by the pressure the calculation and cost regulations exert on costs—to generate 'competition' for current cost and price reductions. Not even the best-performing enterprises are induced to reveal their reserves and thus bring their production standard up to the level of the world market.

New developments which produce savings of materials can even lead to penalization of the enterprise, because the new product shows lower profit and fulfilment of important indicators than the previous one [94, p. 11]: 'because a new price must be set, it naturally allows for a smaller proportion of materials; i.e. the commodity production and labour productivity indicators fall, while the manufacturing work involved remains constant. And what enterprise wants this?'

(g) The extremely complicated procedure for confirming prices of new and improved products is likely to have a very inhibiting effect, especially as the Prices Office is overloaded with the multitude of responsibilities entrusted to it. Owing to the excessive administrative work it is hardly able to implement consistently the desired principles of price-setting.

(h) Inadequate price flexibility remains an important problem of price-setting in the GDR. Enterprises can neither react in the short term to declining demand—e.g. by ceasing to cover fixed costs—nor meet rising demand with price increases in order to finance expansion of capacity. There is no longer scope for adaptation to sudden disturbances now that profit is firmly incorporated into financial planning.

In view of this catalogue of defects one might have expected thoroughly prepared measures to bring about decisive improvements in price-setting methods for the period after 1975. Such expectations seem destined for disappointment, since in April 1974 it was decided to conduct the statistical accounting of production at least for the next five-year plan 1976–80 in constant prices based on those in force on 1 January 1975 [95, pp. 240f.]. This means that the present heavily distorted prices will continue to form the basis of plan accounting.

The theoretical discussions in the GDR on price-setting show that there is thorough awareness of the defects of prices. Thus, according to one article, for example [96, p. 643]:

'Anomalies which result from a marked discrepancy in value and price trends, because there is not a sufficient tendency for prices to be kept close to the changing value of products, can be a *source of wrong planning decisions*, because the cost is not correctly known. They can lead to divergences between physical and financial planning. So-called shadow calculations alongside price are only a stop-gap for planning, above all because they cannot replace the objectively necessary role of price in the economic accounting of VVBs, combines, and enterprises, even if at the level of the economy as a whole they furnish definite insights.'

Yet priority continues to be given to the policy of stable consumer goods prices in the 1976–80 five-year plan. This of course likewise means the further maintenance of prices which are considerably below the actual cost level, such as passenger transport fares, prices for public services, for some basic foods, and for children's outer clothing. This is also true of rents.[1] State subsidies are thus likely to increase further.

For industrial prices there seems to be greater readiness to make price changes, especially as substantial differences in profitability persist between basic materials industries and manufacturing industries: while in recent years manufacturing branches were able to achieve considerable increases in labour productivity and reductions in cost through technical progress, important branches of the basic materials industries have had only limited success in this respect. In addition, deterioration of natural conditions has led to cost increases. Referring to the price changes which are particularly necessary for products of these branches, the working group on problems of improving planning and economic accounting, formed by order of the Scientific Council, explained in May 1974 [96, p. 648]:

'Further work is needed to examine whether necessary industrial price changes for basic materials will be required in the period up to 1980 or only after 1980. To the extent that bringing industrial prices closer to cost maintains the planned proportions of the national economy better and is an effective means for further increasing efficiency, changes should be made in industrial prices. Yet we must be certain that changes in industrial prices can in practice be efficiently prepared and incorporated into the plan and that the state keeps prices firmly under control.'

The working group could hardly suspect that external reasons would soon compel the GDR to make price changes.

The problems of increasing raw material costs

In addition to the sharp domestic price distortions described, the GDR found itself with a quite crucial new external problem: the

---

[1] Thus today—after the rent reduction introduced at the beginning of July 1972 for a certain group of persons—blue- and white-collar worker households with a monthly income up to 2000 Mark pay 1·00–1·25 Mark in East Berlin and 0·80–0·90 Mark elsewhere in the GDR per square metre of living space. Families with a higher income have to pay up to one-third more.

world-wide energy price rises. Although internal and foreign trade prices in the GDR are in principle insulated from each other, the GDR economic leadership had to decide whether and how the substantial increases in the cost of raw material imports should be taken into account in domestic prices. At the same time the deterioration in the geological conditions for extracting brown coal had to be reflected in its price. A simple subsidy policy without price changes was ruled out because it would not have generated any incentives to economize on materials. The aim of obtaining two-thirds of the energy consumption needed for the increment in output up to 1980 by energy saving [97, p. 3] compelled the adoption of a price policy designed to do this: the relative prices of energy raw materials had to be set so as to achieve economies both by reducing their use as fuels through cost increases and by promoting switching to more efficient forms of utilization. In May 1975 therefore a series of orders was promulgated establishing higher prices for raw materials and raw material-intensive products (e.g. oil, electric power, gas, heat, solid fuels, building materials, ferrous and non-ferrous metal products) with effect from 1 January 1976 [98, pp. 369ff.].

The question who should bear the cost increases brought manifold problems: on the one hand, it was thought that the increased costs could not be passed on to the population because the political decision to maintain consumer goods prices constant would no longer have been upheld. On the other hand, changes in the prices of semi-fabricates and finished goods produced by industrial users of raw materials (other than consumer goods industries) could not be allowed immediately because the already seriously disturbed price system would have been in complete confusion. Apart from the difficulty for the state organs of having to review all prices and set new ones in a short space of time, this would also have meant that in the very first year of the new five-year plan for 1976–80 the annual plan for 1976 would have had to be constructed on a substantially different price basis from the five-year plan. In view of this problem the GDR economic leadership decided to make the new raw material prices effective only for industrial users. The cost increases which have occurred are balanced by state subsidies or changes in product taxes for producers of consumer goods and of services for which specific relationships between substitutes are sought. For industrial customers cost increases are primarily to be absorbed by decreases in deductions from net profit as well as by enterprises' efforts to raise productivity. This gave rise to new problems in the additional burden on the state budget and the difficulties of a dual price level where the same products remain cheaper for consumers than for other users.

A substantial additional administrative cost was necessary, for, in order not to let the function of the new prices as incentives for raw material saving fizzle out, these prices had to be incorporated into the enterprise planning process. For enterprise financial planning this meant prior consideration of the financial effects of the planned changes in industrial prices and their compensation, as a rule, by decreases in deductions from net profits [99, pp. 419ff.] or through the so-called price equalization fund [100, pp. 422ff.] when no subsidies or changes in product taxes are envisaged.

This revision of raw material prices was the beginning of a process which contains its own momentum for further improvement: the GDR economic leadership must adapt the prices of products of higher stages of production to the changes in raw material costs. It has therefore set new prices for semi-fabricates, spare parts, and some finished products for wholesale transactions between enterprises with effect from 1 January 1977. In March 1976, 51 orders established higher prices for supplies like metallurgical products, chemical products, wood, building materials, wool, cotton, glass, engineering products, and also design services [101, pp. 264ff.]. These price increases too are not to affect the consumer, nor agricultural and handicraft enterprises. For industrial users, who are affected by the new prices, there are still to be no increases in the prices of their final products in 1977, and probably a complicated procedure of subsidies, decreases in deductions from net profit and compensation by means of the price equalization fund will be used. The appropriate orders have not yet been published.

These price revisions must extend beyond 1977 until—at the beginning of 1978 at the earliest—final product prices are also adjusted to the increased material costs. But even then there will be no certainty that the periodic price revisions which are so disruptive to planning are at an end, for now new changes in import prices for energy raw materials have come into effect. These too are bound to cause renewed revisions of domestic prices.

These regulations have made price-setting in the GDR at present even more problematic than it was in 1974–5: in an environment of severely distorted prices, which are now further disturbed by the present and future planned price changes decreed by the state authorities, which partly aim to reflect costs better, but partly work in the opposite direction too, the uncertainties facing the enterprise have clearly increased. With changing expenditures for raw and other materials and semi-fabricates, which are only inadequately reflected in cost norms, it must hold its product prices basically constant. It can only hope for an increase in its prices in the future, and even then it is bound to fear that part of its additional costs will have to be absorbed by productivity increases.

Price-setting according to the price-performance relationship

Since neither marked cost savings nor greater rises in efficiency were successfully achieved, the state authorities too have no ground for satisfaction. It became more and more clear that, rather than develop new products, enterprises prefer to continue producing obsolete ones, because the latter yield higher profits [*102*, pp. 840f.]. Besides, in spite of the new raw material prices enterprises saw hardly any incentive to economize on materials because with a worthwhile reduction in raw material content the value of their commodity output declined and thus their degree of plan fulfilment deteriorated.[1] Enterprises' continuing practice, in view of the substantial problems of material balancing, of preferring to use important raw materials as means of exchange rather than admitting savings to the state organs, is hardly unfamiliar.

As an emergency solution, because all else was of little help, the GDR economic leadership felt in July 1976 that it must create an incentive for economy of raw and other materials and also for improvement of products by means of new and, in conception, short-term regulations for price setting [*103*, pp. 317ff.]. Both were more the consequence of necessity than of any new theoretical approach. On the one hand, imports of dearer raw materials had to be stemmed by effective material savings and, on the other, innovations had to be induced to raise domestic efficiency and increase exports. According to the new regulations, the enterprise may hold the enterprise price (i.e. industry wholesale price less production tax and/or consumption tax) constant until 1980 when it achieves cost savings; this means that plan fulfilment accounting is no longer adversely affected by cost reductions and the enterprise (e.g. when it saves materials) receives a profit advantage.

For new or improved products prices are set according to the so-called *price-performance relationship*, i.e. in relation to improvements in user qualities *vis-à-vis* comparable products. Starting from the price of the most comparable existing product the improvement in user qualities of the new product is measured and the new price calculated accordingly. As pure cost-based price setting was thus forsaken, the calculation principle which was only developed in 1972 had to be abandoned again and replaced by a new one containing price setting according to the price-performance relationship [*104*, pp. 321ff.]. This calculation principle grants the producer a larger

[1] See also p. 139, point (f).

share in the rise in utility of the new product than the user: as an incentive to quality improvements the producer is allowed 70 per cent of the utility advantage of the new product in the price, so that his profit is also increased. Thirty per cent of the utility advantage goes to the user so that in relation to the overall utility of the product he enjoys a cost reduction.

The GDR central authorities are hoping for twofold advantages from the new price-setting procedure:

(a) A substantial alleviation of the task of checking which falls to them under the extremely bureaucratic price proposal and confirmation procedure. Instead of having to carry out a lengthy and detailed examination of the costs of new products it is thought that new prices can be derived more quickly and simply directly from the already recognized expenditure per unit of performance of comparable products [105, p. 846].

(b) Better integration of new products into the existing assortment. Products with the same or a similar use are to receive coordinated prices based on their price-performance relationship. This means that disruptions of the relative values of similar or easily substitutable products, which have resulted hitherto on account of the distortions due to the existence of prices set on different bases, should now be avoided.

The existence of these advantages must indeed be agreed in principle. Yet the new regulations represent only a small step in the direction of the desired improvements, because they have a number of disadvantages. In essence there are three problems:

(a) The incentive created for enterprises to develop new products or economize on materials is relatively small with the existing rules on the use of profit, since a substantial part of the additional profit must be handed over to the state budget and the remaining part allocated to form funds for prescribed purposes.

(b) Objective yardsticks are frequently lacking for measuring the user qualities of new products, so that inadequate evaluation of expenditure has merely been replaced by inadequate measurement and evaluation of user qualities. Enterprises will try to emphasize all allegedly positive qualities of their new products and at the same time neglect the disadvantages.

(c) Prices for new products based on the price-performance relationship do nothing to end the existing price distortions but only serve to fit new products into the existing product range better. Within the product range new products can be valued in accordance with relative user qualities. But between product ranges the old distortions due to prices set on different principles remain. Thus, for example, it is likely that in capital-intensive branches of industry it will not be possible for a number of years to take capital costs into account and set 'capital-related' prices.

Looking at price setting for new or improved products as a whole, it is clear that the economic leadership's intention of replacing the previous insoluble problem of checking costs—as a precondition for evaluating new products—by a simpler procedure can scarcely be said to have succeeded. The new price-setting mechanism creates substantial new problems which do not ease the lot of the centre, even if it delegates a large part of the administrative work involved to the enterprises. For, in place of problems of cost calculation the centre now faces the still more difficult task of undertaking effective checking and evaluation of user qualities.

In addition to the three existing groups of prices already illustrated a fourth is now added: prices set on the basis of the price-performance relationship for products with improvements in use value which are partly illusory or overvalued.

BANKING AND CREDIT

The banks in the GDR were up to 1974 independent but non-competing state institutions, which followed the 'principle of economic accounting' since then most of the banks may be seen as branches of the State Bank. The *State Bank* is responsible for duties like cash emission, currency management, and the conduct of accounts for the state budget. It is also involved in the preparation of aggregate economic planning decisions in so far as they are expected to have effects in the field of money and credit [*106*, pp. 3ff.]. The branches of the Industry and Trade Bank, the Agricultural Bank, the Foreign Trade and Cooperative Bank, and the savings banks operate as *business banks*. The Industry and Trade Bank is particularly important as, besides the granting of credit and the execution of payments between enterprises, economic organizations, and the state, it exercises significant supervisory functions over the accounts of enterprises and economic organizations.[1] In particular, it checks the implementation of the tasks specified in the investment plan. Because of its importance, the Industry and Trade Bank was incorporated with the State Bank with effect from 1 July 1974.[2]

The granting of credit basically follows the credit plan passed by the Council of Ministers. It is intended to support production which

[1] The banks keep a check on all monetary movements by enterprises and organizations because the latter are obliged to use non-cash transfers and to keep their accounts with the branch of the bank responsible for them. This means, for example, that all funds have to be conducted through the bank and all cash receipts have likewise to be paid in; apart from a few small other cases the only significant cash withdrawals are for wage payments.

[2] This was done in order to centralize financial discipline.

is both efficient and in accordance with the plan. Thus credit policy too is clearly adapted to the planned physical target structure. Yet it cannot be ruled out that within the narrow framework of pre-determined targets enterprises themselves might give preference to goals which were more efficient but perhaps contrary to the plan rather than to tasks which were less efficient but conformed to the plan. For this reason the rights of the banks to check intra-enterprise activities—quite independently of the source of finance—have been substantially reinforced in recent years. According to the new credit decree [*107*, pp. 41ff.],[1] it is the duty of the banks to promote production in accordance with plan and demand and to work to avoid plan violations. This is done through:

■ reporting on draft plans and participating in the process of enterprise plan negotiation;

■ cooperation with the enterprise's chief accountant,[2] whose importance as a checking agent has been increased since 1971, and other control organs;[3]

■ informing enterprise authorities and superior organs of the results of their investigations;

■ imposition of penal rates of interest for violation of the credit agreement or failure to fulfil credit conditions, and reduction or even refusal of credit for the future;

■ declarations that the enterprise has only conditional creditworthiness or is not creditworthy at all, in cases of serious and persistent plan contraventions.[4]

The credit decrees lay down that credits for investment and working capital are tied to a number of conditions:

(a) For *investment credits* not only must the investment project be

---

[1] See also the orders on credit for agriculture in [*108*, pp. 726ff.; *109*, pp. 793ff.].

[2] The chief accountant has a dual function: not only is he responsible, as head of finance and credit and cost accounting, for drawing up the enterprise's balance sheet at the end of the year, profit and loss accounting, and plan accounting, and thus the most important checking agent within the enterprise, but he is also assigned by the superior management organs with supervising plan observance from the standpoint of the central organs, ensuring compliance with laws, and implementing central orders in the enterprise. Thus in the case of important contraventions he has to inform the Minister of Finance and the Minister responsible for the enterprise. In addition, the Minister of Finance has the right to issue direct instructions to him concerning auditing, and to demand reports on their execution [*110*, pp. 137ff.].

[3] Besides the workers' and peasants' inspectorates, which enjoy relatively extensive authority, these also include the 'central permanent production conference' which operates as an organ of the enterprise trade union heads and the 'permanent production conferences' subordinated to departmental trade union heads.

[4] This measure can be cancelled again only after the introduction of a procedure for re-establishment of sound management—the so-called stabilization procedure.

thoroughly prepared and accepted in the plan, but compliance with relevant effectiveness criteria and other values (e.g. investment cost, technical performance, repayment period, construction time) must also be guaranteed. In addition, the banks are to use their influence to see that plants are expanded only using the most up-to-date technology and when the existing capacity is fully employed and sufficient labour is available for the new.

(b) *Working capital credits* are tied to fulfilment of indicators and norms for use of materials and levels of stocks and also to observance of sound payment times by the enterprise. The banks are also supposed to urge enterprises to adhere to stated price groups for consumer goods, to produce sufficient spare parts, and to speed up their stock turnover; they are also to punish use of excess working capital by interest surcharges, unless it is needed for overfulfilment of plan targets, when this is rewarded by reduced interest rates.

Credits are basically granted for a period of five years at an interest rate of 5 per cent. For credits to finance rationalization measures the interest rate can be reduced to 1·8 per cent. For extra-plan credits to surmount temporary liquidity difficulties 8 per cent is charged, and it is a condition of such credits that the enterprise gives an assurance of fulfilment of future plan tasks and repayment of the credit by the end of the following plan year at the latest. If the credit agreement is contravened interest rises to 10 per cent.

Foreign trade enterprises can be granted credits in foreign currency in accordance with plan, and over and above it if additional imports would make overplan exports with a high export profitability possible in a short time.

THE STATE BUDGET

The essential instruments of state economic policy in the GDR include the revenue and expenditure sides of the state budget. The peculiarities of the economic and social system and of the state organization give it a specific function within the state system of economic management. It differs from Western state budgets, and in particular from that of the German Federal Republic, not only in its aggregate economic importance, its volume, and structure, but also in respect of its almost complete secrecy. The minimal data in the GDR Gazette[1] are supplemented by far fewer statistics in the statistical yearbook than is the case with any other Comecon member country.

[1] The 1974 budget law comprises not quite one and a half pages of the Gazette and contains a total of only seventy-four figures, including the data on revenue, expenditure, and central allocations for each of the fifteen regions of the GDR [*111*, pp. 570–1].

The significance of the GDR state budget differs from that of a Western budget, on the one hand, because of the effect of socialist ownership on the relationship between the state and the economy: the state's position *vis-à-vis* the economy is not only as Exchequer, i.e. for the financing of state services, but also as owner of the means of production. In this capacity it demands a share in profit and uses its profits among other things to finance investments. This means that the state budget reflects, for example, essential functions of a capital market, which in a Western economy remain outside the budget. Moreover, within the framework of economic planning the state has numerous possibilities for direct influence to further its interests and is therefore less dependent in this respect than market economies on the conduct of state finances. On the other hand, many state decisions in planning the economy have financial effects and thus affect the volume of the state budget in one way or another.

Altogether, therefore, the size of the budget in East European economies—measured against gross social product or national income—is generally greater than in Western Europe. This effect is accentuated by the state responsibility for and financing of a whole series of functions which in other social systems are performed by non-state groups or bodies (e.g. public legal institutions for broadcasting, scientific or social foundations, churches, etc.). Consequently the expenditure of the state budget or all public budgets as a proportion of gross social product in the GDR was about 49 per cent in 1970 [*112*, p. 277; *113*, p. 311], much higher than in the Federal Republic where in the same year it only amounted to around 29 per cent [*114*, pp. 42, 108].

Table 23: Trends of national income and state expenditure in the GDR 1950–75 (in mlrd Mark)

	National income	State budget expenditure	Expenditure as a percentage of national income
1950	27·2	24·1	88·6
1955	50·3	38·3	76·1
1960	71·0	49·5	69·7
1965	84·2	55·8	66·2
1970	108·7	70·0	64·4
1971	113·6	79·1	69·6
1972	120·1	85·7	71·4
1973	126·8	93·3	73·6
1974	135·0	103·3	76·5
1975	141·7	114·2	80·6

Source: [*112*, pp. 36, 287].

As Table 23 shows, between 1950 and 1970 there was a continuous decline in state expenditure as a proportion of national income—which because it is restricted to net product in the material production sector is naturally less than gross social product. Since 1971 there has been a certain rise in the proportion again, presumably because of the clear centralization of state decisions, especially in the investment field [*116*, p. 1637], which we have repeatedly emphasized.

The structure of the GDR state budget differs from that of the German Federal Republic and other Western European countries principally in that it is a so-called 'uniform' state budget: it includes not only the republic budget but also those of the regions, districts, and parishes, as well as social insurance revenues and expenditures.

The most important functions of the state budget are considered to be [*117*, p. 759]: the *redistribution function*, to supplement physical planning decisions and supplement or correct the primary monetary distribution within the state's prices and incomes policy; the *lever function*, to stimulate producers' performance and to bring about the most economical use of resources; and the *control function*, i.e. checks on the formation, distribution, and use of parts of the total social product and of the state's net income (both centralized, in the state budget, and decentralized, in state enterprises) and capital.

Charges on the state economy make up the largest part of the revenue items in the state budget, accounting for about 55–57 per cent of the total. They include:

(a) the product-linked charge (production charge, services charge, or trade charge), a charge which is differentiated for different kinds of goods and, like the Soviet turnover tax to which it corresponds, is levied principally in the consumer goods sphere. It accounts for about 50 per cent of all revenue from the state economy [*116*, p. 1642];

(b) the production capital charge (and trade capital charge), a levy on enterprise production capital, similar to interest, the main function of which is as an economic lever; it is not included in enterprises' costs, but is rather a minimum deduction from enterprise profits to the state budget. It is therefore closely connected with

(c) the net profit deduction, i.e. the part of enterprise net profit (gross profit less production capital charge) which is not allotted to any enterprise fund but is payable to the state as owner of the enterprise.

The system of charges on the state economy is mostly described as a 'two-channel system', but also occasionally as a 'three-channel system' (production charge, production capital charge, net profit deduction).

Other revenue items are: income from state establishments (e.g. radio and television duties); taxes on cooperatives; taxes on semi-state enterprises; taxes on private entrepreneurs and craftsmen; taxes on the earned incomes of the population; social security contributions.

Owing to the almost complete elimination of private and semi-state enterprises and their transformation into state enterprises in the spring of 1972, taxes from this sector are now insignificant. The same applies to direct taxes on the population, the maximum rate of which is 20 per cent on wages and salaries, 30 per cent on income from free professional activity (non-capitalist—e.g. doctors or artists). These taxes are far less important than the indirect taxes (the production charge).

The expenditures of the state budget, which are also shown in very little detail, include: (a) expenditures on the national economy, in particular for investments, increases in working capital, and subsidies; (b) expenditure on schools, higher education, science, and research; (c) expenditures for social, health, and cultural purposes; (d) military expenditure; (e) state administration and other expenditures; (f) revenue surplus—by law to be spent on financing the national economy and therefore not distinguishable from item (a).

According to the budget laws the trends in revenue and expenditure in the years 1972–4 were as shown in Table 24.

The data available on the actual revenue and expenditure in 1972–5 show some considerable deviations from the plan figures (see Table 25).

Table 24: GDR budget plans 1972-7

Item	in mlrd Mark						as percentages of the total					
	1972	1973	1974	1975	1976	1977	1972	1973	1974	1975	1976	1977
Total revenue	82·3	90·3	99·6	106·5	115·9	122·2	100	100	100	100	100	100
from the state economy	44·2	51·3	57·2	64·9	70·2	77·5	53·7	56·8	57·4	60·9	60·6	63·4
from agricultural cooperatives	1·1	1·1	1·1	1·1	1·3	1·3	1·3	1·2	1·1	1·0	1·1	1·1
Social Insurance contributions												
from state employees	8·8	9·2	9·6	10·0	10·6	11·1	10·7	10·2	9·6	9·4	9·1	9·1
from cooperative members	1·4	1·3	1·3	1·3	1·4	1·4	1·7	1·4	1·3	1·2	1·2	1·1
Other revenue	26·8	27·4	30·4	29·2	32·4	30·9	32·6	30·3	30·5	27·4	28·0	25·3
Total expenditure	82·3	90·3	99·6	106·4	115·9	122·2	100	100	100	100	100	100
for social funds	22·7	24·8	26·7	28·0	31·5	33·2	27·6	27·5	26·8	26·3	27·2	27·2
Subsidy for social insurance	5·7	8·1	8·9	9·0	9·0	11·0	6·9	9·0	8·9	8·5	7·8	9·0
Investment in education and health	1·0	1·0	1·0	1·1	1·2	1·1	1·2	1·1	1·0	1·0	1·0	0·9
Investment in the economy, incl. research and development	3·9	5·2	6·7	1·0[1]	2·8	4·2	4·7	5·8	6·7	0·9[1]	2·4	3·4
Agricultural subsidies	2·2	2·1	2·2	2·1	2·2	2·2	2·7	2·3	2·2	2·0	1·9	1·8
Military	7·6	8·3	8·9	9·6	10·2	11·0	9·2	9·2	8·9	9·0	8·8	9·0
Other	39·1	40·7	45·1	55·6	59·0	59·5	47·5	45·1	45·3	52·3	50·9	48·7
Revenue surplus	0·057	0·063	0·045	0·057	0·063	0·068	0·0	0·0	0·0	0·0	0·0	0·0

[1] Research and development only.

Sources: [118, p. 197; 119, p. 288; 120, p. 570; 121, p. 574; 122, p. 746; 123, p. 535].

Table 25: *Revenue and expenditure of the GDR state budget, 1972–5, plan and actual*

Year	Revenue Plan	Revenue Actual	Deviation	Expenditure Plan	Expenditure Actual	Deviation	Surplus Plan	Surplus Actual	Deviation
1972	82,301·3	86,934·8	+4,633·5	82,244·3	85,747·6	+3,503·3	57·0	1,187·2	+1,130·2
1973	90,261·8	94,946·2	+4,684·4	90,198·8	93,276·7	+3,077·9	63·0	1,669·5	+1,606·5
1974	99,562·9	104,645·2	+5,082·3	99,517·9	103,291·9	+3,774·0	45·0	1,353·3	+1,308·3
1975	106,466·1	114,662·0	+8,195·9	106,409·1	114,160·2	+7,751·1	57·0	502·0	+445·0

Sources: [*118*, p. 197; *119*, p. 288; *120*, p. 570; *121*, p. 574; *124*, p. 287].

Note: a more detailed analysis of the causes and effects of these deviations is not possible because of the lack of data on individual items in the state budget.

References to Chapter IV

1. 'Beschluss des Staatsrats der DDR über weitere Massnahmen zur Gestaltung des ökonomischen Systems des Sozialismus vom 22. April 1968' (Resolution of the GDR State Council of 22 April 1968 on further measures for the development of the Economic System of Socialism), *Gesetzblatt der DDR*, I, no. 9, 1968.
2. *Gesetzblatt der DDR*, II, no. 66, 1968.
3. *Die Wirtschaft*, nos. 18, 19, and 20, 1970, Supplements.
4. '15. Tagung des ZK der SED am 28. Januar 1971' (15th Plenum of the Central Committee of the SED), *Neues Deutschland*, 29 January 1971.
5. 'Richtlinie . . .' (*Principles* . . .), see ref. 6, Chapter I.
6. A. Binz, 'Die Aufgaben der Bilanzorgane zur Sicherung der planmässigen, proportionalen Entwicklung der Volkswirtschaft' (The tasks of the balancing organs to ensure the planned, proportional development of the national economy), *Die Wirtschaft*, no. 12, 1971.
7. *Politische Ökonomie des Sozialismus und ihre Anwendung in der DDR* (Political Economy of Socialism and its Application in the GDR). East Berlin 1969.
8. Heinz-Dieter Haustein, *Wirtschaftsprognose* (Economic Forecasts). East Berlin, 1969.
9. Heinz-Dieter Haustein, *Prognoseverfahren* (Forecasting Procedures). East Berlin, 1970.
10. Gerhard Schürer, 'Zur Vervollkommnung der Planung in der DDR' (On the improvement of planning in the GDR), *Einheit*, no. 1, 1972.
11. M. Jäger, W. Karbstein, G. Rudlich, 'Die Verflechtungsbilanz des Gesamtprodukts in der DDR' (Input–output table of aggregate product in the GDR), *Sozialistische Planwirtschaft*, no. 8, 1960.
12. M. Jäger, W. Karbstein, G. Rudlich, 'Zu einigen Ergebnissen der Verflechtungsbilanz des Gesamtprodukts in der DDR' (On some results from the input–output table of aggregate product in the GDR), *Wirtschaftswissenschaft*, no. 9, 1963.
13. Kurt Scharnbacher, 'Ökonomisch-mathematische Modelle als Instrument zentraler Planung in der DDR' (Mathematical economic models as an instrument of central planning in the GDR), *Ost-Europa Wirtschaft*, nos. 3–4, 1973.
14. H. Fischer, *Modelldenken und Operationsforschung als Führungsaufgaben* (Modelling and Operations Research as Management Problems). Berlin, 1968.
15. 'Anordnung über die Methodik zur Ausarbeitung des Volkswirtschaftsplanes 1973 vom 15. Februar 1972' (Order of 15 February 1972 on the methods for working out the national economic plan for 1973), *Gesetzblatt der DDR*, Sonderdruck no. 726, 14 March 1972.
16. 'Anordnung über den terminlichen Ablauf der Ausarbeitung des Volkswirtschaftsplanes und des Staatshaushaltsplanes 1974 vom 25. April 1973' (Order of 25 April 1973 on the timing of the working out of the national economic plan and the state budget plan for 1974), *Gesetzblatt der DDR*, I, no. 21, 1973.
16a. 'Anordnung über den Ablauf der Ausarbeitung des Volkswirtschaftsplanes und des Staatshaushaltsplanes 1977' (Order on the procedure for working out the national economic plan and state budget for 1977), *Gesetzblatt der DDR*, I, no. 17. 1976.
17. 'Anordnung über die planmethodischen Regelungen zur Durchführung des Volkswirtschaftsplanes 1974 vom 20. Dezember 1973' (Order of 20 December

1973 on the procedural regulations for implementing the national economic plan for 1974), *Gesetzblatt der DDR*, I, no. 59, 1973.

18. 'Vorschläge zur Vervollkommnung der Jahresplanung' (Proposals for the improvement of annual planning), *Die Wirtschaft*, no. 2, 1972.

19. W. Laatsch, S. Vollstädt, 'Wie hoch ist der volkswirtschaftlich begründete Bedarf?' (How high is economically justified need?'), *Die Wirtschaft*, no. 7, 1972.

20. Hans Hackbarth, 'Planmethodik soll besser überschaubar sein' (Planning methods should be clearer), *Die Wirtschaft*, no. 8, 1972.

21. Walter Marx, 'Fragen der Konstanthaltung volkswirtschaftlicher Verzeichnisse und Systematiken' (Problems of the stability of economic schedules and systems), *Statistische Praxis*, no. 11, 1971.

22. 'Beschluss über Massnahmen auf dem Gebiet der Leitung, Planung und Entwicklung der Industriepreise vom 17. November 1971' (Resolution of 17 November 1971 on measures in the field of management, planning, and development of industrial prices), *Gesetzblatt der DDR*, II, no. 77, 1971.

23. Helmut Hesse, 'Hier Überplanbestände und dort Sortimentslücken— woran liegt das?' (Here over-plan stocks and there gaps in assortment— what is the reason for it?), *Die Wirtschaft*, no. 9, 1974.

24. Ernst-Günter Zorn, 'Wie orientieren wir auf die Bedarfsdeckung und auf ein hohes Wachstumstempo der Produktion?' (How do we concentrate on meeting demand and on a high rate of growth of output?), *Die Wirtschaft*, no. 9, 1972.

25. Kurt Erdmann. 'Der Gegenplan 1974—ideologische und ökonomische Aspekte' (The 1974 counterplan—ideological and economic aspects), *Analysen der Forschungsstelle für gesamtdeutsche wirtschaftliche und soziale Fragen*, no. 2, 1974.

26. 'Anordnung zu den Regelungen für die Arbeit mit Gegenplänen in den Betrieben und Kombinaten zur Erfüllung und Überbietung des Volkswirtschaftsplanes 1974 vom 19. Dezember 1973' (Order of 19 December 1973 for the regulations on work with counterplans in enterprises and combines for fulfilling and surpassing the 1974 national economic plan), *Gesetzblatt der DDR*, I, no. 1, 1974. 'Anordnung zu den Regelungen für die Weiterführung der Arbeit mit den Gegenplänen in Betrieben und Kombinaten bei der Durchführung des Volkswirtschaftsplanes 1977 vom 3. Januar 1977' (Order of 3 January 1977 on the regulations for continuing the work with counterplans in enterprises and combines when executing the national economic plan for 1977), *Gesetzblatt der DDR*, I, 1, 1977.

27. Gerhard Schürer, 'Die Weiterentwicklung der Leitung und Planung der Volkswirtschaft' (The further development of the management and planning of the national economy), *Neues Deutschland*, 5 August 1971.

28. 'Verordnung über die Material-, Ausrüstungs- und Konsumgüterbilanzierung vom 20. Mai 1971' (Decree of 20 May 1971 on materials, equipment, and consumer goods balancing), *Gesetzblatt der DDR*, II, no. 50, 1971.

29. Heinz-Jürgen Lorenz, Gerhard Steiner, 'Bilanzieren heisst leiten und planen' (Balancing means managing and planning), *Die Wirtschaft*, no. 28, 1971.

30. 'Anordnung Nr. 2 über die Nomenklatur für die Planung, Bilanzierung und Abrechnung von Material, Ausrüstungen und Konsumgütern zur Ausarbeitung und Durchführung der Volkswirtschaftspläne ab 1972—Bilanzverzeichnis—vom 24. September 1971' (Order no. 2 of 24 September 1971 on the nomenclature for the planning, balancing, and accounting of materials, equipment, and consumer goods for the elaboration and im-

plementation of national economic plans from 1972 onward—Balance list), *Gesetzblatt der DDR*, Sonderdruck no. 688/1.

31. Heinz Uhlig, Günter Müller, 'Einheitliche Artikelkatalogisierung in der Volkswirtschaft' (Uniform item cataloguing in the national economy), *Die Wirtschaft*, no. 9, 1973.

32. Lorena Kiehle, 'Bilanzierung durchdenken und rationalisieren' (Rethinking and rationalizing balancing), *Die Wirtschaft*, no. 8, 1972.

33. Ina Grüning, 'Wie soll es in der Jahresplanung weitergehen?' (How should annual planning proceed?), *Die Wirtschaft*, no. 48, 1971.

34. Ina Grüning, 'Bilanzverantwortung, Bedarfsplanung, Bilanzierungsmethoden' (Balance responsibility, demand planning, balancing methods), *Die Wirtschaft*, no. 4, 1972.

35. Gerhard Schilling, Horst Steeger, 'Proportionalität in unserer sozialistischen Planwirtschaft' (Proportionality in our socialist planned economy), *Einheit*, no, 5, 1971.

36. Hans-Heinrich Dahl, 'Normenarbeit in der chemischen Industrie' (Work on norms in the chemical industry), *Die Wirtschaft*, no. 19, 1972.

37. Friedrich Schiefer, 'Bilanzen, Bedarf und Normenarbeit' (Balances, demand, and work on norms), *Die Wirtschaft*, no. 7, 1972.

38. Norbert Moc, 'Technisch-ökonomisch begründete Normative senken den Materialaufwand' (Technically and economically grounded norms reduce material input), *Die Wirtschaft*, no. 10, 1973.

39. Jürgen Kalatz, 'Materialökonomie weiter verbessern' (Further improving economy on materials), *Die Wirtschaft*, no. 7, 1974.

40. Georg Ebert, Harry Milke, 'Aktuelle Probleme unserer sozialistischen Planung' (Current problems of our socialist planning), *Einheit*, no. 12, 1971.

41. Gerhard Schilling, Horst Steeger, 'Der VIII. Parteitag der SED und die weitere Vervollkommnung der Planung der Volkswirtschaft' (The Eighth SED Party Congress and the further improvement of economic planning), *Wirtschaftswissenschaft*, no. 10, 1971.

42. 'Gesetz über den Ministerrat der Deutschen Demokratischen Republik vom 16. Oktober 1972' (Law of 16 October 1972 on the Council of Ministers of the German Democratic Republic), *Gesetzblatt der DDR*, I, no. 16, 1972.

43. 'Statut der Staatlichen Plankommission—Beschluss des Ministerrates vom 9. August 1973' (Statute of the State Planning Commission—Resolution of the Council of Ministers of 9 August 1973), *Gesetzblatt der DDR*, I, no. 41, 1973.

44. 'Statut des Ministeriums für Glas- und Keramikindustrie—Beschluss des Ministerrates vom 4. Juli 1973' (Statute of the Ministry of the Glass and Ceramics Industry—Resolution of the Council of Ministers of 4 July 1973), *Gesetzblatt der DDR*, I, no. 37, 1973.

45. 'Gesetz über die örtlichen Volksvertretungen und ihre Organe in der Deutschen Demokratischen Republik vom 12. Juli 1973' (Law of 12 July 1973 on local representation and its organization in the German Democratic Republic), *Gesetzblatt der DDR*, I, no. 32, 1973.

46. 'Verordnung über die Aufgaben, Rechte und Pflichten des volkseigenen Produktionsbetriebes vom 9. Februar 1967' (Decree of 9 February 1967 on the tasks, rights, and duties of the nationalized productive enterprise), *Gesetzblatt der DDR*, II, no. 21, 1967.

47. 'Verordnung über die Aufgaben, Rechte und Pflichten der volkseigenen Betriebe, Kombinate und VVB vom 28. März 1973' (Decree of 28 March 1973 on the tasks, rights, and duties of nationalized enterprises, combines, and VVB), *Gesetzblatt der DDR*, I, no. 15, 1973.

48. Angela Rüger, *Die Bedeutung 'strukturbestimmender Aufgaben' für die Wirtschaftsplanung und -organisation der DDR* (The significance of 'structure-determining tasks' for economic planning and organization in the GDR). Berlin, 1969.

49. 'Beschluss über die Durchführung des ökonomischen Systems des Sozialismus im Jahre 1971 vom 1. Dezember 1970' (Resolution of 1 December 1970 on the implementation of the Economic System of Socialism in 1971), *Gesetzblatt der DDR*, II, no. 100, 1970.

50. 'Verordnung über die ökonomische Materialverwendung und Vorratswirtschaft sowie über die Ordnung in der Lagerwirtschaft—Arbeit mit Normen und Kennziffern vom 15. September 1971' (Decree of 15 September 1971 on the economical use of materials and control of stocks and on orderly stock control—work with norms and indicators), *Gesetzblatt der DDR*, II, no. 69, 1971.

51. E. Liberman, 'Plan, pribyl', premiya' (Plan, profit, bonus), *Pravda*, 9 September 1962.

52. 'Verordnung über die Produktionsfondsabgabe' (Decree on the production capital charge), *Gesetzblatt der DDR*, II, no. 4, 1971.

53. 'Finanzierungsrichtlinie für 1972' (Financial guideline for 1972), *Gesetzblatt der DDR*, II, no. 78, 1971.

54. 'Finanzierungsrichtlinie für die volkseigene Wirtschaft' (Financial guideline for the nationalized economy), *Gesetzblatt der DDR*, II, no. 42, 1972.

55. Harry Nick, 'Wissenschaftlich-technischer Fortschritt und wirtschaftliche Rechnungsführung' (Scientific-technical progress and economic calculation), *Einheit*, no. 12, 1973.

56. *Die Wirtschaft*, no. 44, 1971.

57. 'Verordnung über die Planung, Bildung und Verwendung des Prämienfonds und des Kultur- und Sozialfonds für das Jahr 1971' (Decree on the planning, formation, and use of the bonus fund and the cultural and social fund for 1971), *Gesetzblatt der DDR*, II, no. 16, 1971.

58. 'Verordnung über die Planung, Bildung und Verwendung des Prämienfonds und des Kultur- und Sozialfonds für volkseigene Betriebe im Jahre 1972' (Decree on the planning, formation, and use of the bonus fund and the cultural and social fund for nationalized enterprises in 1972), *Gesetzblatt der DDR*, II, no. 5, 1972.

59. 'Anordnung über die Bildung und Verwendung des Betriebsergebnisses aus der Aussenhandelstätigkeit und der finanziellen Fonds der Aussenhandelsbetriebe und der Dienstleistungsbetriebe der Aussenwirtschaft' (Order on the formation and use of enterprise foreign trade results and of the financial funds of foreign trade and services enterprises), *Gesetzblatt der DDR*, II, no. 15, 1972.

60. 'Anordnung über die Finanzplanung in den volkseigenen Betrieben und Kombinaten' (Order on financial planning in nationalized enterprises and combines), *Gesetzblatt der DDR*, I, no. 6, 1973.

61. 'Beschluss über die Anwendung technisch-ökonomisch begründeter Normative bei der Planung des Materialverbrauchs' (Resolution on the use of technically and economically based norms in the planning of materials use), including the relevant order, Sonderdruck (special issue), *Gesetzblatt der DDR*, no. 737, 1972.

62. 'Zweite Verordnung über die ökonomische Materialverwendung und Vorratswirtschaft sowie über die Ordnung in der Lagerwirtschaft' (Second decree on the economical use of materials and control of stocks and on orderly stock control), *Gesetzblatt der DDR*, II, no. 39, 1972.

63. 'Beschluss über die Grundsätze für die differenzierte Erfassung, Normierung und Berücksichtigung der Gemeinkosten bei der Planung und Preisbildung in den volkseigenen Betrieben' (Resolution on the principles for differentiated recording, norming, and accounting of overhead costs in planning and price setting in nationalized enterprises), *Gesetzblatt der DDR*, II, no. 89, 1967.

64. 'Anordnung über die Bildung und Verwendung des Risikofonds' (Order on the formation and use of the risk fund), *Gesetzblatt der DDR*, II, no. 32, 1971.

65. 'Anordnung über die Bildung und Verwendung des Risikofonds im Bereich des Bauwesens' (Order on the formation and use of the risk fund in the construction sector), *Gesetzblatt der DDR*, II, no. 52, 1971.

66. Adolf Polz, 'Verbindliche Preisangebote sind gesetzlich vorgeschrieben' (Binding price quotations are legally prescribed), *Die Wirtschaft*, no. 30, 1971.

67. 'Anordnung über die Finanzierung und Stimulierung wissenschaftlich-technischer Leistungen in der DDR' (Order on the financing and stimulation of scientific and technical achievements in the GDR), *Gesetzblatt der DDR*, II, no. 73, 1972.

68. *Gesetzblatt der DDR*, II, no. 34, 1972.

69. ibid., II, no. 48, 1972.

70. ibid., I, no. 46, 1973.

71. ibid., II, no. 70, 1972.

72. ibid., I, no. 30, 1973.

73. *Berliner Zeitung*, 25 March 1973.

74. 'Anordnung über die Planung, Bildung und Verwendung des Leistungsfonds der volkseigenen Betriebe' (Order on the planning, formation, and use of the performance fund of the nationalized enterprise), *Gesetzblatt der DDR*, II, no. 42, 1972.

75. Siegfried Böhm, 'Leistungsfonds fördern die Initiativen der Kollektive' (Performance funds stimulate the initiatives of the work force), *Presse-Informationen*, no. 79, 1972.

76. Siegfried Böhm, 'Leistungsfonds und andere ökonomische Regelungen fördern die Initiative der Betriebskollektive' (Performance funds and other economic regulations stimulate the initiative of the enterprise work force), *Sozialistische Finanzwirtschaft*, no. 14, 1972.

77. 'Anordnung Nr. 2 über die Planung, Bildung und Verwendung des Leistungsfonds der volkseigenen Betriebe' (Order no. 2 on the planning, formation, and use of the performance fund of nationalized enterprises), *Gesetzblatt der DDR*, I, no. 7, 1974.

78. *Neues Deutschland*, 27 December 1972.

79. *Einheit*, no. 1, 1974.

80. Manfred Melzer, 'Preispolitik und Preisbildungsprobleme in der DDR' (Price policy and problems of price-setting in the GDR), *Vierteljahreshefte zur Wirtschaftsforschung*, no. 3, 1969.

81. *Gesetzblatt der DDR*, II, no. 67, 1972.

82. 'Beschluss über Massnahmen auf dem Gebiet der Leitung, Planung und Entwicklung der Industriepreise' (Resolution on measures in the field of management, planning, and development of industrial prices), *Gesetzblatt der DDR*, II, no. 77, 1971.

83. *Die Wirtschaft*, no. 14, 1972.

84. 'Beschluss über die Bestätigung der Verbraucherpreise für Konsumgüter nach staatlichen Nomenklaturen und zur Erhöhung der Verantwortung des Amtes für Preise' (Resolution on the confirmation of retail prices for

consumer goods according to state nomenclatures and on increasing the responsibility of the Prices Office), *Gesetzblatt der DDR*, II, no. 77, 1971.

85. 'Anordnung Nr. Pr. 92 über das Verfahren bei der Ausarbeitung, Einreichung und Prüfung von Preisanträgen sowie bei der Bestätigung, Einstufung und Bekanntgabe von Preisen, Teilpreisnormativen und Kalkulationselementen—Preisantragsverfahren' (Order no. Pr. 92 on the procedure for working out, submitting, and checking price proposals and for confirmation, classification and announcement of prices, partial price norms, and calculation elements—price proposals procedure), *Gesetzblatt der DDR*, II, no. 24, 1972.

86. 'Anordnung über die zentrale staatliche Kalkulationsrichtlinie zur Bildung von Industriepreisen' (Order on the central state calculation principles for setting industrial prices), *Gesetzblatt der DDR*, II, no. 67, 1972.

87. 'Kalkulationsrichtlinie' (Calculation guide-lines), Annexe to *Gesetzblatt der DDR*, II, no. 67, 1972.

88. 'Anordnung über die Bildung der Industriepreise für Investitionsleistungen und für den Export von Anlagen durch General- und Hauptauftragnehmer' (Order on the setting of industrial prices for investment projects and for the export of plants by general and main contractors), *Gesetzblatt der DDR*, II, no. 32, 1971.

89. Peter Hoss, Gerhard Schilling, 'Die inhaltlichen Fragen der Einheit von materieller und finanzieller Planung' (The substantial problems of the unity of physical and financial planning), *Wirtschaftswissenschaft*, no. 5, 1972.

90. G. Ebert, F. Matho, H. Milke, 'Optimalpreis und fondsbezogener Preis' (Optimal price and capital-related price), *Wirtschaftswissenschaft*, no. 11, 1968.

91. Harry Nick, *Warum fondsbezogener Preistyp?* (Why the Capital-Related Price Type?). East Berlin, 1968.

92. *Wirtschaftswissenschaft*, no. 10, 1972.

93. E. Seifert, H. Pohl, K. Maier, *et al.*, *Gewinn in der volkseigenen Industrie* (Profit in nationalized industry). East Berlin, 1968.

94. *Die Wirtschaft*, no. 50, 1973.

95. 'Anordnung über die Einführung konstanter Planpreise für die Planung und statistische Abrechnung der industriellen Produktion' (Order on the introduction of constant plan prices for the planning and statistical accounting of industrial production), *Gesetzblatt der DDR*, I, no. 23, 1974.

96. 'Fragen der Weiterentwicklung der Preise und der Bewertung volkswirtschaftlicher Ressourcen als wichtige Voraussetzung für die Einheit von materieller und finanzieller Planung (Thesen)' (Questions of the further development of prices and the valuation of national economic resources as an important prerequisite for the unity of physical and financial planning (theses)), *Wirtschaftswissenschaft*, no. 5, 1974.

97. Klaus Siebold, 'Der VIII Parteitag der SED wies realen Weg für eine effektive Energiewirtschaft' (The VIII SED Congress showed the real way to an efficient energy sector), *Neues Deutschland*, 31 May–1 June, 1975.

98. Anordnungen Nr. Pr. 125–139, *Gesetzblatt der DDR*, I, 1976.

99. 'Anordnung über die Planung der finanziellen Auswirkungen aus planmässigen Industriepreisänderungen per 1. Januar 1976' (Order on the planning of the financial effects of planned industrial price changes from 1 January 1976), *Gesetzblatt der DDR*, I, no. 23, 1975.

100. 'Anordnung über die Planung und Bildung von Preisausgleichsfonds im Zusammenhang mit der Ausarbeitung und Durchführung des Volkswirtschaftsplanes und Staatshaushaltsplanes 1976' (Order on the planning and formation of price equalization funds in connection with the elaboration

and implementation of the economic plan and state budget for 1976), *Gesetzblatt der DDR*, I, no. 23, 1975.

101. 'Anordnung Nr. Pr. 210 über Abnehmerbereiche von Erzeugnissen und Leistungen, für deren Industriepreise am 1. Januar 1977 neue Anordnungen in Kraft getreten sind' (Order no. para 210 on groups of customers for products and services for whose industrial prices new orders came into force on 1 January 1977), *Gesetzblatt der DDR*, I, no. 18, 1976. See also *Sonderdruck des Gesetzblatt der DDR* Nr 830–2, 834–7, 839–68 and 875.

102. Helmut Mann, 'Die planmässige Preisbildung als Instrument zur Förderung des wissenschaftlich-technischen Fortschritts' (Planned price setting as an instrument for promoting scientific and technical progress), *Wirtschaftswissenschaft*, vol. 6, 1975.

103. 'Beschluss über die Bildung der Industriepreise zur Durchführung des Beschlusses zur Leistungsbewertung der Betriebe und Kombinate' (Decision on the setting of industrial prices to implement the decision on evaluation of the performance of enterprises and combines), *Gesetzblatt der DDR*, I, no. 24, 1976.

104. 'Anordnung über die zentrale staatliche Kalkulationsrichtlinie zur Bildung von Industriepreisen' (Order on the central state calculation principle for setting industrial prices), *Gesetzblatt der DDR*, I, no. 24, 1976.

105. Theo Banse, Harry Nick, 'Gebrauchswert und Preisbildung' (Use value and price setting), *Wirtschaftswissenschaft*, vol. 6, 1975.

106. Grete Wittkowski, 'Neue Masstäbe für die Leitung und Planung unseres Kreditwesens' (New yardsticks for the management and planning of credit), *Sozialistische Finanzwirtschaft*, no. 22, 1972.

107. 'Verordnung über die Durchführung der Kredit- und Zinspolitik gegenüber volkseigenen Betrieben, konsumgenossenschaftlichen Betrieben und sozialistischen Wohnungsbaugenossenschaften' (Decree on the execution of credit and interest policy towards nationalized enterprises, consumer cooperative enterprises, and socialist housebuilding cooperatives), *Gesetzblatt der DDR*, II, no. 4, 1972.

108. ibid., II, no. 82, 1971.

109. ibid., II, no. 68, 1972.

110. 'Verordnung über die Stellung, Aufgaben, Rechte und Pflichten des Hauptbuchhalters im ökonomischen System des Sozialismus' (Decree on the position, tasks, rights, and duties of the chief accountant in the Economic System of Socialism), *Gesetzblatt der DDR*, II, no. 62, 1971.

111. 'Gesetz über den Staatshaushaltsplan 1974 vom 19. Dezember 1973' (Law of 19 December 1973 on the state budget plan for 1974), *Gesetzblatt der DDR*, I, no. 58, 1973.

112. Deutsches Institut für Wirtschaftsforschung, *DDR-Wirtschaft—Eine Bestandsaufnahme* (The GDR Economy—a Situation Report). Frankfurt and Hamburg, 1971.

113. *Statistisches Jahrbuch der DDR 1973*. East Berlin, 1973.

114. *Leistung in Zahlen '72* (Performance in figures, '72). Bundesministerium für Wirtschaft. Bonn, 1973.

115. A. Birman, 'Gosudarstvennyi byudzhet SSSR v perspektive ekonomicheskogo razvitiya' (The USSR state budget in the perspective of economic development), *Voprosy ekonomiki*, no. 9, 1973.

116. Walter Bielig, Johannes Gurtz, 'Wesen und Bedeutung der Staatseinnahmen aus der volkseigenen Wirtschaft' (The substance and significance of the state's revenue from the nationalized economy), *Wirtschaftswissenschaft*, no. 11, 1973.

117. 'Staatshaushalt' (The state budget)—article in *Wörterbuch der Ökonomie-Sozialismus* (Dictionary of Economics-Socialism). Berlin, 1969.
118. *Gesetzblatt der DDR*, I, no. 11, 1971.
119. ibid., I, no. 20, 1972.
120. ibid., I, no. 58, 1973.
121. ibid., I, no. 62, 1974.
122. ibid., I, no. 46, 1975.
123. ibid., I, no. 47, 1976.
124. *Statistisches Jahrbuch der DDR 1976*. East Berlin, 1976.

CHAPTER V

THE DEVELOPMENT OF THE ECONOMY AFTER THE TERMINATION OF THE REFORM

After surmounting the growth crisis at the beginning of the sixties the economy of the GDR displayed an overall trend of continuous steady growth until 1969 and 1970. Just when the reform model was supposed to come fully into operation, substantial disproportions appeared—bottlenecks, shortages, insufficient reserves, and increasing foreign indebtedness.

In this situation the economic leadership of the GDR decided on a revision of the New Economic System (return to greater centralization) in order, in particular, to counter the neglect of 'non structure-determining' production resulting from the excessive emphasis on 'structure-determining' tasks. The leadership also felt itself compelled to revise both the plan targets for 1970 and its original conceptions for the 1971–5 five-year plan.

V.1 The corrected five-year plan, 1971–5 [1, pp. 85ff.]

In view of the substantial aggregate economic disproportions, the new five-year plan had to aim at consolidation of the economy as a whole, fulfilment of the tasks which fell to the GDR within the framework of Comecon, and also—a politically determined factor— at strengthening the badly neglected consumption sphere, rather than at the fastest possible growth.

The year 1971 started without any long-term plan; a meagre annual plan set out the objectives: building up the power and raw materials base, improving the technical infrastructure, developing the supply industries, and expanding exports to reduce foreign indebtedness. Investment, which had been stagnating, was now concentrated on completion of projects already begun; new construction was to start only for expansion of the power and chemical industries and also housebuilding. Originally, narrow limits were set on private consumption too, but after some months a change of course occurred— under the impact of the political tensions sparked off by prices and incomes policy measures in neighbouring socialist countries. Improvements in income and increases in the supply of consumer goods led to corrections to the 1971 plan. Finally, at the Eighth Congress of the SED in the middle of 1971 'raising the material and cultural living standard of the population' was declared the principal task of the five-year plan, which was published at the end of 1971 [2, pp. 175ff.] together with the plan for 1972.

According to the plan, *national income* (*produced*) was to reach 138 mlrd Mark (at constant prices) in 1975, which corresponds to an average annual growth rate of 4·9 per cent. In view of the fact that production capacity was fully utilized this growth in output was to be achieved primarily by rises in labour productivity. For the *manufacturing industry* an average annual increase in *commodity production* of 6 per cent (1966–70 = 6·5 per cent) was envisaged. The priority areas in industry were:

(a) development of *electric power generation*: output was to be raised to 88–90 mlrd kWh (1970 = around 69 mlrd kWh) and installed capacity to around 19,000MW; the structure of energy use was to shift in favour of liquid and gaseous forms (which provided 23 per cent in 1970 and were to provide 33 per cent in 1975);

(b) construction of new capacity in the *chemical industry* for synthetic materials, artificial fibres, and magnetic tape production, and for production of nitrogenous fertilizers from imported natural gas;

(c) further change in the output structure of *metallurgy*, towards high-quality steel;

(d) strong expansion of output of important *electrical and electronic products*;

(e) development primarily of export-intensive branches of *engineering* and *supply industries*;

(f) priority expansion of export-intensive branches of *light industry*.

For *construction* the plan target was substantially reduced, by an average of 5 per cent annually, compared with the previous five-year period. The chief reasons seem to have been that the planned increases in labour productivity were not even half achieved and the plan was nearly fulfilled only through a marked increase in employment—by 87,000—which could certainly not be repeated during the 1971–5 five-year plan. In addition, there were substantial difficulties, some structural, some the result of planning methods [5], which had to be overcome after 1970. In *agriculture* the rate of growth or state output of cattle was cut back to 2·5 per cent per year—compared with 3·5 per cent in 1966–70. *Transport* too, after the completion of the build-up of shipping, shows a reduction of the plan target for total freight transport to only 4 per cent per annum—during 1966–70 increases of 10 per cent were achieved.

Indicators of the planned economic development of the GDR, 1971–75
(real growth expressed in percentages)

	Actual 1966–70[1]	Plan 1971[2]	1971–75[1]	1975 (1970=100)
tional income (produced)	5·3	4·9	4·9	127
nufacturing industry				
Commodity production	6·5	6·5	6·0	134
Labour productivity	5·7[7]	5·4[9]	6·2[7]	135[8]
Building materials production	6·8[9]	—	6·2	134–136
nstruction output	8·3[10] ⎫	4·1[11]	4·6	125
Construction industry gross output	7·0 ⎭		4·9[12]	127[12]
Labour productivity	3·1	—	4·2	121–124
riculture				
tate yields of				
cattle	3·8	3·0	2·9	115
milk	2·7	1·5	2·1	111
eggs	3·8	—	0·5	103
nsport				
Freight transport output	10·2	7·9	4·2	123
Freight transport (quantity)	4·0	—	2·7	114
t and communications output	7·0	—	4·7	126
ss capital investment[3]	9·9	1·5[13]	3·0	116
nsumption	4·6	—	4·2	123
al retail trade turnover[4]	4·6	2·4[14, 16]	4·1[14]	122[14]
Food and luxuries	4·4	—	3·0[14]	116[14]
ndustrial commodities	5·0	—	5·4[14]	130[14]
eign trade turnover[5]	9·9	8·0	—	—
xports	8·3	16·0	10·5[15]	160–170
mports	11·5	0	—	—
ome of the population[6]	4·0	3·7[16]	4·0	121·5

nual average growth; [2] growth compared with previous year; [3] excl. general repairs; owth at current prices; [5] total imports and exports, incl. intra-German trade, excl. ices, in foreign currency Mark at current prices; [6] net money incomes; [7] gross duction per blue- and white-collar worker (excl. apprentices); [8] basis: commodity duction; [9] gross output of principal group of products 'building materials'; [10] in- ling the output of steel and metal light construction (750 m. Mark annually), uded in volume of construction since 1968; [11] construction revenue; [12] construction repair output of the Ministry of Construction; [13] incl. investment participation oad; [14] commodity deliveries incl. increases in stocks in consumer goods trade, ribution partly estimated; [15] socialist countries only; [16] these planned growth rates 1971 were raised by an unknown amount by resolutions of the Politbureau and ncil of Ministers of 26 and 29 January 1971.

rces: National economic plans, plan fulfilment reports, GDR statistical yearbooks, Eighth Congress materials [3], Directive of the Eighth Congress for the 1971–5 five-year plan. Taken from [4, p. 323].

On the expenditure side the cut-back fell particularly on *investment*. An annual average growth rate of only 3 per cent was envisaged (in 1966–70 almost 10 per cent was attained); taking into account a planned decline of 1·5 per cent in 1971, this gave a figure of 4·2 per cent for the remaining years 1972–5. Out of the total planned investment of 175 mlrd Mark 14 mlrd Mark were to be for the purpose of expanding electric power generation. There were also to be investments in the development of the chemical industry, supply industries, housing construction, and education. The housing programme envisaged the construction of 500,000 dwellings through new building, reconstruction, and extension and modernization of the existing stock, and education was to benefit by the creation of 16,000–17,000 new classrooms, over 25,000 boarding-school places, and 22,000–26,000 work and lecture room places in universities and other higher educational institutions.

Private consumption was to grow faster than investment, even though by less than the national income. Thus an annual rise of 4 per cent was envisaged for the money incomes of the population. The level of equipment of households with consumer durables was to show worthwhile improvements by 1975 with the number of television sets and refrigerators per 100 households reaching 75–80 (in 1970 they were 69 and 56 respectively) and that of washing machines 65–70 (54 in 1970).

As far as *foreign trade* is concerned, one major factor was the 'complex programme' demanding substantial deliveries to the other Comecon countries and thus well above average exports. In addition, the GDR had to participate both financially and with the provision of labour in the opening up of raw material deposits, particularly in the USSR. On the other hand, the great need for Western investment goods, without which the GDR cannot overcome some of her technological gaps, meant that she could not allow trade with the West to stagnate.

V.2 Balance sheet of the five-year plan

By about 1973 the GDR economy succeeded in surmounting the difficulties which were clearly visible in 1970 and 1971 and in achieving a broad measure of consolidation and stabilization of the course of her economy.

In 1971, however, it did not look as though this would be accomplished quickly [6, pp. 3f.]: in agriculture there were marked harvest shortfalls—as in 1969 and 1970—because of unfavourable weather conditions. Demand for electric power—despite the construction of additional capacity—still could not be fully met at peak load periods. There were shortages of materials and of labour.[1]

National income (produced) rose by 4·5 per cent in 1971 (plan: 4·9 per cent); taking into account the fact that the year contained two more working days than 1970, the corrected growth figure was only a bare 4 per cent. Manufacturing industry achieved a 5·5 per cent increase in production, and construction the same, so that they, at least, exceeded the planned figures. Freight transport developed according to plan, though delays did not cease. Expenditure was distinguished by stagnation of investment as planned and by a faster rise in private consumption than the plan envisaged: retail trade turnover climbed 3·9 per cent compared with the planned 2·4 per cent. Numerous gaps in the assortment of goods appeared, which necessitated additional imports of consumer goods. Foreign trade ended up with a small overall surplus, but deliveries from Western industrial countries considerably exceeded deliveries in the opposite direction.

In 1972 real progress was made in consolidation [8, p. 3]: favourable weather conditions enabled agriculture to achieve a record harvest, the bottlenecks in supply industries declined markedly, and, despite evident strains, there were no more major disruptions in the electric power supply. Nevertheless, in many sectors more overtime and holiday working was necessary.

The production results were indeed good:[2] national income (produced) rose by 5·7 per cent, commodity production of the manufacturing industry by as much as 7·2 per cent, construction output expanded by 6·4 per cent, and agricultural output by 12·6 per cent. In transport, on the other hand, the volume of freight carried rose only insignificantly as shortages of spare parts prevented vehicles from being fully used. On the expenditure side investment, as before, showed only modest growth (3·9 per cent), although within industry investment in the coal and power branches and in the consumer goods industry was stepped up. Private consumption, by contrast, achieved large increases: retail trade turnover rose by 6 per cent (8 per cent for industrial goods); net money incomes climbed by a good 6 per cent, partly on account of overtime working, to be sure, but also as a consequence of wage increases and improvements in social benefits. This extra purchasing power, as well as increased purchases by foreign tourists from neighbouring socialist countries, especially Poland, led to renewed shortages despite the expansion of the supply of commodities.

[1] For details see [7].
[2] For precise details see [9].

In foreign trade the export surplus increased to 1·1 mlrd Mark, but at the same time the trade deficit with the Western industrial countries was around 2 mlrd Mark.

In view of the favourable overall development in 1972 the GDR economic leadership decided—despite the continuing bottlenecks in power, the supply industries, and the labour situation—to set the plan targets for 1973 at an appreciably higher level [10, pp. 283f.]. But the result was a plan that was not fully consistent internally, since the planned production increases (e.g. 6·5 per cent for the manufacturing industry) were not sufficient for the ambitious targets on the expenditure side—investment up 9 per cent and retail trade turnover up to 6·2 per cent [11]. The planned figure for production of the manufacturing industry would have had to be 1·5 percentage points higher, in other words, around 8 per cent. Such a high growth rate was nevertheless not reached, despite more overtime working and an increased campaign for enterprises to take on counterplans offering additional output.

The principal results were as follows [12, p. 3]: production of the manufacturing industry rose by 6·8 per cent, somewhat more than planned, but national income (produced), by contrast, lagged slightly behind target (5·5 instead of 5·7 per cent increase); investment expanded almost according to plan by 8 per cent, with the biggest rises in branches of industry close to consumption.[1] Private consumption—measured by retail trade turnover—following the plan closely, rose by almost 6 per cent, and by a full 9 per cent for industrial goods. Pension increases of 20 per cent and other additional social benefits, as well as overtime work showed up here, and caused an increase of 5·6 per cent in the net money incomes of the population, greater than the rise planned. In foreign trade, the outcome was an annual deficit of 1·2 mlrd foreign currency Mark, and 2·9 mlrd with the Western industrial countries. This considerably increased the financing problems of the GDR.

Overall, the following problems continued: the labour supply situation remained very tight and made labour-saving investments necessary; on the other hand, the utilization of new plants, especially in the chemical industry, was often inadequate; despite definite improvements, shortages still occurred in supplies; the engineering industry, which supplies both important exports and also the means of rationalization urgently needed at home, got into a particularly tight situation; there were still gaps in the assortment of consumer goods and defects in their quality.

Since the twenty-fifth anniversary of the founding of the GDR fell in 1974, high targets were once again set and considerable plan

[1] Thus the structural shifts in investment, begun in 1971, continued; see [13].

Table 27: Planned development of the GDR economy 1972–5, according to annual plans
(real percentage increase over preceding year)

	1972	1973	1974	1975
National income (produced)	4·6	5·7	5·4	5·5
Manufacturing industry				
Commodity production	5·5	6·5	6·7	6·3
Labour productivity	5·0[3]	5·7[3]	6·0[3]	5·6[3]
of which: Commodity production of building materials	—	8·1	7·2	7·1
Construction				
Total output of construction	3·5	7·6	5·4	5·0
Construction and repair work by the nationalized construction industry	3·6[4]	4·4[4]	5·1[4]	5·3
Agriculture				
State yields of				
cattle	2·2[5]	7·5	5·6[6]	7·4[6]
milk	−0·4[5]	3·1	3·3[6]	7·6[6]
eggs	—	0·1	2·3[6]	5·2[6]
Transport				
Total freight transport	6·3[7]	4·5[7]	4·1	3·8
Quantity of goods transported	—	—	—	—
Gross capital investment (incl. general repairs)	2·0	9·0	5·3	4·4
Total retail trade turnover[1]	4·0	6·2	5·2	4·6
of which: food and luxuries[1]	3·8	4·2	4·0[8]	3·0
industrial commodities[1]	4·3	8·7	6·0[8]	6·2
Foreign trade turnover[2]	12·5	14·0	10·0	9·1
Exports	11·5	—	—	—
Imports	13·5	—	—	—
Net money incomes	3·9	5·3	4·5	4·4

[1] increase at current prices; [2] imports plus exports in foreign currency Mark at current prices; [3] in the field covered by the industrial ministries (basis: commodity production); [4] Ministry for Construction; [5] these growth rates are calculated by relating the quantitative outputs set for 1972 to the actual results for 1971; the plan growth rates, by contrast, were 2·4 and 0 per cent respectively; [6] related to the plan figure for the preceding year (incl. extra output); [7] see [14, p. 7]; [8] deliveries of commodities for internal trade.

Sources: GDR economic plans and [9] and [11].

over-fulfilments were expected to be achieved through 'socialist competition'. The major plan targets were [15, pp. 563ff.] to increase national income (produced) by 5·4 per cent, commodity production of the manufacturing industry by 6·7 per cent, the output of construction by around 6 per cent and freight transported by 4 per cent. On the expenditure side, investment and private consumption (retail trade turnover) were each to increase by only 5 per cent, but foreign trade turnover by 10 per cent, with priority emphasis on developing the GDR's export capacity.

The results show that [17, pp. 3–4] most of the targets were reached and some substantially exceeded. National income produced rose in 1974 to around 134 mlrd Mark, or 6·4 per cent more than in the previous year. This is undoubtedly a record result, exceeding the plan figure by almost a full percentage point. This result is all the more striking as it occurred in a year when the economies of a number of Western industrial countries were suffering from a strong recession. Commodity production of the manufacturing industry in the GDR rose by 7·4 per cent, (7·7 per cent adjusted for the number of working days) with an increase in labour productivity of 6·3 per cent; the output of the construction industry likewise increased more than planned, with a 6·2 per cent rise. Agriculture was marked by a good harvest.

On the expenditure side private consumption—measured by retail trade turnover—rose, more than planned, by 6·1 per cent, and that of industrial commodities by as much as 8 per cent. The increase in net money incomes of 4·8 per cent was only slightly above plan. Investment on the other hand lagged behind plan, with a growth rate of only 4·2 per cent. Shortfalls occurred particularly in the chemical industry, primarily as a consequence of defects in the preparation and execution of new projects. Great concern was caused as before by the frequently unsatisfactory utilization and efficiency of new plants.

For 1975 a further big increase in growth was planned [18, pp. 3–4], although such great efforts as were made in the 'socialist competition' of 1974 surely could not have been expected again. National income (produced) was to rise by 5·5 per cent to 141 mlrd Mark, commodity production of the manufacturing industry by 6·3 per cent, and construction output by 5 per cent. The growth targets for both investment and private consumption (retail trade turnover) were reduced to around 4·5 per cent each. Even for foreign trade the growth rate envisaged was slowed down somewhat (to 9 per cent).

In view of the world-wide price increases of energy and raw materials the GDR economic leadership had once again laid great emphasis on appeals for material savings. The most important measure, however, was a renewed shift in the structure of investment: around 60 per cent of all industrial investment—more than twice as much as hitherto—was to be devoted to the raw material sector in 1975 (above all, brown coal and electric power) [19, pp. 3f.].

In 1975 [28, pp. 4–5] the growth of national income (produced), 4·9 per cent, lagged slightly behind the planned figure. Commodity production of the manufacturing industry rose according to plan by 6·4 per cent, with an increase of 5·5 per cent in labour productivity.

Table 28: Actual development of the GDR economy, 1971–5
(real increase over the preceding year, expressed in percentages)

	1971	1972	1973	1974	1975
National income (produced)	4·5	5·7	5·5	6·4	4·9
Manufacturing industry					
Commodity production	5·5	7·2	6·8	7·4	6·4
Labour productivity	5·4	4·5[3]	5·5[4]	6·3[4]	5·5
Gross output of construction	6·1[5]	3·5[6]	7·1[5]	9·7	8·3[6]
Construction					
Total output	5·5	6·4	—	—	—
Gross output of construction industry	6·0	—	4·7	6·2	7·7
Construction and repair work by nationalized construction industry	6·1	4·3	4·8	6·4	—
Agriculture					
State yields of					
cattle	3·2	8·8	5·4	8·3	8·1
milk	1·3	6·1	4·2	4·5	0·6
eggs	3·6	0·2	4·9	10·1	2·5
Transport					
Total freight transport	4·6	0·4	7·9	1·4	3·8
Quantity of goods transported	5·5	3·8	1·8	3·3	6·2
Gross capital investment (excl. general repairs)	0·6	3·9	8·0	4·2	3·8
Total retail trade turnover[1]	3·9	6·0	5·8	6·1	3·5
of which: food and luxuries[1]	2·9	4·1	3·2	4·2	3·0
industrial commodities[1]	5·1	8·3	8·8	8·2	4·0
Foreign trade turnover[2]	6·7	10·8	14·4	19·6	16·2
Exports	10·8	12·2	9·4	16·3	—
Imports	2·8	9·2	19·6	22·8	—
Net money incomes	3·4	6·1	5·6	4·8	4·0

[1] increase at current prices; [2] imports plus exports in foreign currency Mark at current prices; [3] estimated; [4] in the field covered by the industrial ministries (basis: commodity production); [5] gross output of the product group 'construction materials'; [6] industrial commodity production of nationalized construction materials industry.

Sources: Plan fulfilment reports, GDR statistical yearbooks, and [*11*], [*16*], [*26*] and [*27*].

Output of the construction·industry, 7·7 per cent higher, exceeded the plan. In agriculture the extreme drought of the summer had an adverse effect on crop production. Transport, on the other hand, sustained smaller losses due to disruption than in the previous year.

On the expenditure side private consumption—measured by retail trade turnover—rose appreciably less (3·5 per cent) than planned; this is particularly due to the failure to achieve the target for turnover in industrial commodities. In the investment sphere too the growth target, which was meagre anyway, was not reached.

On foreign trade, for which only little information is available, the GDR statistics gave the following picture [29, pp. 305–6]: in trade with the Western industrial countries (including intra-German trade) turnover diminished by 2 per cent in 1975. On the other hand, statistics of the Western trading partners show an increase of around 5 per cent. According to the latter, imports and exports rose more or less equally, so that the GDR deficit on commodity trade, which had amounted to around 700m. foreign trade Mark in 1974 increased only slightly (according to the GDR statistics the excess of imports was much higher—around 3 mlrd Mark in 1974).

In trade with the Comecon countries turnover rose by 26 per cent in 1975 according to the GDR statistics. This also corresponds to the trading partners' statistics, which show an increase in GDR imports of around 30 per cent and of exports around 25 per cent. This gives a GDR deficit in 1975 of around 1 mlrd foreign trade Mark (in 1974 an export surplus of 400m. Mark was achieved). This excess of imports originated in trade with the USSR, primarily because of the price rises for raw materials. With other Comecon countries there was a surplus on commodity trade.

If we try to estimate the overall result of the five-year plan period on the basis of the actual results up to 1975 we obtain the following picture:

Table 29: Balance-sheet of the five-year plan

	Overall percentage increase—1975 over 1970	
	FYP target	Actual
National income (produced)	27	30
Commodity production of manufacturing industry	34	37
Investment	16	22
Retail trade turnover	22	28
Net money incomes of the population	21·5	27

This makes it clear that generally substantial overfulfilment of the cautious five-year plan was achieved, though by varying extents: the expenditure side shows an appreciably higher degree of overfulfilment than the production side, though the former's growth rates were set relatively lower in the plan. Obviously this means that in the present GDR economic situation, additional production increases require more than proportionate rises on the expenditure side—in the form of higher investment, higher private incomes, and greater supplies of consumer goods. Holiday working, overtime, and adoption of obligations to additional performance in 'socialist competition' are impossible without clear income incentives even in a socialist society.

Exports were to be increased more than imports. With a rise in foreign trade turnover from 1970 to 1975—at constant prices—of 50 per cent, exports were indeed increased more than imports. The difference in the growth rates of exports and imports varied in individual years, however, and overall was presumably smaller than envisaged in the five-year plan.

As for the development year by year, we have the following picture: the rates of growth of output and expenditure reached the highest levels in the years 1972 to 1974 and fell below the average figures in the first and last years of the five-year period.

Despite the favourable overall development, not all individual targets were successfully implemented. The most important case is the power industry: while it was planned to raise the installed generating capacity to around 19,000MW by the end of 1975 it was in fact only 16,900MW.

In housebuilding, on the contrary, an appreciable overfulfilment occurred, as by the end of 1974 467,000 dwellings had already been completed. The overfulfilment nevertheless relates more to rebuilding[1] and above all to modernization of the existing stock of housing[2] than to new building.[3] Of the 608,700 dwellings completed by the end of 1975, 136,200 were modernized and 72,900 rebuilt; 399,600 new dwellings were built. The number of new houses planned to be built by 1975 was 383,500 so that the new building target was exceeded by 16,100 dwellings.

[1] The maximum expenditure for rebuilding and extension of dwellings was set at 300 Mark per square metre of useful floor area for at least thirty years' extension of the useful life of the buildings [20, p. 5].

[2] Modernization is to bring the equipment of dwellings up to today's requirements. It covers principally the installation of mains water supply, water heating facilities, construction of internal toilets, showers, baths, and the installation of central heating systems. The cost of modernization must not exceed a maximum of 70 per cent of the cost of comparable new building, and the remaining useful life of the houses must be extended by a minimum of thirty years [21, p. 5]. In many cases, where old houses are equipped with mains water and inside toilets, the expense must be far below this maximum.

[3] Here we have assumed that the decision of the GDR authorities in 1972 to plan the additional construction of 25,000 small houses and bungalows for workers [22, pp. 395ff.; 23, p. 3] has been debited to the planned construction of dwellings. Although it has never been made clear whether or not the planned number of dwellings to be constructed was reduced by that 25,000, it seems likely that the targets have not been changed at all.

V.3 Main points of the five-year plan for 1976–80

The 1971–5 five-year plan targets underwent correction during its course—through the individual annual plans; the establishment of future proportions of economic development is therefore uncertain. With the greater complexity of the economic process, its increasing vulnerability, and the higher incidence of unpredictable exogenous disturbances, this problem becomes more and more difficult. Moreover, there is less scope for establishing crucial new centres of emphasis in view of the existing basic targets or those which result from the past; and a switch-over to faster growth is unlikely because of the continuing tightness of the employment position, the high export demands of the other Comecon countries, the burden of financing the greatly increased costs of raw material imports, and the limitation which continued advancement of consumption puts on investment growth as long as there is little progress with innovation. In addition, planning must now take into account regularly occurring price changes and a periodic review of established structural decisions carried out on the basis of the altered price structure, factors which complicate both planning and plan evaluation.

For these reasons not only were the targets in the directives for the 1976–80 five-year plan [30] set more cautiously but, in addition, all the important figures in the five-year plan law, which has meanwhile been published, are set at the lower limits of the ranges in the directives [31, pp. 519ff.]. The GDR economic leadership evidently assumes that economic growth in the years up to 1980 will turn out lower than in 1971–5.

Productivity increases are expected only to a lesser extent than in the previous five-year period, which was in this respect disappointing. On the other hand, in contrast to the situation hitherto, an increasing number of inhabitants of working age means that some additional labour is available for use. An extra 130,000 employees in industry are planned, 36,000 for construction and 23,000 for the transport sector.

For the economy as a whole the previous average annual growth of 5·4 per cent has been cut to 5 per cent (the directives had 4·9–5·4 per cent). In industry the position is exactly the same: the planned growth of 6·0 per cent annually is noticeably below the average annual growth of 6·5 per cent achieved previously. Within industry machine tools and processing machinery are now at the head of the growth table (increase in 1980—compared with 1975—56 per cent), followed by the former leader, electrical and electronics (+45·7 per cent). Then follow the chemical industry (+44·5 per cent), glass and ceramic production (+44·1 per cent), and general engineering (+42 per cent).

Table 30: *Major indicators of the economic development of the GDR up to 1980*
(percentage increases)

| | 1971–5 | | 1976–80 | | |
	Actual	Total increase Plan	Directives	Law	Annual increase
National income (produced)	30	27	27–30	27·9	>5·0
Industrial commodity production	37	34	34–36	34·0	>6·0
Industrial labour productivity[1]	28	35[2]	30–32	30·0	5·4
Construction output	26	27[3]	27–28[4]	27·6[4]	5·0[4]
Foreign trade turnover[5]	48	42[6]	—	—	—
Imports	42	—	—	—	—
Exports	55	60–70[7]	50[7]	50[7]	8·4[7]
Retail trade turnover[8]	28	22	20–22	21·5	4·0
Food etc.	19	16	13–16	13–16	2·5–3·0
Industrial goods	39	30	25–28	25–28	4·5–5·0
Social consumption	46 ⎱	23	21–23	22·5	4·1
Personal consumption	28 ⎰				
Net money incomes	27	22	20–22	21·4	4·0
Gross capital investment[9]	22	16[10]	28–31[11]	28·8[12]	5·3

[1] gross output per blue- and white-collar worker (excl. apprentices); [2] industrial ministries, commodity production basis; [3] Ministry of Construction; [4] whole economy; [5] total imports and exports (incl. intra-German trade); [6] Comecon countries only; [7] socialist countries only; [8] at current prices; [9] excl. general repairs and foreign participation; [10] incl. foreign participation; [11] volume for the whole period: 232–236 mlrd Mark; [12] total volume excl. foreign participation (8 mlrd Mark) for 1976–80: 234 mlrd Mark.

Sources: Five-year plan 1971–5 [2]; Draft directives of Ninth SED Congress [32, pp. 3ff.]; Five-year plan 1976–80 [33, pp. 3ff.]; GDR statistical yearbooks, plan fulfilment reports; DIW calculations.

Structural alterations are not confined to industry either. In utilization of national income, priority is given to exports. In view of the higher raw material costs sharp increases in imports in money terms are unavoidable. Because of a deterioration in the terms of trade, especially *vis-à-vis* the USSR, the GDR must export substantially more in real terms to finance the urgently needed imports. Consequently the plan envisages a rise of 50 per cent in real exports to the socialist countries compared with the 1971–5 results. No data are given on trade with the West. In view of the great need for investment goods and modern technology from Western countries a marked expansion may be expected in this sector of foreign trade too. The expansion of exports as a priority task, however, means that a larger part of domestic production must be taken away from domestic use than before.

The planned growth rate of domestic expenditure, therefore, is below that of exports. Although the period of investment restriction has been ended, it could only be allowed to grow at a moderate pace. Excluding participation in foreign investment in the Comecon area (8 mlrd Mark)—which would be treated as a capital export in Western accounting—the cumulative plan figure for 1976–80 of 234 mlrd Mark corresponds to an average annual growth rate of 5·3 per cent.

The areas of concentration of investment remain industry and housing. In industry (110 mlrd Mark) 60 per cent of the investment is earmarked for the raw materials sector, to strengthen the domestic raw materials base. Forty-five mlrd Mark are planned for the completion of 750,000 dwellings (including 550,000 newly built dwellings) by 1980[1] [25, pp. 5ff.]. At the Ninth SED Congress the housebuilding programme was further expanded when the FDGB (Freier Deutscher Gewerkschaftsbund) [34, p. 4] pledged itself to modernize an extra 100,000 dwellings. This reflects both the unfavourable age structure[2] and equipment of the housing stock and the desired improvement in the regional distribution of the labour force. Thus the existing centres of raw material extraction, engineering, and chemicals in the southern provinces are to be extended but the northern regions are also to be further industrialized—to the extent that conditions there allow.

Last on the list for expenditure—as in 1975—is private consumption. It is to rise by only about 4 per cent annually up to 1980—measured by 'commodity turnover for the supply of the population'. The growth rate for industrial goods is thus reduced to 4–5 per cent: this is paralleled by the planning of a 4 per cent rate of increase in net money incomes; rises in pensions and other social payments are not envisaged, so that the share of wages and salaries in total income will increase. The growing state expenditures on the maintenance of stable prices and for cultural and social purposes are cited as evidence of rises in the standard of living, still as always called the principal objective.

The reasons for setting cautious growth targets must chiefly be seen in the foreign trade burden. Almost all increases in domestic production require increases in the now much more costly raw materials, which in view of the deterioration of the terms of trade with the USSR can only be financed by substantial and in fact almost

---

[1] This programme envisages the construction or modernization of 2·8–3 million dwellings during the whole period up to 1990.

[2] At the beginning of 1971 only one-fifth of all dwellings in the GDR had been built after the Second World War, compared with more than half in the Federal Republic.

impossible rises in exports. Furthermore, on the one hand both the capacity and the readiness of the Comecon countries to supply raw materials are limited, and on the other hand to switch to other countries would cause problems because of the even higher world market prices. As for trade with the West, an additional difficulty is that the slackening in economic growth of major Western industrial countries also affects the traditional export opportunities of the GDR. Consequently, apart from a forced export drive—intensification of Comecon trade by overcoming its present capacity problems and expanding trade with the West through quality improvements— there is nothing left for the GDR but to make savings in the use of materials per unit of output and strive for an undoubtedly costly expansion of its domestic raw material base. It is here that the GDR faces a number of additional problems: savings in materials can only be made to a small extent, despite more precise and tighter materials use norms. Neither will the increases in domestic raw material prices and the improvements in setting the prices of material-saving innovations help very much. For it still frequently appears more advantageous for enterprises to omit to notify savings and to barter the material saved for other raw materials, spare parts and urgently needed goods on the 'grey' market. The expansion of the domestic raw material base is no less problematic. Thus, for example, the specific energy consumption of the electric power sector is particularly high because of the use of obsolete techniques[1]—for the same production level it is reckoned to be 20 per cent higher than in other industrial countries. It is therefore especially serious that electric power generation has grown appreciably less since 1960 than gross industrial output or labour productivity in the manufacturing industry [24, pp. 14–15]. A problem here is that electric power generation is for the most part dependent on brown coal (84 per cent in 1973), which is very susceptible to the effects of bad weather. Four-fifths of total primary energy consumption are met by solid fuels (70 per cent by brown coal); since a marked expansion of imports of oil and gas is extremely difficult, the mining of brown coal must be increased further, amid worsening geological conditions. This in turn pre-empts substantial investments which, because of the long development periods for open-cast mining, are only reflected in production after a long interval. Construction of power stations too proceeds slowly and requires large investment funds. Finally, both are dependent on expansion of the capacity to produce heavy equipment.

The GDR's investment policy has thus got into a situation of conflicting aims: the decision to expand the domestic raw material

[1] Specific energy consumption is consumption of primary energy per unit of output.

base ties up 60 per cent of industrial investment up to 1980, leaving substantially less than hitherto for, in particular, the producers of investment goods (1971–5—22·3 per cent; 1976–80—19 per cent of industrial investment). But it is precisely the capacity of the investment goods industries which would have to be raised sharply in order to be able to satisfy both export needs and desires and also the pressing domestic rationalization requirements.

Another sector which has suffered from starving of investment funds is water supply. This is far from unimportant, for both the increasing water pollution and the rise in the water consumption of manufacturing industry, agriculture and private households from the present 8–9 mlrd cubic metres to an estimated 14 mlrd by 1980 cause substantial problems: because of inadequate reservoir capacity[1] persistent shortages in water supply occur in dry periods and in long periods of rain overflowing is unavoidable.[2] It is only the relatively favourable weather conditions of recent years that have prevented these problems from becoming more obvious.

V.4 Unplanned slowdown in real growth to date

The state central statistical administration's report for 1976 [35] is full of contradictions and puzzles, as it speaks of numerous over-fulfilments although many plan targets were in fact underfulfilled. If we explain this by putting forward the thesis of a downward plan revision during the course of 1976 the question immediately arises of the reason for such a reduction in the annual plan targets. Otherwise we must assume that some of the data in the fulfilment report are incorrect. In that case there has evidently been a structural difficulty which has led to distinct imbalances.

In detail, national income produced showed a rise of only 3·7 per cent in 1976, whereas 5·3 per cent was planned. This considerable slowdown in growth is officially explained by the substantial losses in agriculture. Crop production was severely affected by the extreme drought of the summer of 1976: total crop production—measured in grain units—fell by around 14 per cent. Livestock output, on the other hand, with only a slight decline, was roughly according to plan.

In industry planned and actual growth rates diverge only slightly (6 per cent and 5·9 per cent), yet the fulfilment report speaks of a real increase in industrial commodity production of 14 mlrd Mark as an

---

[1] Although reservoirs for 600 million cubic metres of water have been built in the GDR since 1945, gross fixed capital in water supply has declined as a proportion of the total in industry from 8·4 per cent in 1960 to 6·8 per cent in 1975.

[2] Water supply has been a difficult problem in the GDR for a long time. The level of water use is unusually high in comparison with other countries [4, p. 55].

Table 31: Indicators of GDR economic development, 1976–80
(percentage increases over previous year)

	1976–80[1] Five-year plan	1976 Plan	1976 Actual	1977 Plan
National income (produced)	>5·0	5·3	3·7	5·5
Manufacturing industry				
Commodity production	>6·0	6·0	5·9	5·1
Labour productivity[2]	5·4	5·5	6·0	5·1
Construction				
Construction output	6·5[3]	6·3[4]	6·8[4]	6·2[4]
Labour productivity	5·1[3]	—	5·1	4·7[3]
Agriculture				
State yields of				
cattle[5]	0·1[6]	−1·5[6]	−1·4	—
milk	1·4[6]	−0·5[6]	0·3	—
eggs	0·0[6]	−3·5[6]	1·3	—
Grain production	—	—	−9[7]	—
Investment (excl. general repairs)	5·2	6·5	6·8	6·5
Foreign trade turnover[8]	8·4[9]	9·7	—	8·7
Retail trade turnover[10]	4·0	4·0	4·3	4·0
Food etc.	2·5–3·0	—	3·1	—
Industrial goods	4·5–5·0	—	5·6	—
Net money incomes	4·0	4·0	4·0	4·0

[1] average annual increase; [2] industrial ministries, commodity production basis; [3] Ministry of Construction; [4] construction output; [5] live weight; [6] quantities planned; [7] estimated; yield per hectare fell by 9·3 per cent; [8] total imports and exports, incl. intra-German trade, excl. services, at current prices; [9] socialist countries only; [10] current prices.

Sources: GDR statistical yearbooks and journal; 1976 economic plan [38]; 1977 economic plan [39, pp. 533ff.]; five-year plan 1976–80 [39, pp. 519ff.]; plan fulfilment report for 1976 [36] and [40].

overfulfilment of 2·6 mlrd Mark. It is this contradiction which makes us suspect plan revisions. The reason could well be connected with the raw materials problem: in the first few months of the year it became obvious that materials savings of the extent envisaged were not attainable and therefore that the supplies of materials required to fulfil the planned targets could not be ensured. Even the higher raw material prices did not induce the desired economies. Furthermore, enterprises argued that materials-saving product improvements meant that they incurred the disadvantage of a lower output return for plan fulfilment. All these reasons could have led the economic leadership to make downward plan revisions.

Just how great the slowdown in growth in the industrial sectors was is shown if we make a correction for the number of working days. Since 1976 contained six more working days than 1975 all sectors of

Table 32: *Index of industrial commodity production,*
January to September 1976
(percentage growth over previous year)

	per working day[1]	per calendar month[2]
Fuel and power	6·9	8·5
Chemicals	6·3	7·9
Metals	4·4	6·0
Building materials	4·2	5·9
Water supply	5·3	7·0
Engineering and vehicles	4·0	5·7
Electrical, electronics, and instruments	6·6	8·3
Light industry	4·4	6·0
Textiles	3·7	5·3
Foodstuffs	1·4	3·0
All industry	4·4	6·1

[1] see *Statistische Praxis*, no. 6, 1976; [2] aggregated overall calculation.

Source: [*36*, p. 47].

industry and industry taken as a whole show only modest growth
after this adjustment; for all industry the figure was only 4·4 per cent
[*36*].

In the construction sector output shows an overfulfilment (actual:
6·8 per cent, plan: 6·3 per cent). This result must be attributable to
special efforts both in housebuilding and also to overcome the
difficulties with industrial construction.

On the expenditure side private consumption—measured by retail
trade turnover—with a 4·3 per cent rise grew somewhat faster than
net money incomes (4·0 per cent). Turnover in industrial goods
expanded substantially more (5·6 per cent) than in foodstuffs (3·1 per
cent).

In the investment sector the growth target (6·5 per cent), which was
itself high in comparison with the five-year plan, was slightly
exceeded (6·8 per cent). The planned rate had obviously been set high
because in 1974 and especially 1975 the growth of investment had
faltered. This was attributable above all to a substantial setback in
industrial investment. During 1974 and 1975 increases of 3·2 and
4·6 per cent respectively were planned, but the actual outcome was
−1·6 and −0·8 per cent. All the same, it is unlikely that the industrial
investment target for 1976 (8·7 per cent) was achieved. So despite a
slight overfulfilment, the trend in investment should not be regarded
as wholly positive because, on the one hand, it was caused by
increased costs of individual investment projects and, on the other,
the obsolete capital stock of the GDR only permits sensible combination of old and new parts of plants if substantial extra expenditure is
incurred.

Foreign trade turnover—at current prices—rose by 14 per cent according to the plan fulfilment report; no further data were published.

The plan for 1977 [37, pp. 533ff.], occupying barely two pages of the official gazette, was the shortest for many years (the 1976 plan covered eight pages). This alone implied some uncertainty on the part of the economic leadership about what the future held. For both the increased pressure to export in order to finance dearer raw materials and the promise of constant consumer prices with the consequent rising subsidies (1977 plan: 13·5 mlrd Mark) were and are still substantial economic burdens. In addition to this the unbalanced development in 1976 and in particular the difficulties which arose in industry must have influenced the plan targets set.

For 1977 an increase of 5·5 per cent in national income produced was planned, despite a below-average growth figure for industry of 5·1 per cent. Evidently the plan was based on the assumption of a normal agricultural harvest. The growth rate for industry, which is also reduced in comparison with the five-year plan average, must be mainly attributable to difficulties with the supply of materials and enterprises' uncertainty about the new price regulations.

This picture fits with the economic leadership's decision on the expenditure side to give priority to increasing investment (6·5 per cent), alongside a further rise in exports. This was both to check the slowdown in the growth of industry by an expansion in capacity and also represented an attempt to overcome disproportions in the investment sector. Since a large part of industrial investment must be used for opening up domestic raw material deposits and utilizing secondary raw materials, which are not directly reflected in output increases, in recent years the GDR has tried to have recourse to rationalization measures to expand manufacturing industry production. With the shortage of resources for rationalization, however, this way out is also blocked by the impossibility of fitting rationalization investment smoothly into all sections of the production process in industrial enterprises. This has set constraints on the new industrial growth focus in the GDR, rationalization equipment produced by the engineering industry, which has made it impossible for it to fulfil the qualitative and quantitative targets set for it. This in turn cannot fail to affect export requirements and import financing.

In these circumstances it was already clear at the beginning of 1977 that the prospects for fulfilment of the reduced 1977 plan targets were small. Even the below-average rise in private consumption (increase in retail trade turnover of 4 per cent) could hardly be judged realistic or only on cost of under fulfilment of other targets.

180 ECONOMIC REFORM IN EAST GERMAN INDUSTRY

References to Chapter V

1. Peter Mitzscherling, 'Die Wirtschaft der DDR' (The economy of the GDR) in *Die Wirtschaft Osteuropas zu Beginn der 70er Jahre* (The Economy of Eastern Europe at the Beginning of the Seventies), ed. Hans-Hermann Höhmann. Stuttgart, 1972.

2. 'Gesetz über den Fünfjahrplan für die Entwicklung der Volkswirtschaft der DDR 1971–1975' (Law on the five-year plan for the development of the national economy of the GDR, 1971–1975), *Gesetzblatt der DDR*, I, no. 10, 1971.

3. *Neues Deutschland*, 19 June 1971.

4. DIW. *DDR-Wirtschaft: Eine Bestandsaufnahme* (The GDR Economy: a Situation Report), 3rd revised edition. Frankfurt-am-Main, 1974.

5. 'Die Bauwirtschaft der DDR zu Beginn der siebziger Jahre' (The construction sector in the GDR at the beginning of the seventies), Manfred Melzer, *Wochenbericht des DIW*, no. 24, 1970.

6. 'Über die Durchführung des Volkswirtschaftsplanes 1971' (On the fulfilment of the national economic plan in 1971), *Neues Deutschland*, 14 January 1972.

7. 'Anhaltende Konsolidierungsbemühungen. Die Wirtschaft der DDR am Beginn des Jahres 1972' (Prolonged efforts at consolidation. The GDR economy at the beginning of 1972), Peter Mitzscherling, *Wochenbericht des DIW*, nos. 5–6, 1972.

8. 'Über die Durchführung des Volkswirtschaftsplanes 1972' (On the fulfilment of the national economic plan in 1972), *Neues Deutschland*, 19 January 1973.

9. 'Forcierte Wachstumsbemühungen. Zur Wirtschaftslage der DDR am Beginn des Jahres 1973' (Growth efforts stepped up: on the economic position of the GDR at the beginning of 1973), Peter Mitzscherling, *Wochenbericht des DIW*, no. 5, 1973.

10. 'Gesetz über den Volkswirtschaftsplan 1973' (Law on the national economic plan for 1973), *Gesetzblatt der DDR*, I, no. 20, 1972.

11. 'Vor erneuter Wachstumsabschwächung? Zur Wirtschaftslage der DDR am Beginn des Jahres 1974' (Growth faltering again? On the economic position of the GDR at the beginning of 1974), Peter Mitzscherling, *Wochenbericht des DIW*, no. 4, 1974.

12. 'Mitteilung der Staatlichen Zentralverwaltung für Statistik über die Durchführung des Volkswirtschaftsplanes 1973' (Communiqué of the State Central Administration for Statistics on fulfilment of the national economic plan in 1973), *Neues Deutschland*, 18 January 1974.

13. 'Anhaltender Strukturwandel in der Investitionstätigkeit der DDR?' (A permanent structural change in GDR investment?), Manfred Melzer, *Wochenbericht des DIW*, no. 48, 1973.

14. *Sozialistische Demokratie*, no. 52, 1971, Supplement.

15. 'Gesetz über den Volkswirtschaftsplan 1974' (Law on the national economic plan for 1974), *Gesetzblatt der DDR*, I, no. 58, 1973.

16. *Wochenbericht des DIW*, no. 31, 1974.

17. 'Mitteilung der Staatlichen Zentralverwaltung für Statistik über die Durchführung des Volkswirtschaftsplanes 1974' (Communiqué of the State Central Statistical Administration on the fulfilment of the national economic plan for 1974), *Neues Deutschland*, 15 January 1975.

18. 'Gesetz über den Volkswirtschaftsplan 1975' (Law on the national economic plan for 1975), *Neues Deutschland*, 21 December 1974.

19. Horst Sindermann, 'Mit hoher Schöpferkraft ins letzte Jahr des Fünfjahrplans' (We enter the last year of the five-year plan with great creative power), *Neues Deutschland*, 20 December 1974.

20. *Sozialistische Demokratie*, 7 April 1972.
21. ibid., 28 January 1972.
22. *Gesetzblatt der DDR*, II, no. 35, 1972.
23. *Neues Deutschland*, 3 July 1972.
24. Bärbel Laschke and Christian Czogalla, 'Energiewirtschaftliche Zusammenhänge der Intensivierung' (Implications of intensification for the energy sector), *Die Wirtschaft*, no. 1, 1975.
25. Wolfgang Junker (Minister for Construction), 'Das Wohnungsbauprogramm der DDR für die Jahre 1976 bis 1990' (The housing construction programme of the GDR for the years 1976 to 1990), *Neues Deutschland*, 4 October 1973.
26. *Wochenbericht des DIW*, no. 32, 1975.
27. ibid., no. 33, 1976.
28. 'Mitteilung der Staatlichen Zentralverwaltung für Statistik über die Durchführung des Volkswirtschaftsplanes 1975' (Bulletin of the State Central Administration for Statistics on the fulfilment of the national economic plan for 1975), *Neues Deutschland*, 20 January 1976.
29. 'Die wirtschaftliche Lage in der DDR zur Jahresmitte 1976' (The economic situation in the GDR at the middle of 1976), Doris Cornelsen, *Wochenbericht des DIW*, no. 33, 1976.
30. 'Direktive des VIII Parteitags der SED zum Fünfjahrplan für die Entwicklung der Volkswirtschaft der DDR 1971 bis 1975' (Directives of the eighth congress of the SED for the five-year plan for the development of the GDR economy from 1971 to 1975), *Neues Deutschland*, 23 June 1971, special supplement.
31. 'Gesetz über den Fünfjahrplan für die Entwicklung der Volkswirtschaft der DDR 1976–1980' (Law on the five-year plan for the development of the GDR economy 1976–1980), *Gesetzblatt der DDR*, I, no. 46, 1976.
32. *Neues Deutschland*, 15 January 1976.
33. ibid., 17 December 1976.
34. Harry Tisch, 'Sinn des Sozialismus bestimmt unsere Arbeit' (The feeling of socialism determines our work), *Neues Deutschland*, 21 May 1976.
35. 'Mitteilung der Staatlichen Zentralverwaltung für Statistik über die Durchführung des Volkswirtschaftsplanes 1976' (Report of the State Central Administration for Statistics on the fulfilment of the national economic plan for 1976), *Neues Deutschland*, 22/23 January 1977.
36. 'Anhaltendes Wachstum bei reduzierten Planvorgaben—Die Wirtschaft der DDR an der Jahreswende 1976/77' (Continuing growth with reduced plan targets—the GDR economy at the turn of the year 1976/77), Doris Cornelsen, *Wochenbericht des DIW*, no. 6, 1977.
37. 'Gesetz über den Volkswirtschaftsplan 1977' (Law on the 1977 national economic plan), *Gesetzblatt der DDR*, I, no. 46, 1976.
38. *Neues Deutschland*, 8 December 1975.
39. *Gesetzblatt der DDR*, I, no. 46, 1976.
40. *Neues Deutschland*, 22/23 January, 1977.

CHAPTER VI

BETWEEN SPONTANEITY
AND EXCESSIVE INTERVENTION

Looking back at the GDR economy over the last decade and a half, and in particular at the years since the beginning of the economic reform in 1964, i.e. the seven years of the reform and the post-reform period since 1971, the observer is struck by a remarkable contradiction.

On the one hand, official statements and statistical publications claim continuous economic growth at a comparatively high rate. The difficulties at the beginning of the previous decade were surmounted (growth of national income (produced) in 1961–3: 1·6, 2·7, and 3·5 per cent), and growth rates since the introduction of the New Economic System have apparently been rather constant at around 5 per cent with the maximum variation between 4·5 per cent (1971) and 6·3 per cent (1974) [1, p. 17; 2, p. 3]. Even today this success is still for the most part ascribed to the organizational improvements of 1964 and thereafter. On the other hand, it is not clear what these improvements actually are. The discussions in the GDR periodicals on the planning and management system, explicitly described as the 'management and planning system' since the termination of the reform at the beginning of 1971,[1] show clearly that in the middle of the seventies no solution has been found to the problems which were criticized in 1963 and which provided the justification for reform at that time. Thus the 'Critical Evaluation of the Existing Practice of Planning and Management of the National Economy', which was appended to the 'Principles of the NES' and published in the same issue of the official gazette [4, pp. 481–4], laid the blame for 'losses resulting from friction and violation of economic laws' on the following defects [5, pp. 10–12] which according to current discussion are also prevalent today:

(a) enterprises' clinging to obsolete products which are more profitable than new products because of the fixed price system (1963), or the continuation of production of 'obsolete products . . . because, with the present means of evaluating performance, plan indicators can best be fulfilled in this way' (1974).

(b) the lack of interest of enterprises (because of the system of performance indicators) and workers (because of the wages system)

---

[1] This terminological shift of emphasis was considered so significant that even the constitution of the GDR was changed at eight points on account of it [3].

in quality improvements (1963), or the fact that 'quantitative growth rates have priority in the planning and evaluation of enterprise performance' and that practicable methods have yet to be developed for unified planning of quantity and quality (1974).

(c) enterprises' one-sided concentration on annual plans, with the undesired consequence of the striving for 'easy' plans, and the discontinuities in the course of the economy which result from the lack of scientifically based long-term (five-year) planning (1963), or the necessity to plan the crucial tasks of the national economy and enterprises over a longer period than one year and to apportion greater significance to the five-year plan. At the same time, however, it is pointed out that there are few indications of how the five-year plan and annual plans should be linked together and that 'soundly based skills in planning over different time periods have [yet] to be worked out' (1974).

This list could be expanded without difficulty to cover many more examples. A comprehensive account of these problems at the aggregate level makes the following observation [5, p. 12]: 'The need to increase performance and efficiency everywhere in the economy is undisputed. By no means so clear, however, is where the possibilities of planning, measuring, and evaluating performance and efficiency are to be found.' At enterprise level the same problem exists, in that: 'enterprises' physical plan targets and economic levers do not always operate equally towards the execution of the principal tasks of the five-year plan'. The result is a central conflict for enterprises [6, p. 11]: 'Should they put all their efforts into discharging their social responsibility to meet demand or into fulfilling the financial indicators of the plan?'

This of course raises again the central problem of a state-planned economy, namely the question how far it is possible to translate what the political leadership recognizes or can impose as demand into state plans and enterprise indicators designed to control the activity of individuals and enterprise work forces.

Here it must not be overlooked that while the problems of 1963 and 1974 are the same in principle, in practice the magnitude and importance of the problems have increased. The technical planning difficulties have grown because not only has the volume of production risen but product differentiation has continued and the proportion of more complicated goods, which place a heavier load on planning, has risen. The demands made on planning and especially on the information system have thus increased more than proportionately. Moreover, because of the growing complexity of the economy, the increasingly intricate interdependencies between individual sectors, and the limits which the defects of the information system place on the possibility of a general view of their interrelationships, the process of economic policy formation is becoming more and more difficult and lengthy. This affects not only the coordination of the more technical production and allocation processes within the economic administrative apparatus, i.e. all organs between the GDR Council of Ministers and individual VEB. It applies equally to the both externally and internally declining scope for decision-making on aggregate economic growth and allocation which the political leadership (the SED Politbureau) has reserved for itself. Externally this scope is restricted by the development of the world economy (inflation and raw material price trends) which immediately affected the GDR's trade with the West and after some delay showed up in the Comecon sector too. Internally it is the result of the growing necessity of having regard to the population's desire for income and consumer goods. For this there were both political and economic reasons. Politically the improvement of general living conditions, as a stabilization factor, was unavoidable, both because of the personal change of power after the retirement of Ulbricht and because of the change in East–West relations, in particular between the GDR and the Federal Republic of Germany. The principal economic reasons for the improvement of the standard of living were that even after the end of the NES economic growth could mainly be achieved by intensive means, that is through rising labour productivity, with limited additional investment; but better performance by the working population required correspondingly greater payment by the state. The political leadership was therefore compelled to make concessions to the desires of the population ('more present consumption') in order to pursue its own chief goals ('more growth').

In this situation the inadequacies of the information system had a particularly negative effect. For the less precisely the desires of the population can be ascertained, the greater must be the safety margin in the concessions granted if events such as those which occurred in Poland in 1970–1 are to be avoided. In particular, the defects of the price system—price structure and price-setting—which had already contributed substantially to the collapse of the NES show up here too. While in the NES phase they were supposed to be compensated by numerous corrective measures, which ultimately gave rise to the danger of economic spontaneity ('spontaneous processes'), the attempt to fix prices absolutely after 1970 has to a large extent robbed them of any information and thus guiding function.[1]

The effect of this was especially negative on planning, because here

---

[1] 'At present the influence of prices on the physical decisions of enterprises and economic management organs is still relatively small' [7, pp. 23–6].

it was not the fixed prices of 1970–1 that were used but, until 1975 inclusive, the so-called 'constant 1967 prices' (cP 67) which had been determined as a result of the price review which introduced the reform. These prices were based on a valuation of productive capital in the prices of 1962, but they had not taken into account the subsequent partial conversion of the new prices of 1967 into capital-related prices, which occurred in 1968–70. Therefore, some of the 'constant 1967 prices' diverged very markedly from actual prices (e.g. of the year 1974) [8, p. 10].

In order to avoid the resultant misjudgements of the economic situation and the associated misallocations, new 'constant plan-prices' were introduced from 1 January 1975 (cPP 75), based on enterprise prices in force on 1 January 1975 [9, pp. 240–1]. For the plan year 1975 industrial production was to be calculated both in the old (cP 67) and the new (cPP 75) prices.

The result of this was the following different bases of valuation for the planning and calculation of industrial performance on the basis of the 'industrial commodity production' plan indicator in the year 1975 [8, p. 10]: (a) for purposes of enterprise performance assessment and bonus calculation—actual enterprise selling prices (ESP = prime cost plus planned profit); (b) for purposes of aggregate economic planning and balancing—actual industry selling prices (ISP = ESP plus turnover tax and minus subsidies); (c) for purposes of long-term plan period comparisons—constant 1967 prices (cP 67); and (d) also for long-term plan period comparisons—constant 1975 plan-prices (cPP 75).

If we consider the central position of the commodity production indicator in the enterprise and the aggregate planning and control system and the multitude of other indicators linked to it (e.g. labour productivity, capital intensity, etc.), the problems of this increasing differentiation in planning and accounting, illustrated with a single example here, become clear.

In enterprises there was increasingly severe criticism of the plethora of decrees and regulations, through which even the specialist can often no longer find his way [10; 11, p. 12]: 'Who is supposed to cope with it all? Hosts of planners would be necessary. And it is by no means certain that the plans would be better.' And another complains [12]: 'I have been planning for over fifteen years in a nougat and marzipan factory. During those years the extent and content of the instruments we work with have changed almost continuously, as have the explanations given about them. The one thing that has not changed is that the economic management organs have often had to give "explanations" about the "explanations" at very hastily summoned working conferences.'

At the same time there were demands that the various planning instruments, planning and accounting methods, data collection programmes, forms, processing and evaluation programmes, etc., should remain unchanged for longer periods [*13*, pp. 616–20] and, furthermore, that the times set by the state for working out enterprise plans should be modified to meet the continually growing demands and that the initial planning data should be issued to industrial branches as early as April of the respective year [*14*, p. 12]. The latter evidently proved impossible: after the date for the issue of 'state tasks' for the 1974 national economic plan had been brought forward to 28 April 1973 so as to meet this demand [*15*, p. 189], the following year saw a return to the old date (15 May 1974) [*16*, p. 235]. For the 1977 plan the date was postponed till 24 May [17, pp. 229ff.].

The justification and official recognition of the validity of enterprises' desires and demands, however, are expressed not only in this—unsuccessful—attempt to allow more generous time limits for planning but also in numerous other efforts: thus, after a year and a half of preparation, explanatory commentaries were published on a 'Draft of the basic principles for annual planning in enterprises and combines' [*18*], and two months later a 'Draft order for planning the GDR national economy in 1976–80' followed [*8*]. Both were attempts to introduce order into the more and more complicated and confused processes of enterprise and national planning, to make them more easily supervised, and thus to counteract the dangerous tendency to excessive intervention in the economy, which is ultimately bound to lead to uncontrollability.

The Basic Principles [*20*] passed as a law some time later, together with the Planning Order [*19*] which was likewise given legal force,[1] in effect introduced a new attempt at reform. It differed fundamentally from the 1963 reform, which was one of substance designed to introduce a new conception of steering the economy, in so far as it was exclusively formal in character, intended to stabilize procedures. The associated expectation that it would therefore encounter fewer problems was, however, soon disappointed. The effects of the essential unsolved problems of economic steering, above all those of setting and changing prices and the associated questions of the connection between physical and financial planning and measurement of efficiency, began to show. The planning situation became increasingly complicated by the effects of external economic developments on the domestic economy. The sharp price increases for raw

---

[1] The publications came out as special issues of the official gazette and were only supplied to a limited circle of subscribers. Although they were not officially designated as Secret or Confidential they were not on public sale and none were supplied to Western countries.

materials—initially only those from Western countries but then from the Comecon area too—caused the GDR's general terms of trade to worsen so much that it was no longer possible to check raw material price rises through increased subsidies financed out of the difference between aggregate improvements in productivity and the increases in income granted by the state. The gap between the growth of productivity and that of incomes had shrunk due to increasing pressure for consumption by the population, and was no longer sufficient. This meant that it was no longer possible to carry out the economic and political leadership's intention to stabilize planning and, in particular, only to alter marginally the prices used for planning. On the contrary it proved essential to raise at least a number of raw material prices. This then led, for one thing, to marked changes in plan prices and thus in the entire system of plan calculations and, for another—because initially only raw material prices were altered—to structural inconsistencies: for some enterprises input prices were changed, i.e. increased, without their being allowed to adapt their output prices at the same time. Enterprises were required to absorb the price increases through internal rationalization—although the authorities well knew that only a few would be able to do so.

Thus the 'formal' reform of economic planning in the GDR, introduced in 1975, collapsed after barely a year. It showed once again that formal planning problems cannot be separated and isolated from the problems of substance. Extreme fluctuations in output and great differences in plan fulfilment are the consequences. The authorities are attempting to master these problems with short-term programmes for critical sectors. Yet the contradictions and inconsistencies in the plan fulfilment reports and the new plans show that the GDR too, although at higher levels of productivity and consumption, has to wrestle with the same unsolved problems as the other countries of Eastern Europe.

The crucial difference from the situation in the reform period of the sixties lies in essence in the fact that economic policy in and after the middle of the seventies has comprised only short-term adaptations. While in the sixties economic policy measures were basically oriented to a fairly comprehensive conception—that of the New Economic System—today any such conception is clearly lacking. This means that organizational decisions, which should be orientated towards a clear goal and should determine the structures of the future, are not possible. Since, because of the increasing complexity of the situation, the torrent of interventions through new laws and orders has less and less effect and is therefore ill fitted to bring about a fundamental change, everything points to the probability that the

GDR economy will remain in this difficult position for a considerable time to come.

References to Chapter VI

1. *Statistisches Jahrbuch der DDR 1974* (GDR statistical yearbook 1974). East Berlin, 1974.
2. *Neues Deutschland*, 15 January 1975.
3. *Gesetzblatt der DDR*, I, no. 47, 1974.
4. ibid., II, no. 64, 1963.
5. Ina Grüning, Eckhard Ladwig, 'Zur Diskussion über die Vervollkommnung der Planung' (On the discussion of the improvement of planning), *Die Wirtschaft*, no. 31, 1974.
6. 'Bei der Planung ist konsequent vom Bedarf auszugehen' (Planning should logically start from demand), *Die Wirtschaft*, no. 43, 1971.
7. Helga Blas, Hans-Jörg Richter, 'Verhältnis von Norm und Normativ bei der Preisbildung' (The relationship of norm and normative in price-setting), *Deutsche Finanzwirtschaft*, no. 11, 1973.
8. Lothar Teubel, Heinz Brass *et al.*, 'Zum Entwurf der Ordnung der Planung der Volkswirtschaft der DDR 1976–80' (On the draft order for planning the GDR national economy in 1976–80), *Die Wirtschaft*, no. 21, 1974, Supplement no. 9, 1974.
9. 'Anordnung über die Einführung konstanter Planpreise für die Planung und statistische Abrechnung der industriellen Produktion vom 25. April 1974' (Order of 25 April 1974 on the introduction of constant plan-prices for the planning and statistical accounting of industrial production), *Gesetzblatt der DDR*, I, no. 23, 1974.
10. *Neues Deutschland*, 30 January 1972.
11. 'Vorschläge zur Vervollkommnung der Jahresplanung' (Proposals for the improvement of annual planning), *Die Wirtschaft*, no. 2, 1972.
12. Hans Hackbarth, 'Planmethodik soll besser überschaubar sein' (Planning methods should be more comprehensible), *Die Wirtschaft*, no. 8, 1972.
13. Walter Marx, 'Fragen der Konstanthaltung volkswirtschaftlicher Verzeichnisse und Systematiken' (Questions of the maintenance of stable national economic classifications and systems), *Statistische Praxis*, no. 11, 1971.
14. *Die Wirtschaft*, no. 2, 1972.
15. 'Anordnung über den terminlichen Ablauf der Ausarbeitung des Volkswirtschaftsplanes und des Staatshaushaltsplanes 1974' (Order on the sequence of dates for the elaboration of the national economic plan and state budget for 1974), *Gesetzblatt der DDR*, I, no. 21, 1973.
16. 'Anordnung über den terminlichen Ablauf der Ausarbeitung des Volkswirtschaftsplanes und des Staatshaushaltsplanes 1975' (Order on the sequence of dates for the elaboration of the national economic plan and state budget for 1975), *Gesetzblatt der DDR*, I, no. 23, 1974.
17. 'Anordnung über den Ablauf des Volkswirtschaftsplanes und des Staatshaushaltsplanes 1977' (Order on the sequence of dates for the national economic plan and state budget for 1977), *Gesetzblatt der DDR*, I, no. 17, 1976.
18. *Die Wirtschaft*, no. 11, 1974, Supplement no. 6, 1974.
19. 'Anordnung über die Ordnung der Planung der Volkswirtschaft der DDR 1976 bis 1980 vom 20.11.1974' (Order of 20.11.1974 on the planning of the national economy of the GDR from 1976 to 1980), *Gesetzblatt der DDR vom 15.11.1974*. Supplement no. 775a.

20. 'Anordnung über die Rahmenrichtlinie für die Jahresplanung der Betriebe und Kombinate der Industrie und des Bauwesens—Rahmenrichtlinie—vom 28.11.1974) (Order of 28.11.1974 on the basic principles for annual planning in industrial and construction enterprises and combines—basic principles), *Gesetzblatt der DDR vom 13.1.1975*. Supplement no. 780.

INDEX

accountant, chief, of an enterprise, 146
adaptability of enterprises, 63–5; inadequate price flexibility and, 139; structure-determining priorities and, 79, 81
administration of industry, 15, 114–16; difficulty of coordinating processes in, 183–4; lack of clarity in, 81
Agricultural Bank, 145
agricultural production cooperatives, 5; revenue from, 151
agriculture: collectivization of, 5, 6; cost increase on investment in, at price reform, 39; percentage annual increase in yields of, planned and/or achieved, (1961–5) 11, (1966–70) 77, 80, (1971–5) 162, 165, 167, 168, 169, 177
aircraft production, 18
amortization fund: of an enterprise, 46; of VVB, 47
automation, 63; structure-determining priority for, 68

balance decree (1968), 64
balancing organizations (State Planning Commission, industrial ministries, VVBs, etc.), 25, 64; and draft annual plan, 107; product group leading enterprises as, 19
balancing system, 17, 111–13
banks, 145–7; new tasks of, under NES, 29–30, 41, 55, (problems over) 62; in preparation of annual plan, 107; see also State Bank
basic materials industries: capital revaluation in, 34; depreciation reform in, 35; gross fixed capital of (1955–70), 33; limited success of, in increasing labour productivity and decreasing costs, 140; output of (1972, 1975), xii–xiii; price reform in, 36, 39
Behrens, Prof. Fritz, 8
Benary, Dr. Arne, 8
Berlin, four-power agreement on (1971), xvi–xvii
Berlin wall (1961), 5, 7

bonus fund, of enterprise: linked to net profits under NES, 45, 93, 128; payments to individuals from, 46, 47, 128; plan fulfilment and, 110, 120, 122, 128
bonus fund, of VVB, 47
Brandt, Willy, Chancellor of GFR, xvi
building materials industries: gross fixed capital of (1955–70), 33; output of (1936–70) as percentage of total manufacture, 74; percentage annual increase in output of, planned and/or achieved, (1956–70), 76, (1971–5), 163, (1976 over 1975), 178; price reform in, 39; structure-determining priorities, and supplies from, 75
buildings: price reform and costs of, 38; share of, in capital of industrial enterprises, before and after revaluation, 32; structure-determining priority for development of light-weight construction methods for, 68, 77; see also housing
butter, output of (1972, 1975), xii–xiii

capital, fixed: in enterprise plan, 20; gross, in manufacturing industry (1955–70), 33; interest on, not reckoned in costs of production, 31, 40, 50; obsolete nature of much of, 66; production charge on, under NES, see production capital charge; productivity and profitability of, 32, 88, 91, 134; revaluation of, 31, (distorted by price changes) 84, 91, 134; as scarce factor, 52; type of price related to, see under prices
capital, working: conditions for bank credits for, 147; motive for saving on, under NES, 54; production charge on, under NES, see production capital charge
capital-intensive industry: capital-related prices and, 50, 84; cost-related prices and, 50; problems in, met by reduced deductions from net